Cross-Cultural Psychology

Human Behavior
in Global Perspective

Cross-Cultural Psychology

Human Behavior in Global Perspective

Marshall H. Segall

Syracuse University

Brooks/Cole Publishing Company
Monterey, California
A Division of Wadsworth, Inc.

Printed in the United States of America

10 9 8 7 6 5 4 3 2 1

Library of Congress Cataloging in Publication Data

Segall, Marshall H.
    Cross-cultural psychology.

    Bibliography.
    Includes index.
    1. Psychology. 2. Psychology—Social aspects.
3. Personality and culture. 4. Cross-cultural
studies. I. Title. [DNLM: 1. Cross-cultural
comparison. 2. Behavior. 3. Psychology.
4. Psychology, Social. HM291 S454c]
BF121.S425   155.8   79-12259
ISBN 0-8185-0344-0

Acquisition Editor: *Claire Verduin*
Manuscript Editor: *William Waller*
Production Editor: *Fiorella Ljunggren*
Interior and Cover Design: *Katherine Minerva*
Illustrations: *Ann Geiger, The Design Company*
Typesetting: *David R. Sullivan Company, Dallas, Texas*

Foreword

Writing a foreword to this book must surely come under the head of unnecessary occupations. The author, Professor Marshall Segall, is not in need of any introduction by me or anyone else. He occupies an important chair at Syracuse University, where he succeeded Floyd Allport, one of the founders of modern social psychology. He has made significant contributions in the field of cross-cultural psychology, with which this book is concerned. He is the author, together with Donald Campbell and the late Melville Herskovits, of *The Influence of Culture on Visual Perception*, which has become a classic in this field. His book on *Human Behavior and Public Policy* has contributed to the development of the whole area of political psychology. Most recently his study, with two younger colleagues, of *Political Identity: A Case Study from Uganda* has thrown light on the problem of intergroup relations in a setting very different from that in which this particular issue has usually been approached. When we were all colleagues at Columbia University a number of years ago, Richard Christie and I invited him to write the chapter on "Anthropology and Psychology" for the volume we were editing on *Perspectives in Social Psychology*. This list of his contributions, although far from complete, is sufficient testimony to his place in social psychology in general and in cross-cultural psychology in particular.

And yet, when Segall asked me to write these few words of introduction, I accepted with pleasure for at least two reasons. The first was that he has very kindly included me among those who in his judgment influenced his development and stimulated his interest in looking at psychological problems in cross-cultural perspective. If this is the case, I am indeed very proud. In an autobiographical sketch published in 1974, I wrote "My contact with anthropology affected me somewhat like a religious conversion. How could psychologists speak of *human* attributes and *human* behavior when they knew only one kind of human being? . . . What would our field be like if the books had been written by Hottentots or Eskimos rather than by Europeans or Americans?" It is good to see this idea accepted, enlarged on, and illuminated by my friend Marshall Segall.

My second source of pleasure in writing this foreword arises from my admiration for what has been accomplished in the field of cross-cultural psychology in the 50 years since my own interest in this field began. At that time psychologists had to look mainly to ethnologists for the data on which a comparative (human) social psychology might be based. Relevant psychological research did exist here and there, but it was rare and usually limited in scope and sophistication. Now the significant material would fill a fair-sized library, with contributions by psychologists from many different countries. As Segall indicates, he has had to make a modest selection from what is available, and he wisely gives his readers guidelines on where to find additional literature and how to keep up with this rapidly expanding area. He asks that his own book be regarded as an introduction.

He has succeeded admirably. His book is interesting; the presentation is clear and well written; the material has been wisely selected; and the need for a cross-cultural approach to psychological issues is argued with conviction, well illustrated, and amply documented. I enjoyed the book and learned a lot from it. I believe it should satisfy both students and their teachers. I hope that it will be widely read and that the enlargement of psychological horizons the author advocates will be increasingly accepted.

Otto Klineberg
Professor Emeritus of Social Psychology,
Columbia University
Director, International Center for
Intergroup Relations, Paris

Preface

A course in cross-cultural psychology, a vibrant and rapidly growing field, can be one of the most exciting in the undergraduate curriculum. This book is meant for such a course. It attempts to demonstrate to undergraduate students—beginners and advanced psychology majors alike—that human behavior is both delightfully varied and satisfyingly orderly. That is, human behavior *can* be studied in a systematic, scientific fashion, but, to do justice to this subject, attention must be paid to the diverse ecological and cultural settings in which human beings live.

The issues covered in this book include the traditional topics of human psychology—perception, cognition, and personality development. Also covered are topics that are central to social psychology, including intergroup relations and the impact of changing cultural settings on the persons experiencing those changes. What is different about the book is the manner in which these topics are treated. Throughout, emphasis is on research conducted in numerous societies for comparative purposes, and attention is regularly focused on the impact of the society on the particular behaviors of concern. In short, human behavior is viewed in this book primarily as a product of culture.

As our world effectively shrinks, our curricula must increasingly treat their constituent subject matters in global perspective. The parochialism that has characterized undergraduate teaching must give way to global education—a treatment of fundamental human concerns that acknowledges the interdependence of the various regions of the world. An educated person anywhere must, from now on, cultivate a sense of his or her fellow humans everywhere—who we are, what moves us, and how we cope with problems that all of us share. There is a crucial role for psychology to play in this effort to globalize knowledge. This book, and the courses that might be built around it, will, I hope, contribute to this effort.

This text grew out of my teaching both beginning and advanced courses in cross-cultural psychology at Syracuse University. In writing the book, I have kept two audiences in mind. To accommodate beginners, I have tried to define every concept that a student who has had no more than an introductory course in one of the social sciences is not likely to have previously encountered. To interest advanced students, I have built the book around psychological research that they are not likely to have encountered in the usual mix of courses that constitute a major in psychology.

The book is also interdisciplinary, touching several concerns that are central to anthropology and sociology. Accordingly, it might well be used in a human-behavior or social-relations course or even in introductory courses in anthropology and sociology. At Syracuse University, students in those two disciplines have regularly pursued cross-cultural psychology, and it is my hope that this volume will permit such cross-disciplinary training at other universities.

The book's structure is straightforward. The introductory section describes cross-cultural psychology, its history, its subject matter, and its methods. The second section, composed of three chapters, presents detailed coverage of what is known about cultural influences on the development of human behavioral processes. The third section takes as its springboard the fact that no culture exists in isolation and considers the impact of that fact on our behavior. All three parts can be covered in a semester-long course. The book might also be employed profitably as a supplement to a basic text in a year-long introductory course in psychology. For advanced students, the text might best be employed in conjunction with contemporary journal articles or with the compendium of papers by cross-cultural psychologists that constitute the projected six-volume *Handbook of Cross-Cultural Psychology.*

The work of the many distinguished contributors to the *Handbook* is amply sampled in this text and presented in a manner that makes it accessible to the nonspecialist. Accordingly, if this book works as it was intended to, the field of cross-cultural psychology—not so long ago an exotic specialty—might become a central part of the undergraduate curriculum.

The final draft of this book benefited mightily from reviews by several cross-cultural psychologists who helped me to eliminate errors of fact, faults of interpretation, and imbalances in emphasis. They are: John Berry of Queen's University, Kingston, Ontario, Martin Chemers of the University of Utah, Gordon Finley of Florida International University, and Walter Lonner of Western Washington University. All remaining defects are my responsibility, but, thanks to the reviewers, the book is one for which I happily accept that responsibility. Imbalances in emphasis remain, I am sure, because I have been selective in ways that reflect my own experience as a cross-cultural psychologist. Thus, some topics, like visual perception, and some areas of the world, like Africa, have received particular attention. But the book is, I believe, as broad in coverage as one cross-cultural psychologist can make it. Throughout, I have tried to convey the delights and satisfactions inherent in a science of human behavior that employs the whole world as its laboratory.

The first draft of this book was completed on May 9, 1977, in—appropriately enough for a text on cross-cultural psychology—Nairobi, Kenya. It was begun on a date that is considerably more difficult to ascertain. Perhaps it was started many years ago, at Northwestern University, where the writer, as a student, was encouraged by Donald Campbell and the late Melville Herskovits to indulge his curiosity about human behavior in what were then exotic cultures. Or perhaps it was started at Yale University, where he was inspired by that very perfect model of a pioneer cross-cultural psychologist, Leonard Doob. Or was it at Columbia University, where Otto Klineberg demonstrated that a social psychology that attends to culture is infinitely richer than one that remains laboratory-bound?

It certainly grew over the years at Syracuse University's Maxwell School, where a succession of internationally minded deans—Stephen Bailey, Alan Campbell, and Guthrie Birkhead—allowed the writer frequently to "go on safari" to collect data in distant places and to think about the numerous research reports and summaries of theories and findings that appear in this book.

It is hard to say when the book was begun, but clearly its growth was nourished by all of the agents of development under whose influence I was fortunate enough to fall. As the book began to take shape, numerous younger colleagues—especially John Berry and Mary Stewart Van Leeuwen (in Canada), Jan Hoorweg (in the Netherlands), and Pierre Dasen (in Geneva)—provided new ideas that made it, at first, much harder to finish but, in the end, much more worth finishing. It is their generation of cross-cultural psychologists that has brought the field to fruition, thus making it possible to prepare a textbook composed of substantive findings, sufficient in number and significant in quality, to inform and instruct other generations. To the pioneers who led me to cross-cultural psychology and to the younger psychologists who have contributed so much to the field, I say thanks. To those among my readers who may themselves become cross-cultural psychologists, this book is dedicated.

To move from first draft to publication has been an effort that could not have succeeded without assistance, support, and encouragement. Several students at Syracuse University—most notably Larry Beyna, Caroline Keating, and Julianne Scarchilli—contributed as if the project were as much theirs as mine. The staff at Brooks/Cole Publishing Company—Claire Verduin, Project-Development Editor, Fiorella Ljunggren, Senior Production Editor, and William Waller, Manuscript Editor—disconfirmed all stereotypes attached to publishers and made my participation in the book-production process a pleasure from start to finish. They treated my book with great thoughtfulness, allowing it to say what I wanted it to say, while improving its clarity significantly. Two fine secretaries in the Maxwell School, Liv Myhre and Harriet Hanlon, typed and retyped and retyped again, with degrees of skill, care, and patience that no author should ever take for granted. And a wife, Sally Bennett Segall, despite the demands of her own career as teacher and writer, supported and endured this writer to a degree that no husband has a right to expect but that this husband most gratefully received. To all of these who helped in bringing the project to completion, I offer thanks.

Marshall H. Segall

Contents

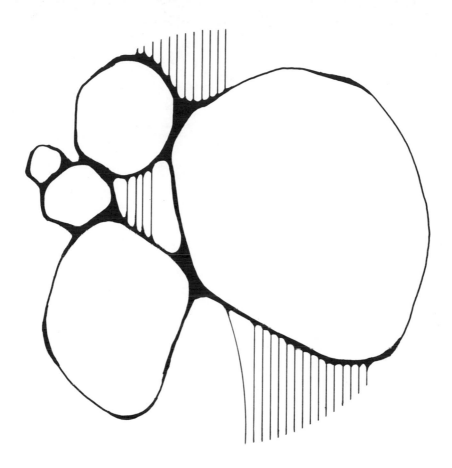

Introduction

Part One

One

The Sociocultural Nature of Human Beings

This book is an introduction to cross-cultural psychology. It aims to introduce you to the scientific study of human behavior, with particular concern for the ways in which that behavior is shaped and influenced by social and cultural forces. The central theme of the book is that human behavior is meaningful *only* when viewed in the sociocultural context in which it occurs. Chapter One introduces this theme by demonstrating that what is often called "human nature" must be viewed as a product of two classes of experience —socialization and enculturation. Without this starting point, one could not possibly understand either the uniformities or the diversities in the behavior patterns of the human animal.

It is beyond dispute that human beings are sociocultural animals. This is not to say, of course, that we are not, first of all, biological creatures. Rather, it is to call attention to what is perhaps the most striking biological fact about humans—namely, that evolution has produced a symbol-using, self-conscious creature, *Homo sapiens,* linked over time and space with all other members of the species. This connection extends to those who preceded or will follow in time and to contemporaries with whom direct contact is impossible. The emergence of language (in its full-blown form, a uniquely human phenomenon) has made possible numerous classes of behavior that no other animal displays. Language, and all that flows from it, is most responsible for what is unique about human behavior.

Behavior and Culture

The many forms of behavior that are distinctly human are also fundamentally social. They all involve to some degree (a) other people, (b) the behavior of other people, and (c) various products of the behavior of other people. These three classes of events affecting human behavior may be referred to as *social stimuli.* We call these categories stimuli because humans respond to them in one way or another. We call them social because they derive from other people.

Among the products of the behavior of other people to which you are probably responding at the moment is a room. This room has a particular shape that resulted from the application of architectural ideas and carpentry skills. The room you are in is most likely rectangular. As you well know, there are places in the world where the probability of your being in a rectangular room at any moment is very low. There are noncarpentered cultures, about which you will be reading as you progress through this book. Within the room, you are probably in a semireclining position that has to do a lot with the fact that a long time ago some other people built objects that we call chairs. To a certain extent, then, your behavior at the moment is in response to that invention. Again, there are parts of the world where the probability of your being in that position would be much lower. There are cultures without chairs.

There are also cultures without classrooms. The fact that you spend time in classrooms, facing persons called teachers (while you think of yourself as a student), also has something to do with another kind of product of individuals who preceded us. For some of the most important kinds of individual creations are institutions. In our culture there is one known as education. This institution has all sorts of aspects, including school buildings and the notion that you go to school from September to May, as well as traditional criteria for evaluation and certification. And the institution provides a whole series of behavioral expectations for all who are a part of it—a series of roles that are to be played. Included in the institution are certain privileges that apply to "teachers" and certain responsibilities that "students" have to shoulder, and vice versa. These, too, are products of the behavior of other people.

A very great deal of our lives as human beings, then, is composed of responses to these kinds of stimuli. Such behavior is social behavior, and it is uniquely human.

Language underlies the uniqueness of human social behavior, because language has permitted the appearance of culture, which is humankind's unique accomplishment in the animal kingdom. The fact is all the more striking in the light of research on communication and intergenerational transmission of learned behaviors in certain primates. What this research underscores is the rudimentary nature of those processes in such close relatives of the human. Clearly, then, how the human animal has created and continues to create cultures is a fit and critically important object for study. So is the manner in which culture, in turn, creates the human animal. Social psychology concerns itself with both of these overarching questions.

To the cross-cultural psychologist, cultures (and the societies they reflect) are seen both as *products* of human behavior and as *shapers* of human behavior. What the human has produced are social environments that continually serve to bring about continuities and changes in life-styles over time and uniformities and diversities in life-styles over space. How the human modifies culture and how various cultures modify the human is what cross-cultural psychology is all about. To all who would understand human behavior, to those who would predict it, and certainly to those who would seek consciously to control or modify it, knowledge of the network of interrelationships between culture and behavior is essential.

In these first few paragraphs we have come close to taking a stand on the question of human nature. It is well to take that stand explicitly.

Human Nature

It is the nature of humans to be socially docile, by which I mean responsive to socioculturally mediated reinforcements. By reinforcements I mean those events that occur after you have made a response and that either strengthen or weaken the response. By socioculturally mediated reinforcements I mean those reinforcements dispensed by other people or otherwise stemming from the behavior of other people.

Consider for a moment the typical college classroom, with 50 or so persons in the room, one of whom does most of the talking. How does it happen that 49 articulate persons spend so much time listening? The typical student has been through a very long reinforcement history in which he or she has learned numerous behavior patterns or role expectations that have to do with being in school. These patterns clearly are customs, and as such they are the product of social learning—the end result of a long reinforcement history in which students were taught to behave like students.

Thus it is the nature of humans to acquire their most significant behaviors through learning. What is to be learned is influenced mightily by social and cultural forces. The details of all of this are what will fill the pages of this book; so, for the present, it is merely asserted. The documentation will be overwhelming, but it will come later. The assertion is made baldly here so that it can be contrasted with a centuries-old, rather tenacious, and completely useless concept—Human Nature, with capital H and N.

A Simple Explanation

In one form or another, Human Nature—taken to mean a set of universally shared, unlearned tendencies, or instincts—has been evoked to "explain" almost every aspect of human behavior that any observer ever considered noteworthy. Among the revered Greek philosophers, Aristotle attributed the very existence of societies to humans' natural instinct to affiliate. Note that this Aristotelian notion may be reduced to "Humans affiliate because they have an instinct to affiliate." In a similar vein centuries later, Adam Smith (1759) pointed to altruism as one of several intrinsic qualities of humans. He assigned it causal status in our observed propensity to cooperate (sometimes) with our fellows: "How selfish soever man may be supposed, there are evidently some principles *in his nature* which interest him in the fortunes of others, and render their happiness necessary to him" (p. 1; italics mine).

Speculation about the nature of humans was central to most prescientific social theorizing, and it continues to the present. But the very notion that there is a distinctly Human Nature and that its specific, unlearned characteristics can be explicated must not go unexamined. Indeed, the way the concept has been used to *explain* behavior can easily be shown to be misleading.

The unsophisticated layperson may invoke Human Nature to explain particular actions. Consider a report of an embezzlement by a bank teller. It is not uncommon for such a report to be explained by the comment that the temptation to take money when so much is handled regularly is just "Human Nature." The frequently observed tendency for people to desire intensely that which is tabooed is also a favorite popular example of Human Nature. But a desire to please authority figures has also been attributed to that same Human Nature. It must be clear that, if a concept explains everything, it must in fact explain nothing!

Instinct Theories

For a time in social-psychological theorizing, the Human Nature line of argument, albeit in a relatively sophisticated form, was dominant. Next to Gabriel Tarde's famous use of humans' tendency to imitate as the "explanation" for social life, the most important modern effort of this kind was that of William McDougall. In his pioneering social-psychology textbook McDougall (1908) argued that instincts are the basis of human behavior. Among the instincts he cited were curiosity, self-assertion, submission, food seeking, mating, acquisitiveness, flight, repulsion, and parental feeling.

Writers after McDougall either added to or subtracted from his list, offering their own inventories in its place. In recent years instinct theorists have told us about such supposedly important, unlearned phenomena as the territorial imperative (Ardrey, 1966) and aggression (Lorenz, 1963). In every such claim the formula is all too simple. Detect a behavioral tendency that appears to be universal, give it a name, invent an instinct that bears that name, and consider the behavior explained.

The first difficulty with such a formula is its logical circularity. One who invokes such a formula necessarily commits the nominal fallacy: the phenomenon is named, and its name is considered to be its explanation. Ponder, for example, the empty statement that a bird flies because it has a flying instinct. It is equally unhelpful to state that mothers protect their children because they have a maternal instinct or that humans create societies because they have an instinct to create societies.

The second difficulty with such pseudoexplanations is that the behaviors to which instincts have so often been attached have seldom been demonstrated to be universal behaviors, although the instinct doctrine itself demands that they must be. Every mother who abandons her children, whatever else we may feel compelled to call her, is an embarrassment to the instinct theorist. So is every war resister a burden to those who contend that all people instinctively rise to the defense of their homeland. To explain such "exceptions," of course, the instinct theorist need only invent new instincts. Not surprisingly, instinct theorists did just that, thereby compounding their original error.

A Critique of Instinct Theories

A most scholarly critique of instinct theorizing has been provided by the experimental psychologist Beach (1955). In it, he considered why it is that "the instinct concept has survived in almost complete absence of empirical validation" (p. 401). The concept is, of course, older than social science. Its roots lie in ancient philosophy and theology. Given the Western theologian's idea of a life after death—an idea that required the postulation of a human soul and that led to a classification system in which humans were set apart from animals—the concept of instinct *had* to be invented. The concept, as it was first used, applied only to animal behavior and was considered its key, just as the rational soul was the key to human behavior. If animals had no soul, then *only* instinct could explain their behavior, which bore so many superficial similarities to human behavior. By attributing instinct to animals and rationality to human beings, the theologian was able to establish humans' unique link with their God and simultaneously assert the rationality of both humans and their God. If God were rational, so must people be rational, and vice versa. In the Judeo-Christian tradition—as in many, if not all, other religions—God and humans were created in each other's image. To keep people close to their supernatural God and apart from animals, the behavior of the latter alone was attributed to their natural instincts. Instinct, then, was originally a rather negative concept, invented almost by a process of elimination.

With the advent of Darwinian insights in biology, the traditional human/animal dichotomy was destroyed. The oft-detected similarities in the behavior of animals and humans were no longer dismissed as merely superficial. Rationality, at least interpreted as a capacity to learn and to adapt, was shown to be shared by humans and other animals. Unfortunately, the Darwinian revolution did not destroy the concept of instinct in the course of destroying the artificial boundary between humanity and animals. Instead, while correctly pointing to humanlike phenomena at many levels of animal behavior, the early post-Darwinians also moved in the opposite direction. They uncritically adopted the instinct notion to explain, in wholesale fashion, great chunks of *human* behavior.

This error was never more obvious than in McDougall's textbook, in which literally dozens of instincts were invented. It was perhaps inevitable that the generation of psychologists who came after McDougall reacted violently against the doctrine of instinct. In the 1920s and 1930s it became fashionable in American psychology to take the position that no behavior as actually performed by *any* animal could be instinctive. This reaction was, according to Beach (1955), a relatively ineffective polemic. It was not based on empirical findings. In denying a role to unlearned patterns of behavior, this line of argument not only may have been incorrect; it also inadvertently perpetuated an unfortunate distinction between heredity and learning and fed fuel to arguments in which "nature" and "nurture" were treated as competing explanations for behavior. In Beach's words, "The implication that all behavior must be determined by learning *or* by heredity, neither of which is more than partially understood, is entirely unjustified. ... The final form of any response is affected by a multiplicity of variables, only two of which are genetical and experiential factors" (1955, p. 405). Beach went on to predict that the concept of instinct would gradually disappear from scientific, if not from popular, attempts to explain and understand behavior.

This is not to say that anyone denies that behavior at any level of the phylogenetic scale is in part a function of a multitude of inherited tendencies. Simultaneously, however, all behavior is shaped by experience, plus numerous other factors that happen to be present in the environment of a behaving organism. All behavior, then, is a product of a complex interaction involving genetic and experiential factors, with both present and past experience weighted heavily in its ultimate determination.

There are also, of course, many reflexive responses at the human level as well as in the behavior of other animals. These responses are mediated by lower centers of the nervous system in a relatively simple way. One of their distinguishing features is considerable stereotypy, or sameness. At the human level, however, such responses account for an infinitesimally small proportion of the total behavioral repertory. Most of human behavior involves the participation of the highest brain centers, notably the cortex. The result is that human responses, even when fundamentally reflexive, lack the characteristic stereotypy of a reflex. For example, sexual behavior, which surely involves reflexive reactions in mouse and human alike, becomes almost bewilderingly convoluted among human beings, whose cortical functions incessantly interact with their glandular secretions.

Human mating behavior can hardly be described as reflexive. Partner preferences are a key feature of human sexual behavior. The bases of these preferences differ widely within societies, across societies, and over time. Our sexual behavior is affected by many rules, standards, values, and laws, with all of these controlling factors in a continuous process of change. This observation, among many others that one could make about learned modification of reflex-based behavior, suggests that we need an answer to the question of the nature of human beings that is very different from that provided by the instinct theorists.

Sociobiology's Perspective

Modern biologists concerned with human behavior have revived interest in genetically based behavioral potentials. Primatologists, especially, have called attention to numerous similarities between the behaviors of various monkeys and apes and those of humans, similarities that are consistent with the view that much of human behavior is rooted in evolutionary developments over millennia. Much of the behavior that has been studied by modern students of sociobiology (see, for example, Wilson, 1975) is basic social behavior, such as courtship and mating, child rearing, dominance and submission interactions, and the like. Some controversy surrounds sociobiology, especially when its findings are applied to very complex social issues. An example is the question of causes of behavioral differences between human males and females (an issue that will be discussed in Chapter Six). And, even in more cautious applications of some of its findings, sociobiology appears to some to have resurrected the old, discredited instinct doctrine. That is an incorrect perception. Rather, sociobiology underscores the continuity of development of biologically related creatures while recognizing the fact that little (or even none) of the behaviors that characterize humans can be attributed solely to biological predispositions. To the sociobiologists, those behaviors are consistent with biological limits but not unaffected by learning.

As the distinguished student of primate behavior S. L. Washburn recently put it:

> I would be the first to agree that the full understanding of the behavior patterns of any species must include biology. But the more that learning is involved, the less there will be of any simple relation between basic biology and behavior. The laws of genetics are not the laws of learning. As a result of intelligence and speech, human beings provide the extreme example of highly varied behavior that is learned and executed by the same fundamental biology. Biology determines the basic need for food, but not the innumerable ways in which this need may be met.
>
> Out of the present controversy, which, on a positive level, has stimulated

renewed interest in human and animal behavior, a new interdisciplinary biologically and socially based behavioral science may emerge. But in applying biological thinking we must take care not to ignore history, sociology, and comparative studies. For if we do, we will be condemned to repeat the scientific errors of the past [1978, p. 75].

A Balanced Approach

Therefore, the preferred answer to the question of our nature as human beings is that we are both sociocultural and animal. Like all other animals, we are first of all biological creatures. We have certain vital needs, and we are structured in such a way that these needs can be fulfilled with some minimum of effort. Before anything else, our behavior must be functional in the sense that it answers those needs. It must enhance our ability to survive in a natural environment. But these survival needs are few in number. The essential ones include oxygen, water, food, rest, elimination of waste products, and, for a time, some kind or kinds of sexual outlet. Our behavioral repertory for fulfilling these needs includes reflexes, which are simple, unlearned, inevitable reactions to specific stimuli, such as sneezing when irritated by dust or pollen. In the actual fulfillment of these needs, however, and in the pursuit of a far more numerous set of unessential, but equally compelling, goals, we hardly behave exclusively by exercising our reflexes. Our sociocultural nature derives from the most highly developed capacity in the entire animal kingdom for behavior to be modified in response to the lessons of experience. Even the manner in which a person drinks, eats, or sleeps reflects to some degree his or her experience in a particular social context.

Thus, as was asserted at the outset of this discussion of human nature, the human being is docile, or, in the original sense of that term, capable of learning. No other animal has this capacity to the same extent that we do. No other animal learns as much as the human or behaves in so many ways that demonstrate the flexibility that this ability to learn makes possible. As a result, we display many forms of behavior that are uniquely human, many of which are part of what we call culture. To attribute human behavior to instinct is to ignore this docility.

The Concept of Habit

If instinct is an unsatisfactory concept, the notion of habit serves us well. If we think of a person as an animal who accumulates habits throughout life, continuously modifying behavior in response to environmental pressures, both natural and manufactured, we are very close to the essence of the human potential.

Early treatments of the habit concept in psychology are to be found in the works of the great philosophers/psychologists who helped found the discipline near the turn of the century in the new American universities. Most notable among these scholars were William James and John Dewey. Both stressed that the human is a creature of habit. Dewey (1896) in particular argued that habits, or learned stimulus-response connections, could account better for behavior than could instincts.

The sociologist George Herbert Mead, a contemporary of Dewey at the University of Chicago during the early years of this century, interpreted human conduct as essentially rational, active, adaptive, and, thus, based to a very great extent on learning. In one of his most provocative contributions, Mead (1934) analyzed the very development of a sense of self as a social product. He constructed a theory that the individual, from the very beginning of socialization, becomes aware of others' responses and that this awareness is the basis of the ego's own evolving conception of itself. In a sense, then, people view themselves as whatever others seem to believe them to be. Mead's idea illustrates how social psychologists after McDougall came to recognize the importance of learning in human life, particularly social learning. In Mead's contribution, even so personal a thing as a self-concept is treated as a product of social learning.

Behaviorism and the Primacy of Learning

By the 1920s behaviorism had established itself as the dominant approach in American psychology. As a result, more attention was directed toward the learning process. A major theme of behaviorism from Watson (1925) onward was that overt behavior takes the particular forms it does because the behaving organism has learned to behave the way it does.

This central tenet of early behaviorism would have remained a simple assertion had it not been that it was so obviously testable. And it was, indeed, put to the test. Literally thousands of experiments demonstrated that behavior can be modified by varying stimulus conditions. In any experiment in which humans acquire new responses or recombine old ones to meet changing environmental conditions, learning is said to have occurred. And from the early days of behaviorism onward, learning has been shown to be involved in the acquisition of all kinds of behaviors, from simple "emotional" responses such as fear on through to complex ideological responses such as attitudes.

The many and fruitless attacks and counterattacks over behaviorism as a philosophy of the science of psychology can be ignored here. Instead, we should acknowledge the behaviorists' concern with the learning process as the most productive approach available to the study of human behavior. I share the view on this subject derived from the tradition established by James, Dewey, Watson, and others. It was developed subsequently by various learning theorists, beginning with Thorndike (1913) and Pavlov (1927), and was refined by such psychologists as Bandura (1969) and Skinner (1974). This view holds that human behavior can best be understood as the product of learning, particularly learning that results from experiences with other people or with ideas, institutions, or other products of the behavior of other people.

Becker: Agreement from Another Quarter

Writing in a very different intellectual tradition from behaviorism, the psychoanalytically oriented anthropologist Ernest Becker (1973) has come to similar conclusions. In his remarkable book *The Denial of Death,* Becker also emphasizes social learning as responsible for most of the unique features of human behavior. His analysis has a very different beginning from mine, but it results in a very similar stand on the question of Human Nature.

Becker built on the ideas of numerous psychoanalysts and philosophers, but especially Rank (1931/1961, 1941/1958), Kierkegaard (1844/1957, 1849/1954), and Brown (1959). He asserted that human beings' ability—obviously mediated by language—to contemplate and fear their own death propels them to deny their mortality, to run from their animalness, and to invent ways to make themselves appear meaningful to themselves and others. Stating it poetically, each of us strives to be a *hero*. To Becker, society is a "codified hero system, . . . a living myth of the significance of human life" (1973, p. 7).* Because we are both animal and symbol user, our terror of death moves us to create institutions, both religious and secular (to Becker, "every society is a religion" [p. 7]), that allow us to repress the unavoidable fact of our impending death. "All culture, all man's creative life ways, are in some basic part of them a fabricated protest against natural reality, a denial of the truth of the human condition, and an attempt to forget the pathetic creature that Man is" (Becker, 1973, p. 33).

Because humans have language, they can give names to experiences and can manufacture and manipulate symbols. They can transmit, receive, and process information, not only about the here and now but also about the there and then. They can even contemplate the merely possible. Using these tools of language, humans become conscious of self and others and aware of their mortality. They come to realize their dependence on others and their need to relate to others in order to live a meaningful existence. Because people start life as helpless, dependent animals, they must learn from others the meaning-imposing myths of human existence. They learn those behaviors that others before them have invented to make them seem more god-like than animal-like. Each personality—or, as Becker terms it, "the lie of character"—is "built up because the child needs to adjust to the world, to the parents, and to his own existential dilemmas" (p. 73).

Thus, propelled by the anxiety of impending death, an anxiety that only a linguistic creature can possess, the human permits self-shaping largely in terms of the image of parents and peers. Whereas prelinguistic children may be in some sense aware of their animalness, their developing humanness involves, in Becker's terms, a "fall from natural perception into the artificialities of the cultural world" (p. 65).

However artificial it may be, culture is what gives meaning to human life,

*This and all other quotations from this source are from *The Denial of Death*, by E. Becker. Copyright 1973 by Macmillan Publishing Company, Inc. Reprinted by permission.

and it is only in culture that we find the forces that shape human nature. Whether or not Becker was correct in his overall view of culture, he succeeded in demonstrating the futility of explaining human behavior as the outward manifestation of instincts. Becker's point of view is compatible with and indeed underscores the need to recognize culturally mediated learning as the process that sets humans apart from their fellow animals. In short, it is the unique nature of humans to be conscious and wary of their animalness and to learn to live as if they were not animals. To live *as* human, man acquires a socially conditioned identity that allows him to "feel that he *controls* his life and his death, that he really does live and act as a willful and free individual, . . . that he is somebody" (Becker, 1973, p. 55).

Human Nature, conceptualized as a set of instincts, is a seriously misleading concept. It is the nature of humans as sociocultural creatures to learn to behave in ways that their predecessors have found useful as defenses against despair, as Becker saw it, and in ways that enhance their existence.

Observing the apparently successful responses of others is one of the most potent of the experiences that lead to learning. Learning from their fellows is what people do best of all—not always, of course, to good effect. But do it we must. Non-symbol-using animals depend less on learning, for they are programmed with behavioral propensities that serve them well. So equipped, they are probably spared the anxieties we derive from the ability to anticipate our own demise. But if we pay a price for our symbol-using ability, what has been purchased is an awesome range of behavioral potential.

Still another way to express the social psychologist's view of humans is to describe them as both culture's creators and culture's creations. As the creation of culture, each human personality is the product of the allied processes of socialization and enculturation.

Socialization and Enculturation

From birth onward, every human being learns to accommodate his or her behavior to that of others. This is the essence of the statement that the human is a social animal. What every person becomes is determined by both biological and social factors, coacting in a complex fashion.

All social animals, including the human, are subject to socialization. We alone are also subject to enculturation. Both of these processes must be understood if we are to have even the most fundamental appreciation of the whys of human behavior.

Socialization

Child (1954) has offered a definition of socialization that underlines our biosocial nature. He described it as "the whole process by which an individual, born with behavioral potentialities of enormously wide range, is led to develop actual behavior which is confined within a much narrower range—the range of what is customary and acceptable for him according to the standards of his group" (p. 655).

This definition has the virtue of reminding us that all humans are capable of a far greater repertory of behaviors than any single person ever exhibits. Each of us, because of the accident of birth, begins life in a particular social context, within which we learn to make certain responses and not others. The most dramatic illustration of this is our linguistic behavior. That one speaks English rather than Russian, even though all languages are possible, aptly demonstrates this fact. Less obviously, socialization also effectively narrows the range of responses each of us habitually makes in many other behavioral domains. The conditions under which we express emotions, and the ways in which we suppress them, are determined by socialization. Our reactions to authority figures, and their reactions to us, reflect the customs of the society into which we happened to be born. Many, if not all, of the behavioral differences that for centuries were attributed to "temperament," such as British coolness and Latin abandon, are attributable to the differential reinforcement of certain responses and the effective elimination of others.

Socialization increases the probability of certain responses in a variety of ways. All of them involve other persons, who for present purposes can be termed *socialization agents*. Any other person who possesses power relative to the individual being socialized can function as a socialization agent. Most often these include parents, teachers, and other elders, who are more knowledgeable in the ways of their society. Under certain circumstances, however, even peers can effect socialization. Whoever can present or withhold reinforcement can socialize.

Whenever interaction with another person results in the shaping or selection of a response that is socially approved, socialization is occurring. Typically, it involves rewarding approved behavior and punishing unwanted behavior. Equally important, although less obvious, is the nonreinforcement of unwanted behavior. This, too, serves to lessen the probability of future occurrences of socially disapproved responses.

The process of socialization often involves conflict between the individual and one or more socialization agents. Not only are some of the individual's responses likely to be punished, some may be blocked by the behavior of others in very subtle, but effective, ways. For example, socialization agents may function effectively by withdrawing opportunities to perform certain responses except at a time and place they consider appropriate. The socialization of feeding behavior during infancy involves this subtle control mechanism to a very great extent.

All examples of socialization have in common the efforts by others to control the behavior of the individual. Socialization, then, consists primarily of deliberate tutelage, with heavy doses of reward and punishment, applied in an effort to produce "acceptable" behavior.

If socialization were not enough to have the impact Child's definition foresees (the narrowing down of behavioral realities as compared with each person's behavioral potential), there is in human life the additional process of enculturation. This process is less direct, but no less effective, than socialization.

Enculturation

Much of what every person learns about the ways of his or her society is learned without interpersonal conflict. When a child struggles with an older sibling, socialization is probably occurring, but what is struggled over and how the struggle is carried on probably reflect enculturation. First employed by Herskovits (1948, pp. 39–42; 1955, pp. 326–329), this term refers to all of the learning that occurs in human life because of the limitations in each society on what is available to be learned. What the child learns to be worth struggling for must be part of the cultural content of his or her society. The manner in which the child expresses a desire for it will be determined by prevalent attitudes toward the expression of desire. The child will learn these as much by emulating others as by being taught deliberately by others. In the latter case, socialization is at work; in the former, the more subtle process of enculturation. Whenever we learn by observation, even in a relatively unconscious way, any part of the content of our society—content that has been culturally shaped and limited during preceding generations—enculturation is occurring.

Although all human beings are enculturated, with the effects obvious to the social scientist, the enculturated individuals are usually unaware of how much of what they do reflects the process. No person is likely to be aware of how much he or she has learned from a society without knowing what was unavailable in the society to be learned. This leads to the apparent paradox that persons who are most thoroughly enculturated are often the least aware of their culture's role in moulding them.

Much of what people learn about their society is learned without direct, deliberate teaching. We all learn particular ideas, concepts, and values, simply because of the differential availability of ideas *to be* learned. We learn, for example, what is music and what is noise. What people learn to identify as music depends primarily on what is there, previously labeled as music, to be learned. Similarly, in every society a high percentage of the people would agree on what is worth fighting for, and not because there is a course in the curriculum on "supreme causes." Instead, such values are widely transmitted, both directly and indirectly, and are learned very well because they are hardly ever questioned.

Much of the actual learning we do involves both socialization and enculturation. Learning a language, for example, can be talked about with both of these concepts. There is a certain amount of direct teaching of the language, as in grammar courses in elementary school. But a lot of the learning of language occurs (apparently) spontaneously, by children who must assume that there is only one language to be learned.

Both processes, socialization and enculturation, result in behavioral similarities within societies and behavioral differences across societies. Both processes involve learning from other people how to behave. In the case of socialization, the learning involves teaching. In the case of enculturation, teaching is not a necessary feature but learning is. Clearly, then, the key to understanding the nature of human behavior is that human beings are the learners par excellence of the animal kingdom. And, since most of what is learned is contained in culture and made available by others, we may take as the beginning point of our exploration of human behavior the premise that human behavior is meaningful only when examined in the sociocultural context.

Social Psychology

One of the pioneers of social psychology in the United States, Floyd Allport, once defined the discipline as "a part of the psychology of the individual, whose behavior it studies in relation to that sector of his environment comprised by his fellows" (1924, p. 4). Some years later, in an introductory textbook on experimental psychology, Keller and Schoenfeld (1950) echoed Allport's statement that social psychology is a part of general psychology in that it deals with social stimuli, which they view as a subclass of all stimuli. An implication of this definition is that there must be much about human behavior that is nonsocial in nature. But further consideration of the concept of social stimulus shows that this is hardly the case.

At this moment you are probably in a room designed, built, and furnished by others of your own species. You are probably clothed in garments of human design and production, however frivolous, which you chose to wear in response to certain social pressures, however nonconformist you believe yourself to be. Indeed, very little in your environment at this moment, or at any other moment, is composed of nonsocial stimuli.

Moreover, even when naturally produced physical stimuli impinge upon you, your relevant behavior is in part determined by simultaneously present social stimuli. Consider a source of light energy reaching the light-sensitive receptors of your eye. This light is clearly a nonsocial stimulus. But your response to it would probably include recognizing its characteristic color. In other words, you would name it and, in a limited sense, "detect" its meaning. The meaning is not inherent in the physical stimulus itself, of course. In fact, your attribution of meaning to the stimulus is a response to the behavior of others. "Others," in this case, are those members of your linguistic community who, ages ago, rather arbitrarily divided the visual spectrum and designated its various parts with labels such as red, fuchsia, and scarlet.

Indeed, it is very difficult to think of examples of human behavior that occur in response to nonsocial stimuli in a pure and simple fashion. Human behavior is almost completely social. Examples of behavior in response to purely physical stimuli, and not at least mediated by social stimuli, are hard to find.

All human behavior, then, that occurs in response to stimuli created by other people, their behavior, or the products of their behavior is the province of the social psychologist. With this in mind, you might wonder if there is any psychology of human behavior that is not, strictly speaking, social psychology. Good.

The Concept of Culture as a Behavioral Determinant

We have thus far stressed that human behavior occurs in a sociocultural context, with most of it being influenced by social stimuli. We must next consider the nature of culture.

Culture is the key concept of anthropology. Like many key concepts (for example, *energy* in physics or *group* in sociology) culture is variously and often ambiguously defined, yet it is used as if its meaning were clear. One anthropologist, White (1947), points to culture as something added to all other forces producing behavior at the human level. As he uses the term, culture denotes all the symbolic behavior, especially language, that makes possible the transmission of wisdom, in the form of techniques for coping with the environment, from generation to generation. Thus, as White sees it, culture is continuous, cumulative, and progressive.

Unfortunately, White's stress on the "extra-somatic character" of culture makes it appear to be a somewhat free-floating, mystical concept. This need not be the case. Moore and Lewis (1952), in a joint philosophical and psychological exercise, culled from diverse anthropological writings what they considered to be the essence of the concept and emerged with a very straightforward account. To them, culture is first of all an abstraction, in the sense that it is merely a convenient label for a very large category of phenomena. It designates knowledge, skills, and information that are learned. More particularly, it refers to that which is learned because it is inculcated. Further, it is social knowledge, in the sense that it is taught to and learned by many individuals and is thus shared. Since it tends to persist over generations, it is more or less adaptive. Finally, it tends to be integrated; that is to say, its contents tend to be mutually reinforcing.

Given these characteristics of culture, it becomes possible to define it simply as the totality of whatever all persons learn from all other persons. Anything one person learns from another, then, is an element of culture, and it is recognized as such to the extent that it is adaptive and persistent over generations.

Following Moore and Lewis, we would note that culture includes language, music, and art forms. It includes preferences, appetites, and aversions. It includes rules, norms, and standards. It includes hopes and fears, beliefs and attitudes, convictions and doubts, at least to the extent that such are shared, inculcated, and transmitted from people to people. To be considered a part of culture, anything, material or symbolic, need only be of human origin.

As Herskovits (1948, p. 17) so aptly put it, culture is the man-made part of the environment.

Culture is thus virtually synonymous with what we earlier designated as the products of the behavior of others. It is useful to retain the term culture, however, because it connotes a set of social stimuli that to a very great extent have existence prior to the individuals on whom they impinge. Put very simply, culture is already there for every individual as he or she begins life. It contains values that will be expressed and a language in which to express them. It contains a way of life that will be followed by most individuals, who through most of their lifetimes will unquestioningly assume that there is no better.

If anthropologists had not invented culture, then social psychologists probably would have. The concept of culture enables the psychologist to account for the fact that social stimuli do not impinge on an individual with equal probability in different places at different times. Some social stimuli are more probable than others. My children are extremely unlikely to greet me by prostrating themselves and kissing my feet. A Swiss peasant is unlikely to be passed on the street by a teenage girl in a miniskirt. A Ganda householder in his East African grass-thatched house is not likely to be confronted with a bowl of cornflakes for breakfast.

These last thoughts carry the important implication that culture and society are roughly coterminous. It is because every society has a culture that behavior patterns tend to be different from society to society. Here, then, is perhaps the best reason for focusing on the concept of culture. It helps to categorize and explain many important differences in human behavior that in the past were erroneously attributed to ill-defined biological differences.

In this introduction to the scientific study of human behavior we have learned that our subject matter can be understood only when viewed in its sociocultural context. Human behavior, we have found, is nearly always influenced by social stimuli. And many of those social stimuli are what we call culture. Thus, a study of human behavior that ignores culture does so at great risk. Accordingly, I will begin the next chapter with a demonstration of the riskiness of ignoring the sociocultural context of human behavior.

The Scope of This Book

Before I embark fully on this introduction to cross-cultural psychology, however, I should note the book's intent and limitations. I intend to range rather widely over this rapidly developing field of endeavor, but I will by no means cover it fully. Although I will review many studies from diverse sources, I will only sample from the many hundreds that are available. The sample I have chosen to present in the chapters that follow is composed of those studies that, for a variety of reasons, struck one cross-cultural psychologist—this writer—as representative and most useful for an introductory survey. Inevitably, biases entered into the sampling.

What is included adds up to a substantial body of material, perhaps more than enough for an introduction to cross-cultural psychology. But what is left out could easily have filled another textbook of this length, designed to serve the identical purpose. Readers of *this* book, then, should understand that from it they will have learned *about* cross-cultural psychology. They will not have been taught cross-cultural psychology in its entirety.

You should know not only that there are many nonreported studies pertaining to the topics discussed but also that there are whole topics, keenly pursued by cross-cultural psychologists, that are scarcely mentioned in this book. Chief among them is psychopathology. Much of the literature on the many forms that psychopathology takes in various cultures has been produced by specialists within the applied field that is coming to be known as transcultural psychiatry. That their work has been left out of this book reflects a somewhat arbitrary decision to limit the book to the study of "normal" behavior. The scholars I cite are predominantly social scientists—psychologists, anthropologists, sociologists, and, to a lesser extent, economists and political scientists—rather than scientists in the clinical, medical disciplines. But even an introductory student of cross-cultural psychology may wish to consult the transcultural psychiatric literature in order to round out his or her introductory knowledge of cultural influences on behavior.[1]

Armed with the introduction to the field that this book aims to provide, the student should be prepared to move on to more sophisticated sources, such as the chapters on linguistics, ethics, esthetics, and other topics, not discussed here, that will be contained in the forthcoming *Handbook of Cross-Cultural Psychology* (Triandis, 1979).

Knowing, then, that there is much more to cross-cultural psychology than can be covered in this introductory text, let us begin to learn about this rewarding approach to the study of human behavior. In the next chapter we will learn why this approach has come to attract so much attention in recent years.

---

[1]Many cross-cultural psychologists share with beginning students in psychology a concern for behavior that deviates from what is considered normal within any culture. What may surprise beginning students is a core finding by the cross-cultural researchers that both the "normal" and the "abnormal" are differently perceived, defined, explained, and treated in different societies. At the same time, despite such differences, there are some fundamental and provocative similarities. Among these are certain features of psychotherapy, whether provided by traditional, non-Western healers or Western-trained psychiatrists. To begin a study of cultural differences in abnormal behavior and its treatment, the student could profitably consult Draguns and Phillips (1972). This paper presents in highly readable form a very comprehensive set of ideas and facts concerning culture and psychopathology. The bibliography appended to the Draguns and Phillips paper provides guides to nearly all the relevant literature published through 1971. The forthcoming *Handbook of Cross-Cultural Psychology* (Triandis, 1979) will contain contributions by Juris Draguns, George Guthrie, Raymond Prince, and Victor Sanua, among others who are active contributors to this topic. Rather than provide here a sample of the major works in this large field of study, I urge the reader to discover them by consulting the few sources cited above.

References

Allport, F. H. *Social Psychology*. Boston: Houghton Mifflin, 1924.

Ardrey, R. *The Territorial Imperative*. New York: Atheneum, 1966.

Bandura, A. *Principles of Behavior Modification*. New York: Holt, Rinehart & Winston, 1969.

Beach, F. The descent of instinct. *Psychological Review*, 1955, *62*, 401–410.

Becker, E. *The Denial of Death*. New York: Free Press, 1973.

Brown, N. *Life against Death: The Psychoanalytical Meaning of History*. New York: Viking, 1959.

Child, I. L. Socialization. In G. Lindzey (Ed.), *Handbook of Social Psychology* (Vol. 2). Cambridge, Mass.: Addison-Wesley, 1954. Pp. 655–692.

Dewey, J. The reflex arc concept in psychology. *Psychological Review*, 1896, *3*, 357–370.

Draguns, J. G., & Phillips, L. *Culture and Psychopathology: The Quest for a Relationship*. Morristown, N.J.: General Learning Press, 1972.

Herskovits, M. J. *Man and His Works: The Science of Cultural Anthropology*. New York: Knopf, 1948.

Herskovits, M. J. *Cultural Anthropology*. New York: Knopf, 1955.

Keller, F., & Schoenfeld, W. N. *Principles of Behavior*. New York: Appleton-Century-Crofts, 1950.

Kierkegaard, S. *The Sickness unto Death* (W. Lowie, trans.). New York: Anchor, 1954. (Originally published, 1849.)

Kierkegaard, S. *The Concept of Dread* (W. Lowie, trans.). Princeton, N.J.: Princeton University Press, 1957. (Originally published, 1844.)

Lorenz, K. *On Aggression*. New York: Harcourt Brace Jovanovich, 1963.

McDougall, W. *Introduction to Social Psychology*. London: Methuen, 1908.

Mead, G. H. *Mind, Self and Society* (C. M. Morris, Ed.). Chicago: University of Chicago Press, 1934.

Moore, O. K., & Lewis, D. J. Learning theory and culture. *Psychological Review*, 1952, *59*, 380–388.

Pavlov, I. P. *Conditioned Reflexes* (G. V. Anrep, trans.). London: Oxford University Press, 1927.

Rank, O. *Beyond Psychology*. New York: Dover Books, 1958. (Originally published, 1941.)

Rank, O. *Psychology and the Soul*. New York: Perpetua Books, 1961. (Originally published, 1931.)

Skinner, B. F. *About Behaviorism*. New York: Knopf, 1974.

Smith, A. *The Theory of Moral Sentiments*. London: A. Miller, 1759.

Tarde, G. *The Laws of Imitation*. New York: Holt, 1903.

Thorndike, E. L. *Educational Psychology*. New York: Teachers College Press, 1913.

Triandis, H. C. (Ed.). *Handbook of Cross-Cultural Psychology*. Boston: Allyn & Bacon. Six volumes, projected for 1979 and later, including: Triandis, H. C., & Lambert, W. W., Vol. 1: *Perspectives*; Triandis, H. C., & Berry, J. W., Vol. 2: *Methodology*; Triandis, H. C., & Lonner, W., Vol. 3: *Basic Processes*; Triandis, H. C., & Heron, A., Vol. 4: *Developmental Psychology*; Triandis, H. C., & Brislin, R., Vol. 5: *Social Psychology*; and Triandis, H. C., & Draguns, J. G., Vol. 6: *Psychopathology*.

Washburn, S. L. What we can't learn about people from apes. *Human Nature*, 1978, *1*(11), 70–75.

Watson, J. B. *Behaviorism*. New York: Norton, 1925.

White, L. A. Culturological vs. psychological interpretations of human behavior. *American Sociological Review*, 1947, *12*, 686–698.

Wilson, E. O. *Sociobiology*. Cambridge, Mass.: Harvard University Press, 1975.

Two

The Cross-Cultural Perspective in Social Psychology: A Brief History

The Need for a Cross-Cultural Perspective

At this juncture in its short history, social psychology is a U.S.-dominated discipline. Most teachers and students of social psychology reside in U.S. universities. Most social psychology research is done in the United States, and most of the publications, journal articles, and books that report this research are produced there.

This is a matter of serious concern. The concern stems not from the fact of U.S. domination; it would be as serious if any other nation enjoyed a similar near monopoly. The problem is the culture-bound nature of the discipline. There is a very real danger that psychologists, by limiting their attention to the behaviors of individuals in a single culture (however complex that culture might be), lose sight altogether of culture itself. The scientist, no less than the most unsophisticated layperson who knows only his or her own society, becomes prey to ethnocentric judgments. Behaviors that may in fact be heavily influenced by cultural forces may appear to the psychologist to be manifestations of "Human Nature."

A Dream Exercise

To appreciate this point, you should proceed deliberately through the following intellectual exercise.[1] Imagine that you are a clinical psychologist, whose professional role is to help people who are troubled by their own behavior.

Into your office comes a 14-year-old boy, who, at your request, relates a dream he recalls as profoundly disturbing. In it, he and his father were traveling together on a bus toward the science and technology museum, where both the boy and his father anticipated wandering through the exhibits of machinery. Suddenly, the bus swerved on the wet pavement and crashed headlong into a tractor-trailer. Amid grinding metal and shattering glass, the passengers were helplessly tossed about into the flesh-tearing projections of the wreckage. As the twisted hulk came finally to rest, the boy, miraculously unharmed, searched about frantically for his father. Groping his way over mangled bodies, the boy finally came upon his father's body, sprawled and bloodied, his legs crushed, his eyes staring at the boy in a piercing, accusing gaze of death.

His dream told, the boy breaks into sobs and tells you how painful it is even to talk about the dream, how saddening it is to contemplate the loss of his beloved father.

Your Interpretation. What do you make of it? What might this dream tell you about the dreamer? What might it tell you about the psychology of adolescent boys?

Since you are a clinical psychologist, you will probably want to put together a few assumptions about human behavior and some ideas about human relations in general in an effort to develop an interpretation of this puzzling dream. To assist you in this process, here are some questions for you to ponder. If you know anything about Sigmund Freud, you are aware that he had a way of interpreting dreams. You may give answers that seem reasonable to you, whether or not they are answers that Freud might have given had he been in your position.

1. What psychological purpose might a dream—any dream—serve?

2. If a dream can reveal to the dreamer a wish or desire that the dreamer is not consciously aware of, what does the boy who reported this dream want to happen to his father?

[1]The exercise, prepared by the present author, is part of a learning package entitled "The Cross-Cultural Research Strategy in Psychology," issued by Learning Resources in International Studies (Copyright 1975 by the Consortium for International Studies Education of the International Studies Association).

3. Since the boy obviously loves his father, what else must he feel in order to wish to be rid of him?

4. Could the boy's simultaneous love and hate (a condition known as *ambivalence*) toward his father have anything to do with the boy's sex drive? If so, what?

5. *If* the sexual stirring of adolescence is involved, how does it relate to the boy's feelings toward his father?

6. Unspeakable as it may seem, might this sexual urge have something to do with the boy's mother (who wasn't even in the dream)? Might it also have something to do with the boy's perception of his father's relationship with her?

7. By the way, wasn't there in ancient Greek literature a story about a boy who loved his own mother and murdered his own father?

8. And isn't that story—a play, actually—still read and performed. And don't modern audiences react with profound emotion?

9. Might it not be, then, that this young man represents only a single instance of a universal human phenomenon? Isn't he typical of the adolescent male groping his way through a developmental stage? Doesn't every boy emerge from a preadult infatuation with his own mother and a jealous hatred for his own father, who seems to enjoy exclusively the sexual favors that the boy wants bestowed on himself?

You have by now probably recognized several things about the foregoing exercise. Firstly, the questions posed were rather rhetorical; that is, they were framed in a way designed to lead you down a predetermined path of interpretation. Secondly (and now we explicitly consider Freud), the path of interpretation was essentially the one that Freud himself followed, in late-19th-century Vienna, when he treated psychologically disturbed, upper-middle-class patients.

Freud's Interpretation. Confronted with a dream report similar to the one you have just analyzed—one in which an adolescent boy told of terrible things happening to his beloved father—Freud would probably have reasoned roughly as follows:

1. A dream is a wish-fulfilling mechanism. We all have wishes and desires that are difficult to confront openly. We suppress them, forcing them to reside in our unconscious. But they reveal themselves to us in indirect ways, including dreams, since our defenses are relaxed when we are asleep.

2. If the boy's dream revealed a subconscious wish, that wish must have been for his father to be obliterated, since the father's death was the critical incident in the dream and the source of greatest discomfort to the boy as he related the dream.

3. In the dream, or at least in its telling, there were numerous reminders that the boy loved his father. This suggests that the boy felt a strong need to assert that love, either because he actually loved his father less than he thought he should or hated him while simultaneously loving him. Since it was the boy's

own dream in which this terrible thing happened to his beloved father, the boy must feel ambivalent toward him, loving and hating him at the same time.

4. A boy's love for his father probably needs no ingenious effort at explanation. On the other hand, why the boy might feel hostile toward his father is a harder question. It must have something to do with the boy's perception of his father's behavior. But what? Boys' fathers in late-19th-century Viennese upper-middle-class society did many things. As a sociologist or social psychologist might say, boys' fathers in that setting performed many different roles. One role that might be particularly salient to adolescent boys, thought Freud, is the father's role as lover of the boy's mother. A big jump in the argument? Perhaps, but not altogether unreasonable. After all, . . .

5. Adolescent boys tend to feel strong and diffuse sexual urges as they approach manhood. As a result, they might well be exceedingly concerned with sexual matters. The boy's father is a significant male model who clearly has adult prerogatives, including—and especially—sexual ones. The boy might well, therefore, emulate his father and wish to be in his shoes, even in his bed. But . . .

6. The sex object in his father's bed is the boy's own mother! She is, properly, the sexual partner of the father, not of the boy. The boy seems to desire his own mother as a sex object. (After all, she was the first and most significant female in his life and was, from the start, warm, loving, and nurturant.) His desire for her necessarily leads to the felt need to be rid of his father, in order that the father be displaced by the boy as mother's lover. Besides, . . .

7. Western literature contains stories like the powerful play about Oedipus, who killed his father and married his mother. That such stories are retold and reacted to by generation after generation of audiences suggests that the mother-son-father triangle comprises a timeless and universal set of feelings, such that . . .

8. All males probably go through a psychosexual development that involves falling in love with mother and developing jealousy toward father, with the emergence of a hostile wish to destroy and displace him. This developmental process might appropriately be labeled, given the well-known Greek play, the *Oedipus complex.*

Thus might Freud have reasoned. The boy's dream may be understood as an expression of his unresolved Oedipus complex. The dream is understandable as a revelation of the dreamer's suppressed hatred for his simultaneously beloved father, with the hatred based on sexual jealousy of the father as mother's lover.

Quite plausible and persuasive, isn't it? There are only a few assumptions in the argument, and it does hold together well. Certainly, several generations of psychologists and other intelligent and educated persons have found Freud's line of argument very acceptable. Some people are so profoundly persuaded by it that they even speak of Freud's *discovery* of the Oedipus complex, rather than describing it as an invention, which of course it is.

By calling the Oedipus complex a discovery, one implies that it was there for Freud to stumble onto. It should, however, be clear to you that Freud created the Oedipus complex as an explanatory *concept*, in much the same way that you may have invented a similar concept when you worked your way through the dream-interpretation exercise a few pages ago.

The problem we must now deal with is *why* Freud—and perhaps you —invented the concept he did. Why didn't you both invent a different concept?

Might Freud—and you—not have come up with a different explanation because he—and you—did the psychologizing solely within the confines of a single cultural setting? Did it matter that the data you considered were limited to individuals and events characteristic of Western society? Let's see how that might very well be so.

A Different Dreamer. What would you say if you were now confronted with an adolescent boy from a faraway island culture, who reported to you a dream in which his *uncle*, with whom he was hunting, stumbled on his spear and was disemboweled? Does the theory that Freud developed fit such a dream? Or does this dream force you to search for an alternative theory that would fit both dreams?

At this point, before reading any further, you should try to construct an alternative explanation for both dreams. Your new theory should account for hostility toward father in one case and hostility toward uncle in the other.

Malinowski's Contribution. One such theory can be derived from some interesting observations that were part of an eminent anthropologist's fieldwork in the 1920s. Malinowski (1927) had read Freud's interpretation of male adolescents' ambivalence toward their fathers. Armed with that knowledge, Malinowski collected dream reports from adolescent boys in the Trobriand Islands, where disciplining of boys is the responsibility of the boys' maternal uncles (mothers' brothers). (This is a cultural feature of societies known to anthropology as *avuncular*, so-called because of the importance of uncles in the kinship and socialization systems.) In the Trobriand Islands Malinowski found *no* instance of nightmares in which fathers suffered but several in which misfortunes befell uncles. The second dream you analyzed could well have been dreamed by a Trobriand Island boy. You must have noted that it was similar in content to the dream you analyzed earlier, except that in the Trobriand dream the accident victim is the dreamer's uncle. What did you make of this second dream? You could have gotten through the first three steps of the original Freudian argument without a hitch. Thus, you could have argued:

1. The dream reveals a suppressed wish
2. to be rid of the uncle, so
3. the boy must feel hostile toward his uncle.

But then you would have to wonder why a boy might feel hostile toward his uncle. Not being the boy's mother's lover, the uncle could not possibly be the object of the boy's sexual jealousy. So you had here to depart from the earlier theory.

The clue you are seeking may be found in the fact that the Trobriand Island society is an avuncular society (note that this word has the same root as *uncle*), a society in which boys' fathers are mothers' lovers but boys' uncles are the boys' *disciplinarians*. Could it be that adolescent boys anywhere wish terrible things would happen to their disciplinarians, who are fathers in many societies and uncles in a few?

Your revised argument would then be that both dreamers were reacting to whoever plays the adult male role of disciplinarian. We would end up with an efficient, four-step argument (compared with the much longer original one) that fits the dreams from both societies. Our new theory, in summary, would be:

1. The dreams reveal a suppressed desire
2. to be rid of a powerful, male, adult figure
3. toward whom the dreamer feels hostile,
4. because the male adult figure has and uses the power to enforce his will on the dreamer, to administer sanctions, and otherwise to control his behavior.

This revised theory, which is very parsimonious (a characteristic of a theory that handles multiple facts and makes few assumptions), accounts for both dreams. It fits two sets of facts, two different dream reports that originated in two different cultures.

The Underlying Principle

This brings us to the essential point of the exercise, which is a principle about the strategy of research, not a substantive point about the meaning of dreams. In other words, we are not primarily interested here in learning how to understand dreams. We are interested in the process by which psychologists try to comprehend the meaning of any behavior, including dream reports.

To illuminate that process and uncover the principle about research strategy that we are seeking, let us consider what Freud did when he invented the Oedipus complex. Recall that the critical problem for Freud was to explain a Viennese boy's hostility toward his father. In seeking an explanation for that, Freud focused on the fact that (most) boys' fathers were (often) the boys' mothers' lovers. But it was also true that in that same setting, as well as in some others, fathers were their sons' disciplinarians. (Indeed, there is some reason to speculate that Viennese fathers tended to be more diligent in the role of disciplinarian than in that of mother's lover!) In any event, for our present purposes the essential fact is that, in Vienna, *both* roles were performed by the same person—the boy's father. A technical way to state this fact is to say that the two roles were *confounded*, or inextricably linked.

Freud chose to ignore one of these confounded roles—that of disciplinarian—and he chose to focus on the other—that of mother's lover. Had
Freud chosen instead to focus on the disciplinary role of the father, he
probably would have come up with our second explanation of adolescents'
suppressed hostility. But even if he had, ambiguity would still have prevailed.
Let us see why.

Suppose Freud had suggested that adolescent boys hate their fathers
because their fathers punish them. Couldn't we then have challenged Freud and
said, for example, "Now, wait a minute. You've overlooked the far more
interesting possibility that fathers, because of their sexual relationship to their
wives, are the objects of their sons' sexual jealousy"?

Of course we could have said that, but we still would have been missing
the most critical point. As long as we had available only the Viennese dream
reports, collected in a single culture in which the two roles were confounded,
there would really be no empirical (grounded-in-fact) way to choose between
the two explanations.

The importance of data like Malinowski's, then, is that they permit an
"unconfounding" of what was confounded in the single-culture data. In the
Trobriand Islands the two roles that compete for our attention are performed
by two different persons, either of whom could be the leading figure in a
nightmare. So, if Trobriand boys had nightmares about their fathers, we would
have good reason to retain the sexual-jealousy theory. But with Trobriand boys
having nightmares about their uncles, the sexual-jealousy theory is challenged
—technically, it is no longer *tenable*. Likewise, the tenability of the resentment-
of-discipline theory is strengthened. The value of having the Trobriand Island
data lies in their permitting us to choose between the two competing explanations. It is a choice neither we, nor Freud, could have made on the basis of the
Viennese data alone.

You should understand that the point of all this was not to criticize Freud
for having made the wrong choice. Rather, it was to show how he lacked the
necessary data even to make a choice.

The principle that you should now have grasped is that it is sometimes
necessary to collect data in more than one culture in order to disentangle certain
facts that are intertwined in a single culture. We may label this principle the
unconfounding function of cross-cultural data. Because some events that might be
influencing the behavior we seek to explain covary in a particular society, we
have to collect data in other societies in order to separate those events and
thereby determine which of them matter.

The exercise you have just performed and the principle that has been
derived from it are based on the teachings of an eminent social-science
methodologist, Donald T. Campbell (1961). In a recent revision written with
Raoul Naroll, another eminent methodologist, the point is made as follows:

> Freud validly observed that boys in late Hapsburgian Vienna had hostile
> feelings toward their fathers. Two possible explanations offered themselves—the

hostility could be due to the father's role as the disciplinarian, or to the father's role of the mother's lover. . . . Freud chose to emphasize the role of the mother's lover. However, working only with his patient population there was no adequate basis for making the choice. The two rival explanations were experimentally confounded, for among the parents of Freud's patients the disciplinarian of little boys was usually the mother's lover. (Remember that in Freud's day it was the morality of one's parents more often than their immorality that drove one to choose the analyst's couch over other couches, so that Freud got a biased sample.) Malinowski (1927) studied a society in which these two parental roles were experimentally disentangled, in which the disciplinarian of young boys and the mother's lover were not one-and-the-same person. And in this society, the boys' hostility was addressed to the disciplinarian, not to the mother's lover. This outcome makes the Oedipal hostility more easily encompassed within the framework of a simple hedonistic learning theory [Campbell & Naroll, 1972, p. 437].*

It should be made clear that we are not saying that research done in only one society necessarily results in errors of explanation. Generalizations derived from any single case may, of course, hold true for all cases. But, given the cultural complexities of human life and the importance of culture as a behavioral determinant, it obviously behooves psychologists to test the cross-cultural generality of their principles before considering them established. It is obvious, then, that the scientific study of human behavior requires that we employ a cross-cultural perspective. The history of social psychology shows that this obvious need, while not recognized by every social psychologist, has been acknowledged by many.

Cross-Cultural Concerns in the History of Social Psychology

Herman Ebbinghaus, one of the founders of modern experimental psychology, was quoted by Boring in his classic *A History of Experimental Psychology* (1929) as having said that "psychology has a long past, but only a short history" (p. vii). This observation applies particularly well to social psychology. From classical Greek scholars onward, we find philosophers, political theorists, and even creative artists treating topics that in one form or another are part of the domain of contemporary social psychology. Still, most psychologists now date the beginning of social psychology from 1908. That year saw the almost simultaneous publication of two textbooks with "social psychology" in their titles, one by the psychologist William McDougall (1908), the other by the sociologist E. A. Ross (1908).

*From "The Mutual Methodological Relevance of Anthropology and Psychology," by D. T. Campbell and R. Naroll. In F. L. K. Hsu (Ed.), *Psychological Anthropology* (Rev. ed.). Copyright 1972 by Schenkman Publishing Co. Reprinted by permission.

German Roots

If social psychology as we know it today is a 20th-century phenomenon, its roots lie in the 19th century. These roots were nourished mostly in Germany, largely because of the intellectual atmosphere generated there by such works as J. F. Herbart's influential *Lehrbuch zur Psychologie* (1816). Herbart's ideas reveal that a concern for culture as a behavioral determinant was present in social psychology from its beginning. He argued that psychology must free itself from metaphysics and embrace the methods of science. If it is to explain our mental life, it must recognize the importance of experience. Further, psychology must recognize that experience is shaped by the temper of the *Völksgeist*, which can be revealed to the psychologist only through ethnography, the systematic description of ethnic groups. In ethnographic work will be found the forces that shape human psychology.

Herbart's call was answered by the launching in 1860 of a scholarly journal, *Zeitschrift für Völkerpsychologie und Sprachwissenschaft*, which was devoted to the study of "national psychology" with an emphasis on language and other customs and institutions. In spite of residual mysticism, metaphysics, and even racism in the works of most 19th-century students of human behavior, there were some anthropologists in Germany calling for empirical research on the "mentality of primitive peoples." Whatever the reasons for their interest in this topic, it gave impetus to the development of a cross-cultural social psychology.

Even Wundt, who in 1879 had founded the first laboratory ever called a psychology laboratory, displayed an active and incredibly productive interest in cross-cultural research. Best known for his experimental analyses of sensation and perception, Wundt was also the author of the ten-volume *Völkerpsychologie* (1900–1920). In that work he discussed topics such as language, myth, and custom.

Early Cross-Cultural Concerns in Britain and the United States

The psychology of primitive peoples was a concern elsewhere in Europe, too. In Britain, psychologists and anthropologists together launched programs of research in which some of the best quantitative techniques of the new experimental psychology were applied in studies of non-Western peoples. Classic examples of such works are those of Rivers on sensation and perception in India (1905) and in the Pacific (1901).

In the United States toward the end of the 19th century, interest in cross-cultural psychology was exemplified best in the work of William Graham Sumner, a sociologist at Yale University. Perhaps his most significant contribution was to go beyond the German concept of *Völksgeist*, which was based on the assumption that the characteristic traits of a people are biologically transmitted. Sumner (1906) argued that folkways are habits of the individual and customs of the society that arise from efforts to satisfy needs. They become regulative for succeeding generations and take on the character of a social force.

French Offshoots

At about the same time, in France, there were other developments that influenced social psychology. While these unfortunately did not emphasize cultural forces, they left their mark on social psychology to such an extent that to ignore them would be to distort its origins. That culture was not a major concern of the 19th century French sociologists may, in fact, go a long way toward explaining why most social psychologists during the first half of the 20th century paid scant attention to cultural variables. The French influence was greater than the German and the British. Wundt, Rivers, and Sumner had a lesser impact on the new social psychology than did Tarde, Le Bon, and Durkheim.

French developments depended largely on interest in the phenomenon of suggestion, the object of much research in French medical circles during the 19th century. While perhaps few realized it at the time, this study was perfectly respectable social psychological research, concerned as it was with the behavior of one individual as a stimulus for the behavior of others. Its medical implications, particularly with regard to hypnotism as a therapeutic technique, were enormous. Among those young physicians influenced by this medico-psychological research was Freud. It also had an impact on social theorists such as Tarde and Le Bon, and it is their work to which we now turn.

Gabriel Tarde sought to explain human social behavior in terms of a single process, imitation. His classic work, *The Laws of Imitation* (1903), erred seriously by treating imitation as an explanation, rather than as something itself needing explanation. But it did call attention to this fundamental social phenomenon. We still ask the question Tarde asked, which in essence is "Why do people tend to behave so much like other people?"

An answer was given by Le Bon, one that must also have been influenced by the French research on suggestion. In *The Crowd* (1895/1896) Le Bon helped to perpetuate the deceptively simple notion of a "group mind"—or a common manner of thinking, feeling, and willing—as the cause of uniformities in behavior. It would not be difficult to translate this idea and others like it into a perfectly acceptable statement about shared values and attitudes leading to shared behavioral patterns within social groups. As such, Le Bon's thesis would be seen as good, contemporary social psychology. But his own statements of his thesis led many to take him almost literally, and the resultant mysticism has not yet been wholly purged from popular treatments of social psychology.

The works of Tarde and Le Bon also helped perpetuate the view, long held rather conveniently by the European aristocracy, that the mass of people are fundamentally irrational, suggestible, and easily duped. In this regard it is interesting to note that until quite recently the journal of the American Psychological Association, which was the major outlet for social-psychological research, was entitled *The Journal of Abnormal and Social Psychology*. (In 1965 this was replaced by two journals, treating these two fields separately.) That abnormal psychology, as exemplified by the work of Freud and his followers, and social psychology, derived from the work of Tarde and Le Bon, were both influenced by 19th-century work on suggestion probably explains the traditional linking of these two disciplines. This association was made to seem reasonable by the undue emphasis given by the first generation of social psychologists to the apparent irrationality of social behavior.

While it would be foolish to deny that people often behave irrationally, particularly when responding to social pressures, it is also apparent that this particular emphasis led to some theoretical excesses. It also diverted attention from other equally intriguing questions. And it probably accounted in part for the disproportionate attention paid by social psychologists to social problems and to behavior that reveals man at his worst. In the extreme, the orientation derived from the early French work led to a virtual equation of social with abnormal psychology. As has already been implied above, the basic premise of this book is that nothing is more normally human than social behavior.

If the trend deriving from German folk psychology emphasized intercultural differences, the trend deriving from French sociology emphasized intracultural similarities. Together, these two trends would have added up to a complete social psychology. With few exceptions, however, social psychology during the first half of the 20th century followed the French and ignored the rest. Many of Tarde's ideas were repeated rather uncritically by Ross in his textbook (1908), and several generations of sociologists perpetuated them. These men were also influenced by Emile Durkheim (1897), who, although conversant with other cultures, was mostly concerned with the influence of forces within a society and their deleterious effects on individual behavior—for example, suicide. The specter of irrationality was a theme of McDougall's textbook (1908), which listed numerous "instincts, sympathies, and sentiments" as explanations of the feelings of individuals behaving in relation to others. (Recall the discussion of instinct in Chapter One.) So, social psychology in its early years tended to be imbalanced. It focused mostly on intracultural studies, leaving the study of culture per se to the anthropologists.

U.S. Influences

During the first half of this century social psychology developed both as a social science and a behavioral science. Because that development occurred mostly in U.S. universities, its distinguishing features reflected the dominant values of science in the United States: empiricism, quantification, and, wherever possible, experimentation. To uphold these values, it was obviously necessary for social psychologists to focus on problems that could be treated rigorously, and this meant in practice dealing with relatively molecular issues.

The products of their efforts were extremely valuable ones. Among them were numerous important advances in methodology, such as techniques for the precise measurement of individual attitudes. Research also yielded knowledge about some very basic social processes, such as how judgments are affected by the expressed judgments of others. And these scientists achieved numerous theoretical insights, such as the concepts of status, role, and reference group. All of these developments greatly enhanced our understanding of human behavior. In the pursuit of these values, however, most social psychologists looked inside their own society. Only a few retained an active interest in culture.

One important center was the Institute of Human Relations at Yale University. There, during the 1930s and '40s, an interdisciplinary group of anthropologists, sociologists, and psychologists concerned themselves with the study of human behavior in the broadest of terms. At the same time the Yale group maintained a standard of scientific rigor that was unsurpassed anywhere. The dominant theoretical emphasis at Yale during those exciting years was a neo-behavioristic learning theory, empirically grounded in laboratory experimentation and mathematically sophisticated. This theory was exemplified by the work of Hull (1943), the most famous learning theorist of his time. The major goal of the Yale group was to apply this rigorous stimulus/response learning theory to the study of complex social behavior. While they looked to the psychologist for principles of how an organism interacts with its environment, they looked to the anthropologist for information about the nature of that environment. Only by integrating the two could the social scientist explain human behavior. This was their faith, and their research mirrored it.

A most significant development at Yale during this period was the establishment of the Human Relations Area Files, a compilation of ethnographic reports arranged in such a manner that quantitative, cross-cultural testing of hypotheses became a real possibility. A classic example of such work was the study by Whiting and Child (1953) of child-rearing practices in many different societies and their concomitant effects on adult personality.

The concern for relations between culture and personality, as exemplified by Whiting and Child's work and that of others at Yale in the '40s, was also shown by a few other groups. These groups were composed mostly of anthropologists and psychologists, many of whom found inspiration at first in the theoretical contributions of Freud and later in the more behavioristic psychology of the Yale variety. Anthropologists who participated in this movement included Malinowski, Mead, Benedict, Sapir, Du Bois, Kardiner, Linton, and Kluckhohn.

Textbooks in social psychology that stressed cultural determinants were rare during the first half of the century. And, with very few exceptions, they were produced by social scientists who were not primarily identified as social psychologists. A most important textbook, which appeared toward the end of this period, was by Kluckhohn and Murray (1953). It was built around a simple premise: "Every man is in certain respects like all other men, like some other men, like no other man" (p. 53). With these words Kluckhohn and Murray expressed the need for a social psychology that encompassed anthropology, sociology, and psychology.

One of the few textbooks by a psychologist to stress anthropological content was that of Klineberg (1940). His text summarized well what little was known about human behavior at the time and viewed even that knowledge with a healthy skepticism. Klineberg's examples drawn from ethnography underlined the diversity of human behavior patterns and forced the student to question the validity of existing principles of behavior that purported to be universal. Perhaps the book's most important contribution was its challenge to prevalent ideas of biological determinism, particularly those of a racist variety.

These, then, were the major efforts that can be described as cross-cultural social psychology during that half-century of rapid growth in psychology. I have tried to make clear that a cross-cultural emphasis was not the dominant trend of this period. At the same time I have shown that there were those who obviously believed that a social psychology that ignored culture and an anthropology that ignored individual behavior were both incomplete.

Modern Developments in Cross-Cultural Psychology

In the decades following World War II, cross-cultural psychology grew, much as an adolescent grows, in spurts. By the 1970s, cross-cultural psychology had come of age.

The postwar decades were marked by the decline of colonialism, the birth of many new nations, and competition between political and social ideologies for the attention of the populations of the less developed new nations. As a consequence, opportunities became available for psychologists in unprecedented numbers to break loose from their laboratories and board jet planes headed for (sometimes literally) greener pastures. Also contributing to the rapid growth of cross-cultural research were the vastly enhanced funding for psychological research, by public and private agencies alike, and the growing numbers of young psychologists with foreign experience as military personnel, Peace Corps volunteers, or exchange students. Faster means of transportation were also a factor.

Once a rather exotic subspeciality, cross-cultural psychology became an established, thriving intellectual enterprise peopled by hundreds of scholars from many parts of the world. By 1973, there were 1125 cross-cultural psychologists listed in a published *Directory of Cross-Cultural Research and Researchers* (Berry, Lonner, & Leroux, 1973) and presumably more who were not listed. Although most of them are in departments of psychology in North American and European universities, many are to be found in the newer universities in Africa, Asia, and Latin America. Wherever they may be, they are linked by a variety of institutions. In large numbers they belong to several newly established professional organizations—including the International Association for Cross-Cultural Psychology (founded in 1972), the Society for Cross-Cultural Research (1972), and the International Studies Association (1959). Many others belong to older, more traditional organizations such as the American Psychological Association and the American Anthropological Association. The increasing cadres of cross-cultural psychologists now enjoy a diversity of journals in which they publish their research findings. These include the *Journal of Cross-Cultural Psychology* (founded in 1970) and the *International Journal of Psychology* (1966). In addition, the older journals in psychology, anthropology, and some related fields are publishing more and more cross-cultural studies, with the *Journal of Social Psychology* encouraging such studies by providing priority publication.

The proliferation of reports on cross-cultural research that fill these journals has prompted the publication of numerous reviews and overviews of work accomplished just in the past decade or two. The most recent and comprehensive reviews include a chapter in the 1971 *Biennial Review of Anthropology* (Triandis, Malpass, & Davidson, 1971), another by the same authors in the 1973 *Annual Review of Psychology*, five chapters by various authors in the multivolumed *Handbook of Social Psychology* (Lindzey & Aronson, 1968 and later years), and a chapter in the *Handbook of Personality Theory and Research* (Borgatta & Lambert, 1968).

Numerous books of readings in which articles reporting cross-cultural psychological data have been reprinted, excerpted, or glossed appeared during the late 1960s and early 1970s. These include volumes edited by Price-Williams (1969), Al-Issa and Dennis (1970), Hsu (1961, 1972), Lambert and Weisbrod (1971), and Berry and Dasen (1974). Two volumes on cultural influences on perception and cognition also appeared in the early 1970s (Lloyd, 1972; Cole & Scribner, 1974).

Later in that decade a brief introduction to cross-cultural psychology for beginning students of psychology was written by Serpell (1976). And a series of edited volumes dealing with research issues was begun by Warren (1977). Both of these served to draw attention to the field among students in England.

Although primarily concerned with research methodology, a book by Brislin, Lonner, and Thorndike (1973) contains numerous summaries of significant cross-cultural studies, most of them conducted during the 1960s. The bibliographies in these several review volumes attest to the virtual explosion of interest and activity in cross-cultural psychology.

Conferences devoted largely or even exclusively to cross-cultural psychology are now frequent occurrences. In recent years, the International Association of Cross-Cultural Psychology has met in Hong Kong (1972), Kingston, Ontario (1974), Tilburg, the Netherlands (1976), and Munich, Germany (1978). Many regional meetings have also taken place, such as the Second Pan-African Psychology Congress in Nairobi, Kenya, in December 1975. The proceedings of most such conferences are also published, thus adding to the materials available for study by cross-cultural psychologists. For examples, see Dawson and Lonner (1974) for the 1972 Hong Kong meeting; Brislin, Bochner, and Lonner (1975) for a 1973 Hawaii Conference; Berry and Lonner (1975) for the 1974 Kingston meeting; and Poortinga (1977) for the 1976 Tilburg meeting.

In addition to communicating with one another at international conferences, cross-cultural psychologists have a newsletter. They also periodically conduct workshops (at the East-West Center in Hawaii, for example) at which they try to improve cooperation in their expanding international data-collection efforts.

As this history is being written, a team of cross-cultural psychologists is preparing a *Handbook of Cross-Cultural Psychology* (Triandis, 1979), which will attempt to compile some of the many theories and facts generated by their colleagues during the remarkably prolific postwar era.[2]

Apparently, it is no longer necessary to preach the need for a cross-cultural perspective in social psychology. Psychologists in various cultures are now quite aware of the discipline's culture boundedness and the inappropriateness of psychological theories and findings when applied to particular societies (see, for example, Moscovici, 1972, and Faucheux, 1976). More and more psychological research is being done cross-culturally. Now the problem is not encouraging its doing but ensuring that it is done well. That is the issue to which we will turn in the next chapter.

References

Al-Issa, I., & Dennis, W. (Eds.). *Cross-Cultural Studies of Behavior.* New York: Holt, Rinehart & Winston, 1970.

Berry, J. W., & Dasen, P. R. (Eds.). *Culture and Cognition: Readings in Cross-Cultural Psychology.* London: Methuen, 1974.

Berry, J. W., & Lonner, W. (Eds.). *Applied Cross-Cultural Psychology.* Amsterdam: Swets & Zeitlinger, 1975.

Berry, J. W., Lonner, W. J., & Leroux, J. *Directory of Cross-Cultural Research and Researchers.* Bellingham, Wash.: Department of Psychology, Center for Cross-Cultural Research, 1973.

Borgatta, E., & Lambert, W. W. (Eds.). *Handbook of Personality Theory and Research.* Chicago: Rand McNally, 1968.

Boring, E. G. *A History of Experimental Psychology.* New York: Century, 1929.

Brislin, R. W., Bochner, S., & Lonner, W. J. (Eds.). *Cross-Cultural Perspectives on Learning.* Beverly Hills, Calif.: Sage, 1975.

Brislin, R. W., Lonner, W. J., & Thorndike, R. M. *Cross-Cultural Research Methods.* New York: Wiley, 1973.

Brislin, R. W., & Segall, M. H. *Cross-Cultural Research: The Role of Culture in Understanding Human Behavior.* (Learning Resources in International Studies, No. 16.) New York: International Studies Association, 1975.

[2]It is impossible to predict whether the rapid growth of cross-cultural psychology will continue. As this chapter is being written, the field is confronted with two serious obstacles: a scarcity of funds to subsidize necessarily expensive cross-cultural research and a diminishing access to some parts of the world, where foreign scholars are sometimes perceived as foreign agents. These constraining factors are somewhat offset by the growth in numbers of indigenous scholars, especially psychologists, in universities in many of the newer nations in the Third and Fourth worlds of Africa and Asia.

Campbell, D. T. The mutual methodological relevance of anthropology and psychology. In F. L. K. Hsu (Ed.), *Psychological Anthropology*. Homewood, Ill.: Dorsey, 1961. Pp. 333–352.

Campbell, D. T., & Naroll, R. The mutual methodological relevance of anthropology and psychology. In F. L. K. Hsu (Ed.), *Psychological Anthropology* (Rev. ed.). Cambridge, Mass.: Schenkman, 1972. Pp. 435–463.

Child, I. L. Personality in culture. In E. Borgatta & W. W. Lambert (Eds.), *Handbook of Personality Theory and Research*. Chicago: Rand McNally, 1968.

Cole, M., & Scribner, S. *Culture and Thought: A Psychological Introduction*. New York: Wiley, 1974.

Dawson, J. L. M., & Lonner, W. J. (Eds.). *Readings in Cross-Cultural Psychology*. Hong Kong: University Press, 1974.

Durkheim, E. *Le Suicide: Étude de Sociologie*. Paris: Félix Alcan, 1897.

Faucheux, C. Cross-cultural research in experimental social psychology. *European Journal of Social Psychology*, 1976, *6*, 269–322.

Herbart, J. F. *Lehrbuch zur Psychologie*, 1816. (Translated by Margaret K. Smith. New York: Appleton & Co., 1897.)

Hsu, F. L. K. (Ed.). *Psychological Anthropology*. Homewood, Ill.: Dorsey, 1961.

Hsu, F. L. K. (Ed.). *Psychological Anthropology* (Rev. ed.). Cambridge, Mass.: Schenkman, 1972.

Hull, C. L. *Principles of Behavior*. New York: Appleton-Century-Crofts, 1943.

Klineberg, O. *Social Psychology*. New York: Holt, 1940.

Kluckhohn, C., & Murray, H. A. (Eds.). *Personality in Nature, Society, and Culture*. New York: Knopf, 1953.

Lambert, W. W., & Weisbrod, R. (Eds.). *Comparative Perspectives on Social Psychology*. Boston: Little, Brown, 1971.

Le Bon, G. [*The Crowd*]. London: Benn, 1896. (Originally published, 1895.)

Lindzey, G., & Aronson, E. (Eds.). *Handbook of Social Psychology* (2nd ed.). Cambridge, Mass.: Addison-Wesley, 1968.

Lloyd, B. B. *Perception and Cognition: A Cross-Cultural Perspective*. Hammondsworth, England: Penguin, 1972.

Malinowski, B. *Sex and Repression in Savage Society*. London: Humanities Press, 1927.

McDougall, W. *Introduction to Social Psychology*. London: Methuen, 1908.

Moscovici, S. Society and theory in social psychology. In J. Israel & H. Tajfel (Eds.), *The Context of Social Psychology*. London: Academic Press, 1972.

Poortinga, Y. *Basic Problems in Cross-Cultural Psychology*. Amsterdam: Swets & Zeitlinger, 1977.

Price-Williams, D. R. (Ed.). *Cross-Cultural Studies*. Baltimore: Penguin, 1969.

Rivers, W. H. R. Introduction and vision. In A. C. Haddon (Ed.), *Reports of the Cambridge Anthropological Expedition to the Torres Straits* (Vol. 2, Pt. 1). Cambridge, England: University Press, 1901.

Rivers, W. H. R. Observations on the senses of the Todas. *British Journal of Psychology*, 1905, *1*, 321–396.

Ross, E. A. *Social Psychology*. New York: Macmillan, 1908.

Serpell, R. *Culture's Influence on Behaviour*. London: Methuen, 1976.

Sumner, W. G. *Folkways*. Boston: Ginn, 1906.

Tarde, G. *The Laws of Imitation*. New York: Holt, 1903.

Triandis, H. C. (Ed.). *Handbook of Cross-Cultural Psychology*. Boston: Allyn & Bacon. Six volumes, projected for 1979 and later, including: Triandis, H. C., & Lambert, W. W., Vol. 1: *Perspectives*; Triandis, H. C., & Berry, J. W., Vol. 2: *Methodology*; Triandis, H. C., & Lonner, W., Vol. 3: *Basic Processes*; Triandis, H. C., & Heron, A., Vol. 4: *Developmental Psychology*; Triandis, H. C., & Brislin, R., Vol. 5: *Social Psychology*; and Triandis, H. C., & Draguns, J. G., Vol. 6: *Psychopathology*.

Triandis, H. C., Malpass, R. S., & Davidson, A. R. Cross-cultural psychology. In B. J. Siegel (Ed.), *Biennial Review of Anthropology*. Stanford, Calif.: Stanford University Press, 1971. Pp. 1–84.

Triandis, H. C., Malpass, R. S., & Davidson, A. R. Psychology and culture. *Annual Review of Psychology*, 1973, *24*, 355–378.

Warren, N. (Ed.). *Studies in Cross-Cultural Psychology* (Vol. 1). London: Academic Press, 1977.

Whiting, J. W. M., & Child, I. L. *Child Training and Personality*. New Haven, Conn.: Yale University Press, 1953.

Wundt, W. *Völkerpsychologie* (10 vols.). Leipzig: Englemann, 1900–1920.

Three

How Research in Cross -Cultural Psychology Is Conducted

In the preceding chapter we saw that cross-cultural psychology became, during the third quarter of the 20th century, a thriving intellectual enterprise. In this chapter we will survey the conduct of that enterprise in broad overview. We will first consider the scope of the discipline, looking at the kinds of questions addressed in cross-cultural research and the way these questions relate to each other. Their interrelationship will be placed within a framework of ideas that links the natural environment, culture, and individual behavior. Then we will consider some of the difficulties of doing behavioral research cross-culturally and, finally, some solutions to those difficulties.

The Scope of Cross-Cultural Psychology: The Kinds of Questions It Seeks to Answer

Cross-cultural psychologists try to understand human behavior through the ways in which sociocultural variables influence it. In pursuit of that understanding, sometimes they focus on behavioral differences across cultures and sometimes on universal patterns of behavior. But the ultimate goal is always to discover how culture and individual behavior relate.

There are many different approaches to uncovering the relationships between culture and behavior. To appreciate what these diverse approaches might accomplish, it is helpful to consider first an overall framework of ideas within which all cross-cultural studies can be classified.

Berry's Framework: An Ecological Model

A useful framework has been developed by the Canadian cross-cultural psychologist John W. Berry (1971, 1975, 1976). Berry's basic premise is that ecological forces are the prime movers and shapers of culture and behavior. As he sees it, ecological variables constrain, pressure, and nurture cultural forms, which in turn shape behavior. Thus, Berry's framework comprises three classes of variables: ecological, adaptive, and behavioral. We will consider them in turn.

Ecological Variables. These include climatic and other natural factors—such as water supply, soil conditions, temperature, and terrain—that combine to influence, among other things, a given society's food-production system. By ecology, then, Berry means any combination of natural conditions that affects food-production techniques, which are clearly fundamental to the functioning of society.

Underlying this emphasis on ecological factors is the assumption that over a long period basic decisions about how a society feeds its members are influenced by natural forces. A decision to feed primarily on meat from large animals depends on their availability, which in turn depends on climate, water supply, type of ground cover, and the like. Herding as a way of producing food depends on the availability of conditions favorable to animal husbandry. Fishing demands that one live near water.

A convenient way to categorize different food-production systems is by the degree of accumulation. At the low extreme are societies that pursue hunting and gathering as a primary feeding technique. Food is not stored for later consumption but is merely out there to be got when needed. It is sometimes abundant and sometimes in short supply, but it is seldom accumulated. Societies at the high extreme include those that employ agriculture, accumulating food by producing, storing, and planting seeds. Such societies typically store much of their food for later needs. Animal-husbandry societies are also high in food accumulation, investing resources in meat on the hoof that may not be needed for months.

There are well-replicated anthropological observations indicating that a society's degree of food accumulation is correlated with certain of its other characteristics. For example, high-food-accumulating societies, including most technologically developed societies, tend to be sedentary and relatively dense in population. Low-food-accumulating societies tend to be composed of less dense, migratory populations.

Adaptive Variables. These include what Berry calls sociocultural and organismic characteristics of populations. Sociocultural characteristics include all inventions that are adaptive to the pressures of ecology. Another way to refer to such inventions, of course, is to call them "culture," since culture consists of all human institutions that in the long run help populations survive in a given ecological niche. These include political systems, kinship systems, and socialization emphases. In any particular environment there are forces that make it likely that certain socialization practices are emphasized more than others, that certain kinship systems are organized rather than others, and so forth.

Without going into great detail one can see how that seems plausible. If, for example, ecological forces influence food accumulation, which in turn is related to the probability of a society's being migratory or sedentary, that in turn will probably lead to a cultural invention that is compatible with being either sedentary or migratory. A migratory society is likely to have a different kinship system from one that is sedentary. A sociocultural variable such as kinship is thus an "adaptive" variable.

Berry's second subcategory of adaptive variables, organismic variables, includes any adaptive response a population makes over many generations that is basically genetic or physiological. Such evolutionary changes are responsive to the press of ecology. Thus, genetic differences across subpopulations of the human race are treated in Berry's framework as organismic adaptations to ecological pressure. These differences may show up as differential susceptibilities to disease; populations will thus differ in characteristic levels of health. These organismic differences do not reflect only genetic predispositions, of course. Health and nutritional status may also vary across populations because of cultural differences in diet and hygiene. But whatever the cause of these differences, they are differences in organismic status that are the result of different adaptations to ecological conditions.

These two subcategories of adaptive variables, sociocultural and organismic, may also interact with one another. For example, cultural taboos regarding foods may reflect a society's experience in ages past with negative consequences of a food, consequences that may have had a genetic basis. Thus, there are ethnic groups in Africa that suffer an organic inability to digest milk. These groups also have a culturally sanctioned aversion to milk. Their diet is less than adequate in protein, giving them a nutritional status that may have behavioral consequences. Their nutritional status is probably a product of both sociocultural and organismic variables, in some complex interaction. However it came about, the complex of dietary practices and prevailing physical condition of a population is a part of that population's adaptation to its environment. Its adaptation is both sociocultural and organismic.

Behavioral Variables. In Berry's framework these may also be called psychological variables or individual-development variables. They include all measurable aspects of individual behavior that can be shown to be linked to ecological or adaptive variables or both.

This framework is thus a conceptual system in which ecological forces are viewed as influencing human behavior, either directly or through the intervening adaptive variables, both sociocultural and organismic. But the direction of relationship is not exclusively from ecology to culture to behavior. Obviously, individual behavior can also influence culture. Indeed, individual behavior can influence ecology. People do go out and cut down the forest or divert water or use up natural resources. The framework, then, is a feedback system, or a network of relationships. Its ultimate usefulness lies in its calling attention to the possible relationships to look for among any combination of ecological, adaptive, and behavioral variables.

Illustrated in Figure 3-1, a version of Berry's model provides a convenient, abstract framework for the concepts of cross-cultural psychology.[1] A sociocultural adaptive class of variables that is singled out for special attention is "socialization," the techniques by which the older generation conveys its norms and standards to the young. Socialization is such an important aspect of how culture influences individual development that it is worthy of special attention. Highlighting it, as Berry does, reminds us to expect certain relationships among, say, population density, socialization practices, and individual personality. The framework suggests that socialization practices tend to be designed to produce those behaviors that are maximally adaptive, that lead to enhanced survival under whatever ecological conditions prevail.

The basic feature of this heuristic device—this model that suggests relationships to be sought and tested—is its stress on functionality, a Darwinian assumption that human behavior is ultimately adaptive. People behave more in ways that enhance their survival than in other ways. According to Berry's framework, in each ecological setting behaviors evolve that produce institutions, life-styles, and shared beliefs and values that influence the way children are reared. These socialization methods, in turn, tend to produce succeeding generations who behave in ways that work, in ways that maximize their probability of survival.

As a heuristic device this framework can lead cross-cultural psychologists to search for all kinds of relationships. For example, we might look for the connections between specific ecological variables and specific cultural variables. Or we might seek out relationships involving any other combination of ecological, adaptive, and individual-development variables.

Let me give you a concrete example. Research might be designed to test the hypothesis that variations in family structure (nuclear family versus extended family, for example) relate to the degree of food accumulation (see Nimkoff & Middleton, 1960). As it turns out, nuclear families (husband, wife, and their children) tend to be found more often in sedentary, high-food-accumulating societies such as our own.

Or research might focus on ecology and socialization techniques (see, for

---

[1]Figure 3-1 presents a simplified version of Berry's model. In its most developed form, and in his own terms, the model appears in Berry, 1976 (p. 41).

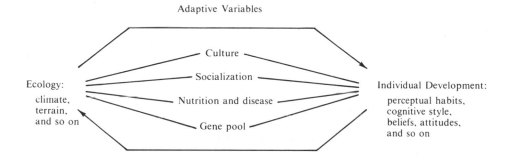

Figure 3-1. A framework for thinking about cross-cultural study. (Adapted from "An Ecological Approach to Cross-Cultural Psychology," by J. W. Berry, *Nederlands Tijdschrift voor de Psychologie,* 1975, *30,* 51–84. Used by permission of the publisher, Van Loghum Slaterus BV, Deventer, The Netherlands.)

example, Barry, Child, & Bacon, 1959). As we shall see in considerable detail later in this book, economic systems are related to the degree to which populations stress obedience and compliance among their children. Or differences in perceptual processes across different cultures might be suggested on the basis of certain natural and human features of the environment in which people happen to be raised (see, for example, Segall, Campbell, & Herskovits, 1966). Or cognitive style (the manner in which persons characteristically approach analytic problems) might be predicted to vary either with socialization practices or with degrees of food accumulation or both (Witkin & Berry, 1975).[2]

Any study, then, that includes the collection of individual behavioral data and seeks to relate that behavior to ecological and sociocultural variables is a study in cross-cultural psychology and can be incorporated into Berry's framework. All such studies, assuming that they are well done, tell us something about the way in which nature, culture, and behavior interrelate.

In some respects Berry's formulation is similar to an earlier conception that long influenced the conduct of cross-cultural research, a conception that was a product of the culture-and-personality school of anthropology. But that conception is also different enough from the more contemporary framework created by Berry that we ought to examine it in some detail and consider the kinds of research that flowed from it.

The Culture-and-Personality School

For several decades, beginning in the 1930s, considerable anthropological research was guided by a formulation that asserted axiomatically that culture and personality are interrelated. Influenced largely by a major emphasis in

---

[2]As will be seen later in this book (Chapter Five), Berry's ecological model has been applied most fruitfully to an analysis of cultural differences in performance of tasks representative of Witkin's concept of psychological differentiation.

Freudian theory on early experience as a primary determinant of adult personality, some anthropologists came to think of culture as a set of conditions that determines the kinds of experience a person has early in life. Thus culture is a major shaper of the personality that develops. For example, Kardiner (1945) and Linton (1945a) suggested that different societies develop different *basic personality types*. Their argument, as summarized by Linton in his foreword to the 1945 volume by Kardiner, is presented here in some detail, so that its flavor can be grasped.

The concept of basic personality types requires four postulates: (1) individuals' early experiences exert a lasting effect on their personalities, especially on the development of basic values; (2) similar experiences tend to produce similar personality configurations in the individuals who are subjected to them; (3) the techniques that the members of any society employ in child rearing are culturally patterned and tend to be similar, although never identical, for various families within the society; and (4) the culturally patterned techniques for the care and rearing of children differ from one society to another.

According to Linton, (1945b), it follows from these postulates that (1) the members of any given society have many elements of early experience in common; (2) as a result of this they have many elements of personality in common; (3) since the early experience of individuals differs from one society to another, the personality norms for various societies also differ; and (4) every society has a basic personality type.

It's that fourth step that I hope you feel a little uneasy about. What does he mean by basic personality type?

> The basic personality type for any society is that personality configuration which is shared by the bulk of the society's members as the result of the early experiences which they have in common. It does not correspond to the total personality of the individual but rather to the "projective systems" or the value-attitude systems which are basic to the individual personality configuration. Thus, the same basic personality type may be reflected in many different forms of behavior, and may enter into many different total personality configurations [Linton, 1945b, pp. vii-viii].

In other words, because of socialization pressures, certain communalities in individual development are produced within members of a society. This is not to say that everybody has the same personality—each total personality differs from every other total personality. But somehow at the core of that personality is something shared by the bulk of the society—some basic values and attitudes —and that is called the *projective system*. This term requires elucidation.

The projective system refers to underlying values and attitudes that are susceptible to observation, presumably by the use of specialized psychological measuring instruments known as projective tests. These instruments were developed initially in clinical settings for use by psychiatrists and psychologists as diagnostic devices in treating neurotic and psychotic individuals. Such instruments (for example, the Rorschach ink blots and the Thematic Apperception Test, or TAT) attracted the attention of anthropologists partly because the instruments *seemed* applicable in any cultural setting and partly because they were linked conceptually with various new and exciting theories of human development.

The most notable of these theories was psychoanalysis—which in many respects constituted the most attractive new way of understanding behavior that had appeared on the intellectual scene in centuries. That psychoanalytic theory purported to be a universally applicable system for understanding human development made it attractive to adherents and skeptics alike.

The Impact of Clinical Psychology. Clinical psychology in the 1920s and 1930s was, then, in some respects the best psychology of its day, and it is little wonder that its themes and techniques (especially the allegedly penetrating projective tests) attracted anthropologists and contributed to the emergence of a culture-and-personality school of thought.[3]

From Freudian theory, many field workers were led to look for relations between child-rearing practices and certain aspects of adult personality. Many studies spawned by this expectation yielded interesting empirical findings, some of which will be reviewed later in this book. But clinical psychology had some effects on anthropology that were not so salutary. (These will be discussed shortly.)

Nonetheless, like Berry's more modern conceptual framework, the culture-and-personality approach carried the implication that there is a reciprocal relationship between social systems and personalities. As one anthropologist (Spiro, 1961) put it, a social system creates "the personality needs which, in turn, are satisfied by and motivate the operation of the social system" (p. 121). (This formulation was derived, as Spiro noted, from the Kardiner

---

[3]Kardiner (1945, p. 15) said "If we are to make psychology one of the social sciences, what aid is it ready to give us and which of the techniques of modern psychology can help us in our task at the present moment? Will the hope sustain us that the animal psychologies can formulate principles that we can confidently follow? The classical psychologies made that promise and came to naught. There are several reasons why this hope is slim. Granted that animal psychology has a definite place and that certain types of learning processes can be accurately studied on lower animals and applied without change to man, this is a very narrow province, and one which plays a small role in human life. The conditioned reflex established a valuable series of data; but the behaviorists did not make good their claims to devise a scientific psychology without the aid of direct experience. They had to use the direct experience of the experimenter. ... In short, we have no psychological technique today that satisfies all requirements, either because its techniques or conclusions are not ready for adoption by the social sciences in any large scale or because the relevancy to these problems is dubious. There remains only psychoanalysis—and by this is meant the significant relations into which the phenomena of direct experience and behavior can be ordered." (From *The Psychological Frontiers of Society*, by A. Kardiner. Copyright 1945 by Columbia University Press. Reprinted by permission.)

model discussed above.) In other words, culture somehow induces people to want to behave in ways that sustain the culture. Every society has developed cultural norms and the devices by which its members come to conform with these norms. Much of that conformity is manifest willingly by individuals because their personalities include internalized motives, role demands, and other acquired behavioral tendencies that are compatible with the norms. To behave otherwise would be to court not only externally administered negative sanctions but also self-administered anxiety, an inevitable cost of nonconformity.

As a general conception of the manner in which culture and personality interrelate, this point of view is hard to fault. The research that it stimulated, however, had some serious deficiencies.

Shortcomings in Research. A major difficulty with research done by adherents of the culture-and-personality school was its relative disregard of individual differences within societies. Researchers set out to find core personalities, those personality characteristics that "had to be" shown by all members of a given society. Criticism of this tendency has been expressed frequently in recent years, but probably no more urgently than by A. F. C. Wallace (1961). Wallace found in the research output a widespread proneness to conceive of societies as culturally homogeneous and to expect individuals in them to share a uniform nuclear character. But Wallace reminded us that there is much diversity not only across cultures but also within them. To him, diversity is the natural order of things and is not pathogenic, or nonfunctional, as some of the culture-and-personality theorists seemed to him to argue.

As Wallace saw it, the "core personalities" produced by this research tradition were either abstractions gleaned from descriptions of individual personalities—with nonshared characteristics simply ignored—or, worse, deductions from cultural descriptions. As such, they hardly constituted *facts*. Many studies thus resulted in "discoveries" of the core personality traits that were demanded by some logical analysis of the culture.

Another difficulty with much of the older culture-and-personality research derived from its heavy dependence on projective techniques. During the 1940s and 1950s numerous studies of national character and modal personality[4] employed the Rorschach test. A typical work is Cora DuBois's *The People of Alor* (1944). This study included the analysis (by a Swiss expert on the Rorschach test) of about 50 Rorschach protocols collected from the Alorese, an Indonesian-island group. "Findings" led the author to describe the core personality as characterized by fearfulness, suspicion, distrust, egocentricity, greed, shallowness of personal relations, lack of emotional responsiveness, but—surprisingly, perhaps, in light of the foregoing—"no evidence of neurotic conflict."

---

[4]Modal personality is a construct that denotes culturally induced central tendencies in the variations of individual personalities in any society.

In Lewis's study on Tepoztlan, Mexico (1951), a chapter by Abel and Calabresi was based on an analysis of about 100 Rorschach protocols. The generalizations derived from these tests included the assertion that the typical person in the community could be characterized as unfriendly, rigid, and unlikely (or unable) to engage in fantasy.

Lindzey (1961, especially Chapter 6) reviewed these and many other studies that employed Rorschach tests cross-culturally. He concluded, to put it bluntly, that they were typically so full of methodological faults that their findings could simply not be evaluated. Among the criticisms Lindzey succinctly summarized were these:

1. The technique imposes the language of pathology; thus modal personalities that emerge from a scoring of Rorschach protocols almost necessarily appear more or less sick.

2. The data are difficult to quantify and treat statistically. The studies seldom specified the nature of the sampling procedures used, so that whatever description emerged was of an unknown degree of applicability to the population in question.

3. By searching for supposedly "deep-seated, underlying personality traits," whatever they may be, the culture-personality researchers usually ignored overt behaviors.

4. The use of projective techniques in the culture in which they were devised—the Euro-American regions of the world—is difficult enough. Their use requires the detection of subtle linguistic cues, the validity of their scoring procedures is dubious, responses may reflect structural variables, such as recent experiences, attitudes toward test taking elicited by the behavior of the tester, and so on. Every one of these problems is simply exacerbated when such instruments are employed in a culture that is foreign to the investigator.*

For these and other reasons, the employment of projective tests in cross-cultural research dwindled virtually to the vanishing point.[5] So did studies seeking modal personality. Such research is no longer fashionable, largely because it resulted in very little solid information about human behavior and how it is shaped by sociocultural forces. Still, the basic doctrine of the culture-and-personality school of thought—that there are shared personality traits or characteristic ways of behaving among members of a society and that those traits are compatible with the society's values—is tenable. It merely expresses an expectation of finding functional relationships among elements of culture and aspects of behavior. As such, this expectation is still held by most students of culture and behavior. And it is, as we have seen, part of the conceptual framework recently developed by Berry. But, whereas Berry's

---

*Adapted from *Projective Techniques and Cross-Cultural Research*, by G. Lindzey. Copyright 1961 by Appleton-Century-Crofts, a division of Prentice-Hall, Inc. Used by permission of the author.

[5]This is not to say that cross-cultural psychologists have abandoned projective techniques. See Holtzman, Díaz-Guerrero, and Swartz (1975) for a modern example of empirical research employing such material.

framework seems heuristically quite valuable, the culture-and-personality conception did not produce a viable research offspring.[6]

Berry's framework suggests that we ought to examine all conceivable aspects of human behavior and try to discover whether and to what degree any aspect is influenced by the ecological and cultural contexts in which it occurs. And that is what contemporary cross-cultural psychologists, for the most part, are doing.

Doing it, however, is harder than saying one will do it. The methodological problems inherent in cross-cultural psychological research are formidable ones. It is to some of these problems that we now turn.

Methodology in Cross-Cultural Research: Some Problems and Some Solutions

Designing a study of human behavior that will produce unambiguous findings is very difficult. This is true even when that study is done in the investigator's own society—where he knows the language, is knowledgeable about the prevailing attitudes, is using measuring instruments of known reliability, and is able to detect subtle cues in the behavior of his subjects. Psychologists who work only in their own societies know full well that despite these advantages their research is always subject to numerous threats to validity. Imagine, then, the problems confronting cross-cultural psychologists.

First, they may not know the language and will probably be unable to read subtle cues that are familiar to insiders. In addition, theories, concepts, research methods, and measuring instruments developed in one society may not be applicable to the behaviors of individuals in any other society.

Three methodological worries especially acute in cross-cultural research are measurement problems, sampling problems, and administrative problems. Each of these categories raises several interesting issues.

Measurement Problems

What to Measure. The primary measurement problem in cross-cultural research is, simply, *what* to measure. That this is a problem may not at first be obvious (which, incidentally, compounds the problem!).

Suppose you begin with an interest in aggressive behavior among

[6]Although acknowledging that "the study of culture and personality occupies an extremely uncertain place in social anthropology, sociology and other 'institutional' social sciences," LeVine (1973, p. vii) noted that these group-level social sciences have rediscovered the need for social and personality psychology to help account for behavior. Whereas LeVine reintroduces psychology to social scientists, my use of Berry's framework forges the same link but from the opposite direction. By the same token, LeVine's ideas and those developed here are often parallel and are never incompatible. Thus, I am in accord with LeVine's expressed hope that "a new psychosocial rapprochement may be drawing near" (1973, p. x).

adolescents in diverse cultures. Don't you simply go to various cultures and observe adolescent aggression? Of course, but what kinds of behaviors are valid indexes of aggression? Aggression, after all, is only a theoretical concept, not a behavior. It is a name that we give to a class of behaviors, and even in our own society we are not sure which kinds of responses should be counted as part of that class. If somebody hits somebody else on the back, that is probably an aggressive response, but not always—it depends on the context in which the hitting occurs.

When we go outside our own culture, we may be confronted with responses that would be accepted as indexes of aggression in our own society but that might have a quite different meaning in some other society. Thus, in a cross-cultural study of aggression it might be inappropriate to study exactly the same behaviors in two or more different cultures, because those behaviors might mean very different things. We might, in fact, have to study different behaviors in order to study the "same phenomenon."[7]

A striking example concerns affirmation or agreement, which in many societies is manifested by moving one's head up and down (nodding). In our society, nodding communicates "yes," "OK," "I agree," or "I'm in favor of what you've just said." But there are some societies where that same information is communicated by a side-to-side motion of the head—which in our society, of course, means just the opposite. If a concept as basic as affirming or negating can be communicated in two such opposing ways, it is obvious that something as subtle as aggression will be manifested in very different ways in different cultures.

How to Measure. Closely related to the problem of deciding *what* to measure is the problem of *how* to measure it. To grasp the essence of this problem, consider a classic study by an English psychologist named Gordon (1923), who was interested in a particular subcultural group within his own society. The group consisted of very poor people who eked out a livelihood on boats that plied the canals of England. The children of these canal-boat people hardly ever went to school, and if they did they went irregularly.

This group's life-style generated hostility and disdain on the part of members of the more affluent core culture. The canal-boat people were considered lazy and stupid, and their failure to behave like middle-class English was attributed to a basic lack of intelligence. That, as you know, is a common reaction of core-cultural people to anyone who, for whatever reason, is not achieving what the society's myths say everyone could achieve.

Gordon doubted the validity of that interpretation; he doubted that the

---

[7]Related to this concern is the "emic/etic" controversy, or the opposing merits of viewing behavior either within its own cultural context or from an outsider's perspective. This is a complex issue on which several writers have commented (for example, Berry, 1969, and Lonner, 1979). It will be discussed in Chapter Five in reference to cross-cultural research on cognition, the topic to which the "emic/etic" distinction is most directly pertinent.

canal-boat people were behaving the way they did because of some inherent deficiency in intelligence or motivation. So he set out to discover just how intelligent canal-boat children really were.

Binet's IQ test had recently been translated into English. Gordon obtained a copy of the American version, amended the language to make it conform to English English, and administered it to a sample of canal-boat children of various ages. He found two significant results.

First, Gordon found an average, or mean, score that was equivalent to an IQ of 60, clearly below average. Even more interesting, he found a decline of IQ with age. The older the children, the "less intelligent" they appeared to be. Gordon was intrigued by this second finding because it said to him that the children must have been subject to negative influences on their intellectual performance that accumulated with age. He concluded, then, that the children's test performances were more a reflection of the cultural deprivation to which their canal-boat environment subjected them than a measure of their potential intellectual abilities.

Given what we know about the diverse determinants of performance on an IQ test, Gordon was probably right. And he deserves praise for being so right so early in the history of psychological testing. But I think we have to go further than Gordon; I think we have to go one more step. He didn't consider the possibility that the test he employed might not even have been appropriate to demonstrate the negative impact of the social environment on intellectual performance. Perhaps the test wasn't even measuring intellectual performance very well.

Perhaps the test, for example, was measuring the children's willingness to answer what might have seemed to them very silly questions put to them by a somewhat bizarre stranger. Or maybe what Gordon was actually measuring was the degree of patience the children had with the kind of tasks that he was asking them to perform. Or maybe the test was, more than anything else, a measure of the familiarity the children had with the content of a culture other than their own, a familiarity that would also decline with increasing immersion in their own subculture, rather than in the host culture. Or maybe the test was measuring all of those things.

What I'm suggesting, then, is that there are really two lessons to learn from Gordon's classic study. The first point is that any test that may in one culture be a reasonably good index of some construct—such as intelligence—may not be an index of that construct within another culture. It may merely measure the kind of performance that usually, but not in this case, serves well as an indicator of capacity or potential. The second lesson is that the test may not even be a good measure of the performance. It may be measuring something entirely different, such as motivation, patience, or sheer willingness to perform. The first point was made by Gordon himself when he said, in effect, "I don't think I'm actually measuring innate, potential capacity." The second point he failed to make.

The first point has been made often, by the way, by a lot of people, perhaps best by Robert LeVine (1970): "Standard intelligence tests measure [only] the current capacity of individuals to participate effectively in Western schools" (p. 581). That much, IQ tests do measure; whether they measure anything else is very dubious.[8] Most psychologists accept this limitation on what an IQ test does. An IQ score is simply a shorthand expression for an individual's level of performance relative to other individuals on a sample of tasks chosen because they predict school performance quite well (but not perfectly, of course).

If you remember the history of IQ tests, that's what they were meant to do in the first place. Binet constructed his test in response to a request from the Board of Education of Paris, which felt that the city could not afford to send everybody to school. The board members wanted to be able to detect in advance the children who were likely to fail. They asked for a test that would find those children who were unlikely to succeed in the Paris school system. That's all the IQ test was designed to do in the beginning, and that is probably all it has ever been able to do, despite the fact that for a long time a lot of people believed that it was really measuring some internal quality of people called intelligence. In fact, an IQ test is a scholastic aptitude test.

That point is well known and widely accepted, at least by psychologists. But the second point—that an IQ test applied in a culture other than the one in which it was developed may not even measure intellectual performance—is less widely accepted, although it is being made with increasing frequency by cross-cultural psychologists.

It is hardly a new discovery that IQ tests are biased against those whose cultural background differs from that of the test's original normative sample. In 1927 the anthropologist Melville Herskovits commented:

> Environmental background, cultural as well as natural, plays a tremendous part in whatever manifestations of innate intelligence an individual may give us through . . . standardized tests. . . . Thus it has been found that the American Indians usually rate somewhat lower in psychological tests than whites, and that this holds true when the tests are of a nonlanguage variety, where the use of words is reduced to a minimum. But the consideration of the fact that the tests ordinarily used have been constructed by persons of a background different from that of the subjects is usually overlooked; and were there to be presented, for consideration as to what is wrong with a given picture, a six-clawed bear rather than a net-less tennis court, one wonders whether the city-dwelling white might not be at a loss rather than the Indians [p. 3].

Over the decades since Herskovits warned that intergroup differences in intelligence test scores might tell much more about the tests than about the

---

[8]A popular misinterpretation of IQ scores—that they reveal the inborn intellectual capacity of individuals or even whole groups—has dangerous political implications. See Kamin (1974) and Segall (1976) for discussions of the political consequences of this conceptual error.

groups, psychometricians have come gradually to acknowledge that this is so. Several attempts have been made to produce "culture-free" or "culture-fair" IQ tests, but none of these has been totally successful. Clearly, culturally mediated experience interacts with test content to influence test performance.

DeVos and Hippler (1969), who reviewed many cross-cultural studies, have made it clear that the once so-called culture-free tests—such as the Raven Progressive Matrices and the Goodenough Draw-A-Man Test—are unavoidably biased in favor of urban, advantaged, Western peoples. As educational and economic conditions anywhere come to resemble those characteristic of the West, test scores reach Western norms. See, for example, Husén (1967), who showed this to have happened in Japan. For some examples from Africa, see McFie (1961), Price-Williams (1961), and Vernon (1965, 1967). And for a comprehensive discussion of the interrelationships between culturally mediated experience and features of testing see Biesheuvel (1949). All these writings refer to one or more of the many ways in which the testing situation and the tester's materials or demeanor are likely to elicit performances from nonadvantaged non-Westerners that yield invalidly low scores.

The kind of evidence that convinces us of IQ tests' cultural bias includes studies cited years ago by Klineberg (1954, pp. 263–269). These studies showed that, among Northern-urban-dwelling Blacks who had been born in Southern-rural settings, there was a positive correlation between length of time in the less deprived environment of the North and IQ scores. Clearly, the more exposure there was to the kind of culture in which the tests were first developed, the better the performance on the tests.

In one recent discussion of the culture-boundedness of tests (Frijda & Jahoda, 1966), a distinction was drawn between *culture-free* and *culture-fair*. The culture-free label would be applied to an instrument that actually measures some inherent quality of human capacity equally well in all cultures. Obviously, there can be no such thing as a culture-free test, so defined.

A culture-fair test could be either of two things. It could be a set of items that are equally unfamiliar to all possible persons in all possible cultures, so everyone would have the same possibility of passing the items. This is—as Brislin, Lonner, and Thorndike (1973, p. 109) put it—a virtual impossibility. Secondly, a culture-fair test could consist of multiple sets of items, modified for use in each culture to ensure that each version of the test would contain the same amount of familiarity. While one would be faced with multiple versions of the same test, it would be culturally fair in that members of each culture would have about the same probability of being able to deal with one version of it.

Culture-fair tests, at least those of this second variety, are quite possible in theory. In practice, they are difficult to construct. And it is extremely difficult, once they have been constructed, to assess their degree of culture fairness.

Let's say, for example, that an investigator is trying to assess the ability of children of various ages in a non-Western culture to grasp a certain concept. She has chosen the concept of conservation of volume—that is, that a given amount of material remains the same when transferred from a tall, thin container to a short, fat one. In her test the investigator uses materials familiar to the tested children rather than materials that were used in similar studies in other cultures—a device employed by Price-Williams (1961). As a result, she will very probably have enhanced the culture fairness of her test. She will at least believe that she has if she finds that the children's performance is better than it was when unfamiliar materials were employed (as Price-Williams found). And her belief will be strengthened if her research produces findings that some theory about psychological processes had led her to expect to find, provided she was measuring the right thing. If she gets such findings, it is plausible to assume that she was indeed measuring the right thing.

Even when that kind of evidence for culture fairness exists, however, there remains the possibility—and a likely one at that—that different things are being measured in different cultures and to an unknown degree.

Returning to our central comment that the primary methodological problem in cross-cultural research is deciding *what* to measure, it should now be apparent that the problem of *how* to measure it stems directly from the first problem. The root of all measurement problems in cross-cultural research is the possibility that the same behaviors may have different meanings across cultures or that the same processes might have different overt manifestations. As a result, the "same" test might be "different" when applied in different cultures. Therefore, the effort to devise culture-fair testing procedures will probably never be completely successful for all of the behavioral traits we might want to measure. The degree to which we are measuring the same thing in more than one culture, whether we are using the same or different test items, must always worry us. We must always assume the worst while hoping for the best.

In the long run, of course, we will acquire confidence that we are measuring truly comparable phenomena if we accumulate evidence that they relate to other variables in a predictable, understandable fashion. But, until such evidence has been accumulated, we cannot be sure of the comparability of what we are measuring when we apply a test—any test—in more than one culture.

One more point about this measurement problem: its importance varies somewhat depending on the purpose for which performance scores in any test are accumulated and the interpretation made of those scores. This point has been made by Vernon (1965, 1967), who himself has used various aptitude tests with samples of students in East Africa and the Caribbean.

The problem is most serious when a test is used to assess some presumed-to-exist inherent ability or some other presumably "fixed" personality trait. To put it bluntly, with no test—not an IQ test, not a Rorschach test—can we be sure that we are measuring what the test purports to measure. For any number of reasons other than differences in the ability or the personality trait, any two cultural groups are very likely to perform differently.

When we are not disposed to interpret performance differences as manifestations of inherent qualities of personality, the problem is less severe but still serious. For we are seldom interested in demonstrating differences *induced by* some feature of the test itself. We want to uncover differences in behavior that can be measured by tests other than the one we happen to be using. So, in this category of studies, too, we must ensure that the differences we find are not merely a product of different reactions to being tested or some other irrelevancy.

The problem is even less severe when we intend merely to assess the current capacity of individuals to perform some task and don't care at all what that current capacity reflects. An example is the use of an aptitude test to select workers who will require the least amount of training to perform a task. In this case the problem of culture fairness almost disappears. *Almost*, but not quite. Even here we might not get a valid assessment if the testing procedure itself somehow inhibits the persons being tested from displaying their current skills.

So, there is really no avoiding the problem. Cross-cultural psychologists need to be constantly vigilant to the possibility that they are not measuring what they intend to measure, regardless of the instrument they use and regardless of the purpose for which they are using it.

Sampling Problems in Cross-Cultural Research

That sampling problems abound in cross-cultural psychology has been noted by many (see, for example, Frijda & Jahoda, 1966; Campbell, 1961; Naroll, 1970; and Brislin, Lonner, & Thorndike, 1973). Of course, sampling is a problem in all psychological research. We have to worry in general about the representativeness of a sample—to what population our findings can be generalized. And, whenever we are comparing two or more samples, we have to worry about their comparability. In cross-cultural psychology the latter worry is obviously common, since so much of the research consists of comparisons of the performance of two or more groups.

Obtaining Comparable Samples. There is a seeming paradox here. Whenever we do a cross-cultural study we presumably want to work with samples that are *different* from each other. Yet we do want them to be comparable. How can they be both comparable and different at the same time? The point is, of course, that we want differences in some respects—for example, the dietary practices of two or more cultures—and commonalities in other respects—for example, years of formal education—so we can investigate the hypothesized effect of some difference on people who are *otherwise* comparable.

Say we have a hypothesis about the long-term consequences of a protein-deficient diet on problem-solving ability. We want to test this hypothesis by comparing cultural groups whose childhood diet is rich in animal protein with groups that feed their children mostly vegetables. We would try to compare groups that have had roughly equal amounts and kinds of schooling, because formal schooling provides some training in problem-solving skills.

Unfortunately, when we move from culture to culture, we find that age and years of schooling are highly correlated in some places but not in others. In other words, whereas in Culture A persons who are, say, in their sixth year of schooling are likely to be within a year or two of 12 years of age, in Culture B they might represent a much wider range of ages and probably be higher in average age. Certainly, if Culture B were in a traditional, less-developed, non-Western society, persons with six years of schooling would be older, would range widely about the average age, and would be relatively rare persons within their own societies. They would probably be richer, disproportionately male, and so on.

So, when we hold one variable constant, we are almost inevitably confronted with variations along some unknown number of other variables.

The aspect of the sampling problem that we have just discussed—the virtual impossibility of obtaining samples from more than one society that are truly comparable—is the major reason that D. T. Campbell has warned (first in 1961 and again in 1972, with Raoul Naroll) that all studies that consist solely of single pair comparisons are uninterpretable. The example Campbell used was Malinowski's material on Trobriand Island dreams compared with Freud's material on Viennese dreams. As we saw in Chapter Two, this comparison demonstrated the need for cross-cultural testing of hypotheses spawned in a single culture. Campbell asserted, however, that such a comparison would *not* reveal the process underlying male adolescent hostility:

> Between Trobriand and Vienna there are many dimensions of differences which could constitute potential rival explanations and which we have no means of ruling out. For comparisons of this pair, the *ceteris paribus* [other things being equal] requirement becomes untenable. But data collection need not stop here. Both the avunculate and the European arrangement are so widely distributed over the world that if testing Oedipal theories were our purpose, we could select a dozen matched pairs of tribes from widely varying culture areas, each pair differing with regard to which male educates and disciplines the boy, but as similar as possible in other respects. Assuming that collections of dreams from boys showed the expected differences between each pair, then the more such pairs we had, the fewer tenable rival hypotheses would be available and, thus, the more certain would be our confirmation [Campbell, 1961, pp. 344–345].

Clearly, then, our sampling objective in any cross-cultural study must be to obtain a large number of societies (certainly more than two) that may be different in some respects (or we wouldn't be interested in them) but similar enough in other respects that they can be meaningfully compared. The objective is, of course, easier to state than to achieve. But it is always worth knowing what our objective is, if only to know how much any study falls short of achieving it.

We turn now to a sampling problem of special concern to those cross-cultural researchers who seek functional relationships among societal characteristics.

Avoiding False Findings. Whiting (1968) attached the label "*the* cross-cultural method" (my italics) to the research strategy in which a number of cultures are employed as if they composed an unbiased sample of all the world's cultures. The degree of covariation around two or more "traits" of these sample cultures are determined by a statistical test (usually a chi-square test or a correlational analysis). A typical application of this method—which clearly is *a* cross-cultural method (only one among many)—may be found in numerous studies that have employed ethnographic data codified in the Human Relations Area Files. Such data consist primarily of reports of typical practices, institutions, and other characteristics of whole societies (rather than facts about individual behaviors). The objective of this kind of cross-cultural study is to find functional relationships between two or more traits that in the Berry framework are classified as "adaptive variables."

For example, a classic study of socialization practices by Whiting and Child (1953) examined, among other things, the relationship between the typical emphasis on aspects of training during childhood and the typical prevalence of certain shared beliefs about the causes of illness. That there might be such a relationship was suggested by the authors' reading of Freudian theory, reinterpreted in the light of contemporary learning theory. To determine whether such a relationship existed, the authors sampled a large number of societies for which information was available about both traits. In essence, they dichotomized both variables, which made it possible to assign all societies in their sample to one of four quadrants in a matrix, as shown in Figure 3-2.

Once the societies are assigned, the question becomes to what degree the societies cluster in some systematic fashion. If, for example, about as many societies that emphasize oral training hold the belief that illness is caused by ingesting "bad" foods as do not hold that belief—and the same is true of societies that do not emphasize oral training—we would conclude that those traits are not functionally related. In contrast, if a preponderance of societies fall in cells 2 and 3 of Figure 3-2—showing that most societies that emphasize oral training hold the belief, whereas most that don't emphasize the training don't hold the belief—we would have evidence for a functional relationship. The relationship would be attested to by a statistically significant chi-square or a statistically significant positive correlation or both.

Incidentally—but not unimportantly—this "functional" relationship would not be taken to mean *necessarily* that the socialization emphasis *causes* the illness-causation belief. It would be understood that it is also possible that the latter influences the former or that both are influenced by some other variable. But a statistic that indicates that the two traits are not independent of each other, that they covary, would be accepted as evidence of a functional relationship.

Belief that illness is caused by oral activity

	Absent	Present
Emphasized	1	2
Unemphasized	3	4

Figure 3-2. Socialization of eating behavior

In order to conclude that a functional relationship has been demonstrated, however, it has to be assumed that the societies in the sample are independent units. The societies must be not only representative of the universe of societies—a necessity if we want to assert that the relationship probably holds for the human species; they must also be truly separate instances of societies. This is so first of all because our statistical test assumes it is so. The significance of a chi-square or of a correlation coefficient of a given magnitude depends on the size of the sample or the number of units in it. (For example, a correlation coefficient of .30 or larger with a sample of 50 units would be significant, while that same size of correlation with a sample of 10 units would not be significant.)

There is one sense in which a sample of, say, 50 societies might really be a much smaller sample. Suppose, for example, that at some time in the distant past Society A came to emphasize oral training *and* to hold the belief that eating could make one ill. These two developments might have been linked functionally—it doesn't matter for this argument. Then suppose that Society A came into contact with Society B in trade or conquest and influenced Society B gradually to adopt *both* traits. In technical language, the two traits would be said to have diffused together from Society A to Society B.

Suppose further that this codiffusion spreads to Societies D, E, and so on through Society L. Finally, suppose that our sample of *n* societies is composed of these particular societies, A through L, plus two others. We would "discover" with such a sample that the two traits are highly correlated, and with a sample size *n* the correlation might well be significant. But, as we have just described the situation, our sample size would, in effect, be only three, because Societies A through L were not independent of one another.

This sampling problem was first recognized by the great British statistician Francces Galton (1889, p. 272) during a meeting of the Royal Anthropological Institute. It was revived during the 1960s by the American anthropologist Raoul Naroll, who has also proposed a number of sampling strategies and statistical techniques for dealing with the problem (Naroll, 1961, 1964; Naroll & D'Andrade, 1963). These several solutions have also been discussed and critically analyzed by Chaney and colleagues (Chaney & Revilla, 1969; Chaney, Morton, & Moore, 1972).

The Naroll solutions are based on the notion that diffusion is more likely among neighboring societies. This notion leads to the argument that, the more geographically dispersed a sample of cultures, the more likely it is that a relationship between two traits within such a sample is functional rather than diffusional or historical. Naroll's argument underscores the need to select samples from various regions of the world in ways that reduce the likelihood of finding pseudorelationships, those that appear functional but are merely diffusional.

Naroll's argument can be generalized into a warning that improper sampling can produce "findings" that are merely artifacts of the sampling procedure employed. This is a warning that cross-cultural researchers must take seriously, because so much of their sampling is done neither systematically nor randomly, but "haphazardly" and conveniently. Putting it bluntly, cross-cultural researchers often take what they can get, employing data that happen already to be available or collecting data in societies they are able or willing to visit.

The sampling problems highlighted by the Galton, Naroll, and Chaney arguments are essentially problems inherent in the Whiting cross-cultural method; but the generalization of the argument applies to all cross-cultural studies of a hypothesis-testing nature. We simply cannot be sanguine about the validity or the generalizability of a cross-cultural finding when the sampling procedures permit sampling artifacts to occur.

Finding Representative Subjects. This brings us to a third aspect of sampling difficulties in cross-cultural research, which may be termed the *accessibility* problem.

Much intracultural psychological research, especially the vast majority of social-psychological experiments conducted in the U.S. university laboratories, employs student subjects who are invited, expected, and induced to volunteer. They are a kind of captive audience. As a result, accessibility is a minimal problem in such research.

In cross-cultural studies, by contrast, merely locating, reaching, and inducing to participate the kinds of persons needed as subjects or respondents is difficult, time consuming, and expensive. As a result, there may well be subtle pressures on the investigator to recruit relatively accessible subjects. These are likely to be persons *on* the beaten track. They are likely to have had relatively high degrees of previous contact with outside cultures. They may be of above-average wealth and education and have linguistic skills or other characteristics that make them unrepresentative of the population they are (erroneously) taken to represent.

Moreover, it seems exceedingly plausible to argue that, the more unaccessible a foreign population is, the more likely a sample drawn from it will be unrepresentative. This is because the greater the difficulties are, the more the investigator will be willing to settle for people with whom he can most conveniently interact. Thus, a cross-cultural study employing cultures that vary in accessibility may reduce to a study in which the samples are highly representative in the accessible cultures and unrepresentative in the inaccessible ones.

The accessibility problem in cross-cultural sampling has an interesting parallel in traditional ethnographic research. Sometimes an anthropologist employs a member of a society as an "informant" about the customs and institutions of that society. The anthropologist is likely to need as an informant someone with whom he can communicate. And persons likely to apply for such a job are in some ways—linguistically, educationally, or otherwise—different from the mass of their own society. Thus, it is probable that an informant will be a member of the elite and, as such, have a specialized atypical knowledge about the society.

As a result, what the anthropologist learns from the informant about the society may be true enough, but it may not be the most *generally* true set of facts that the anthropologist hoped to be acquiring. Thus, what is ultimately "known" about the culture—as in the records of the Human Relations Area Files, for example—has been filtered not only through a foreign observer but also through an unrepresentative and possibly narrow-viewed insider.

To the extent that such data enter into subsequent studies, there is one more threat to the validity of those studies. We have examined the sampling problems of cross-cultural research in some detail. Although we have by no means exhausted the types, enough has been said to make clear that it matters not only what we study and how we study it but also whom we study.

We have seen that measurement problems and sampling problems present cross-cultural research with large hurdles to overcome. And there is still a third category of methodological problems that are particularly acute in cross-cultural research. These we will call administrative problems, and it is to some of these that we now turn.

Administrative Problems in Cross-Cultural Research

Administrative problems refer to threats to the validity of a study that derive from the interaction between the investigator and those whose behavior he or she is investigating. Obviously, people in other cultures will be very different from the investigator in many respects. (That is why, after all, he wants to study them.) From these differences some intriguing methodological problems emerge.

For instance, there are likely to be serious impediments to communication—so serious that the subjects may misinterpret the task they are supposed to perform or the investigator may misinterpret the performance. There may be certain misperceptions by the subjects of the investigator's role and status, and these misperceptions may affect their performance in any variety of unknown ways. The subjects may be frightened, awed, cowed, or otherwise placed in some state of mind that will affect their motivation to perform. They may say or do whatever they think they have to in order to please, placate, or get away from someone they perceive as a tax collector, census enumerator, or policeman.

Once again, if these difficulties are more prevalent in some societies than in others included in a single study, there will be the problem of differential meaningfulness of the behaviors observed in the societies. In some, the behaviors may be typical of what occurs when subjects are relaxed. In others, the behavior may be that which occurs when people are frightened out of their wits. Needless to say, comparability will have been threatened.

Some of these problems—notably those pertaining to the attitudes and motivation of people while being tested—were dealt with earlier when we examined measurement problems. (Further discussion of factors surrounding testing cross-culturally are found in Brislin, Lonner, & Thorndike, 1973; Biesheuvel, 1949; and Frijda & Jahoda, 1966.) We will be concerned here with communication problems and how these can be minimized.

Assuring a Proper Translation. A basic step in all cross-cultural studies that transcend language groups is the translation of tests, tasks, questionnaires, or other instruments. The different language versions must obviously be equivalent. Once again, this is easier said than done. Brislin and his colleagues have recently offered twelve guidelines merely for writing English versions of psychological instruments in a manner that will permit them to be translated into another language (Brislin, Lonner, & Thorndike, 1973, pp. 32–40). They also provided three techniques for translation (pp. 40–47) and five procedures for evaluating the resultant equivalence of translated instruments (pp. 51–80)!

Following Werner and Campbell (1970) and Brislin (1970), Brislin, Lonner, and Thorndike strongly recommend back-translation as the single best technique for producing equivalent versions of an instrument. Starting with, say, an English-language form that is potentially translatable, an English-speaking investigator employs two native speakers of the target language who are themselves bilingual. One translates from English to the target language, and the result is then translated by the second bilingual speaker back to English. If identical English versions result, the target version is likely to be of satisfactory equivalence. Even then it may not be, note Brislin, Lonner, and Thorndike (1973, p. 41). This is because the translators may share erroneous translation rules, among other reasons.

Hence, Brislin (1970) has developed five corroboration techniques. These include the "ultimate" test: employing bilingual subjects randomly assigned to one of four groups, each of which performs the actual task called for by the instrument. One group is administered the source-language version. The second gets the target-language version. And the third and fourth groups get split versions; either the first half of the test is in the source language and the second half in the target language, or vice versa. If all groups earn roughly equal scores and if correlations within the last two groups between scores earned on source and target versions are high, it may be concluded that the two versions are equivalent.

These ultimate performance criteria provide the best possible test of the equivalence of translated instruments. The complexity of the procedures attests to the difficulty of the translation problem. It is a manageable problem, however, as shown in a volume edited by Brislin (1976). Brislin's recommendations should clearly be followed. Not to do so invites differences in behavior across cultures that may be nothing more than the product of non-equivalent instruments.

Avoiding Misunderstanding. D. T. Campbell (1964) has pointed out a further task-communication problem that can plague cross-cultural research. Even when we feel confident that the best possible translation has been achieved, there remains the possibility that the task we have set for our respondents is misunderstood. Suppose, as is so often the case in cross-cultural research, that respondents in one society perform the task one way and respondents in another society do it a different way. This is another way of saying that they give different responses and earn different scores. We would like to be sure that this difference across groups represents a "real" difference. But what if the two (or more) groups merely understood the tasks differently and were, in effect, performing different tasks.

Campbell dealt with this general problem by linking it to a concrete instance of a cross-cultural study of visual perception (Segall, Campbell, & Herskovits, 1966). This study will be discussed in detail in the next chapter of this book. For our present purposes it suffices to know that the study yielded striking differences among a large number of societies in the degree to which they seemed susceptible to a number of optical illusions. That is, whereas in one society subjects tended on the average to indicate that two lines appeared equal when one line was actually 8% longer than another line, in some other society subjects tended to indicate equality of length when one line was 15% longer. Apparently and, for theoretical reasons, preferably, such a difference in performance would be interpreted as evidence that these two groups were actually seeing things differently. But how can we tell when we are communicating well enough to know that people are seeing things differently?

In dramatic fashion, Campbell (1964) elucidated the problem:

> Suppose that we parachuted an anthropologist and a test booklet into a totally isolated New Guinea tribe and that the anthropologist had first to learn the language without the help of an interpreter. The process of language learning would then become a part of the operations which we would have to detail. It would become obvious that no person ever learns another's language perfectly; that the existence of "interpreters" should not be taken for granted; that here is a problematic situation in which the cues and presumptions of communication need to be specified. It turns out that the anthropologist's main cue for achieved communication is similarity between the response of the other to a stimulus and the response which he himself would make. Disagreement turns out to be a sign of communication failure. How then can disagreement on an optical illusion test item be taken instead as a difference in perceiving the world? [p. 317].*

*This and all other quotations from this source are from "Distinguishing Differences of Perception from Failure of Communication in Cross-Cultural Studies," by D. T. Campbell. In F. Northop and H. Livingston (Eds.), *Cross-Cultural Understandings: Epistemology in Anthropology.* Copyright 1964 by Harper & Row, Publishers, Inc. Reprinted by permission.

In the case of the Segall, Campbell, and Herskovits (1966) study, the problem was confronted in a variety of ways, but we will here present only one. This involved the use of four preliminary stimuli, the first items shown to each respondent. They were all prepared in such a way that, if the respondent did not respond exactly as the anthropologist (or you or I) would have, it could only be assumed that misunderstanding of the task was involved. For example, one such item was composed of a *very* short black line and a *very* long red line. The question asked was "Which line is longer, the red or the black one?" If (as almost never happened) someone were to have said "black," we would not have concluded that to that person the black line appeared longer. Rather, we would have concluded that he had misunderstood one or a combination of the words "line," "longer," "black," or "red" or something else about what he was being asked to do.

Yet for the real test items, of course, we were prepared to interpret whatever responses we received at face value. The key to understanding this is to recognize that our preliminary items required comparisons of such extremely exaggerated line differences that anyone would find it incredible to interpret an incorrect response as indicating anything other than a failure of communication. Once it is shown that communication is not failing on the preliminary items, the assumption of achieved communication may then be confidently carried over to the test items.

Because nearly all persons everywhere had behaved alike on the preliminary items, we could treat instances in which they did behave differently as genuinely interesting and not merely artifacts of miscommunication. That the various groups in the study behaved similarly enough in certain respects made it possible to treat the differences that did show up as meaningful differences.

As Campbell (1964) has put it, the preventions taken by Segall, Campbell, and Herskovits

> illustrate one important general principle: Discrepancy can be noted and interpreted only against the background of an overwhelming proportion of nondiscrepant fit, agreement, or pattern repetition. This principle is found in operation in knowledge processes as varied as binocular vision and astronomy. Again and again in science, the equivocal interpretations are available: separate entity vs. same entity changed, moved, or perceived from a different perspective. And in all such instances where the second interpretation occurs, it is made possible by the overwhelming bulk of stable nonchanging background. Consider the reidentification of a single planet on successive nights, plus the inference that the planet migrates in an eccentric backtracking manner. Had Jupiter been the only star in the sky, this might never have been documented, certainly not by a nomadic people. Had all the stars been planets, it would also have gone unascertained. Had the oscillations in the locations of the fixed stars been so great as to subtend several degrees of visual angle, the backtracking would not have been observed. It was the recurrent "fixedness" of 99.9 percent of the stars which made the wanderings of the few planets interpretable as such [p. 327].

Applying this principle to cross-cultural research, then, the dictum is obvious. Design the research in such a way that you ensure finding identical behaviors as well as different ones. For differences alone can only be ambiguous. A difference is interpretable only when embedded in a context of sameness.

We have seen enough in this chapter to understand, in a rather abstract fashion, how cross-cultural research ought to be done. We have not, of course, discussed all the methodological issues that confront cross-cultural psychologists in the detail that those issues require. Fortunately, such discussions are accessible (see, for example, Triandis & Berry, 1979). However, we now have an appreciation for problems of comparability, equivalence, and the like and are ready to look at some research and begin to learn about some of the substantive issues that our methodological sophistication helps us to appreciate. In the next chapter, appropriately enough, we will focus on the substantive research from which Campbell's discussion, reviewed in the immediately preceding section, was drawn. Do people in different cultures really see things differently?

References

Barry, H., Child, I. L., & Bacon, M. K. The relation of child training to subsistence economy. *American Anthropologist*, 1959, *61*, 51–63.

Berry, J. W. On cross-cultural comparability. *International Journal of Psychology*, 1969, *4*, 119–128.

Berry, J. W. Ecological and cultural factors in spatial perceptual development. *Canadian Journal of Behavioural Science*, 1971, *3*, 324–336.

Berry, J. W. An ecological approach to cross-cultural psychology. *Nederlands Tijdschrift voor de Psychologie*, 1975, *30*, 51–84.

Berry, J. W. *Human Ecology and Cognitive Style: Comparative Studies in Cultural and Psychological Adaptation*. Beverly Hills, Calif.: Sage, 1976.

Biesheuvel, S. Psychological tests and their application to non-European peoples. In G. B. Jeffrey (Ed.), *The Yearbook of Education*. London: Evans, 1949. Pp. 90–104.

Brislin, R. W. Back translation for cross-cultural research. *Journal of Cross-Cultural Psychology*, 1970, *1*, 185–216.

Brislin, R. W. (Ed.). *Translation: Applications and Research*. New York: Gardner Press, 1976.

Brislin, R. W., Lonner, W. J., & Thorndike, R. M. *Cross-Cultural Research Methods*. New York: Wiley, 1973.

Campbell, D. T. The mutual methodological relevance of anthropology and psychology. In F. L. K. Hsu (Ed.), *Psychological Anthropology*. Homewood, Ill.: Dorsey, 1961. Pp. 333–352.

Campbell, D. T. Distinguishing differences of perception from failure of communication in cross-cultural studies. In F. Northop & H. Livingston (Eds.), *Cross-Cultural Understandings: Epistemology in Anthropology*. New York: Harper & Row, 1964. Pp. 308–336.

Campbell, D. T., & Naroll, R. The mutual methodological relevance of anthropology and psychology. In F. L. K. Hsu (Ed.), *Psychological Anthropology* (Rev. ed.). Cambridge, Mass.: Schenkman, 1972. Pp. 435–463.

Chaney, R. P., Morton, K., & Moore, T. On the entangled problems of selection and conceptual organization. *American Anthropologist*, 1972, *74*, 221–230.

Chaney, R. P., & Revilla, R. R. Sampling methods and interpretation of correlation. A comparative analysis of seven cross-cultural samples. *American Anthropologist*, 1969, *71*, 597–633.

DeVos, G. A., & Hippler, A. E. Cultural psychology: Comparative studies of human behaviors. In G. Lindzey & E. Aronson (Eds.), *Handbook of Social Psychology* (Vol. 4). Reading, Mass.: Addison-Wesley, 1969.

DuBois, C. *The People of Alor*. Minneapolis: University of Minnesota Press, 1944.

Frijda, N., & Jahoda, G. On the scope and methods of cross-cultural research. *International Journal of Psychology*, 1966, *1*, 110–127.

Galton, F. Comment on E. B. Tylor. On a method of investigating the development of institutions: Applied to laws of marriage and descent. *Journal of the Royal Anthropological Association of Great Britain and Ireland*, 1889.

Gordon, H. *Mental and Scholastic Tests among Retarded Children.* (Educational Pamphlet No. 44.) London: Board of Education, 1923. (Reprinted in abridged form in I. Al-Issa & W. Dennis (Eds.), *Cross-Cultural Studies of Behavior.* New York: Holt, Rinehart & Winston, 1970. Pp. 111–119.)

Herskovits, M. J. *The Negro and Intelligence Tests.* Hanover, N. H.: Sociological Press, 1927.

Holtzman, W. H., Díaz-Guerrero, R., & Swartz, J. D. *Personality Development in Two Cultures: A Cross-Cultural Longitudinal Study of School Children in Mexico and the U.S.* Austin: University of Texas Press, 1975.

Hsu, F. L. K. (Ed.), *Psychological Anthropology.* Homewood, Ill.: Dorsey, 1961.

Hsu, F. L. K. (Ed.), *Psychological Anthropology* (Rev. ed.). Cambridge, Mass.: Schenkman, 1972.

Husén, T. *International Study of Achievement in Mathematics: A Comparison of Twelve Countries* (Vol. 1). New York: Wiley, 1967.

Kamin, L. J. *The Science and Politics of IQ.* Potomac, Md.: Erlbaum, 1974.

Kardiner, A. *The Psychological Frontiers of Society.* New York: Columbia University Press, 1945.

Klineberg, O. *Social Psychology* (Rev. ed.). New York: Holt, 1954. Pp. 263–269.

Klineberg, O. Negro-White differences in intelligence test performance: A new look at an old problem. *American Psychologist*, 1963, *18*, 198–203.

LeVine, R. A. Cross-cultural study in child psychology. In P. Mussen (Ed.), *Carmichael's Manual of Child Psychology* (Vol. 2) (3rd ed.). New York: Wiley, 1970. Pp. 559–612.

LeVine, R. A. *Culture, Behavior and Personality.* Chicago: Aldine, 1973.

Lewis, O. *Life in a Mexican Village: Tepoztlan Restudied.* Urbana: University of Illinois Press, 1951.

Lindzey, G. *Projective Techniques and Cross-Cultural Research.* New York: Appleton-Century-Crofts, 1961.

Linton, R. *The Cultural Background of Personality.* New York: Appleton-Century-Crofts, 1945. (a)

Linton, R. Foreword to *The Psychological Frontiers of Society*, by A. Kardiner. New York: Columbia University Press, 1945. (b)

Lonner, W. J. Issues in cross-cultural psychology. In A. Marsella, R. Tharp, & T. Ciborowski (Eds.), *Perspectives on Cross-Cultural Psychology.* New York: Academic Press, 1979.

McFie, J. The effect of education on African performance on a group of intellectual tests. *British Journal of Educational Psychology,* 1961, *31,* 232–240.

Naroll, R. Two solutions to Galton's problem. *Philosophy of Science,* 1961, *28,* 15–39.

Naroll, R. A fifth solution to Galton's problem. *American Anthropologist,* 1964, *66,* 863–867.

Naroll, R. Cross-cultural sampling. In R. Naroll & R. Cohen (Eds.), *A Handbook of Method in Cultural Anthropology.* New York: American Museum of Natural History, 1970. Pp. 889–926.

Naroll, R., & D'Andrade, R. G. Two further solutions to Galton's problem. *American Anthropologist,* 1963, *65,* 1053–1067.

Nimkoff, M. F., & Middleton, R. Types of family and types of economy. *American Journal of Sociology,* 1960, *66,* 215–225.

Price-Williams, D. R. A study concerning concepts of conservation of quantities among primitive children. *Acta Psychologica,* 1961, *18,* 297–305.

Segall, M. H. *Human Behavior and Public Policy.* Elmsford, N.Y.: Pergamon, 1976.

Segall, M. H., Campbell, D. T., & Herskovits, M. J. *The Influence of Culture on Visual Perception.* Indianapolis: Bobbs-Merrill, 1966.

Spiro, M. E. Social systems, personality, and functional analysis. In B. Kaplan (Ed.), *Studying Personality Cross-Culturally.* Evanston, Ill.: Row, Peterson, 1961. Pp. 93–127.

Triandis, H. C., & Berry, J. W. (Eds.). *Handbook of Cross-Cultural Psychology.* Vol. 2: *Methodology.* Boston: Allyn & Bacon, 1979.

Vernon, P. E. Ability factors and environmental influences. *American Psychologist,* 1965, *20,* 723–733.

Vernon, P. E. Abilities and educational attainments in an East African environment. *Journal of Special Education,* 1967, *1,* 335–345.

Wallace, A. F. C. *Culture and Personality.* New York: Random House, 1961.

Werner, O., & Campbell, D. T. Translating, working through interpreters, and the problem of decentering. In R. Naroll & R. Cohen (Eds.), *A Handbook of Method in Cultural Anthropology.* New York: American Museum of Natural History, 1970. Pp. 398–420.

Whiting, J. W. M. Method and problems in cross-cultural research. In G. Lindzey & E. Aronson (Eds.), *Handbook of Social Psychology* (2nd ed.). Cambridge, Mass.: Addison-Wesley, 1968.

Whiting, J. W. M., & Child, I. L. *Child Training and Personality.* New Haven, Conn.: Yale University Press, 1953.

Witkin, H. A., & Berry, J. W. Psychological differentiation in cross-cultural perspective. *Journal of Cross-Cultural Psychology,* 1975, *6,* 4–87.

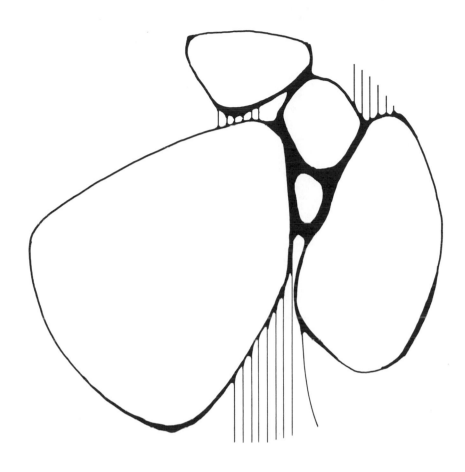

Cultural Influences
on Basic Psychological
Processes

Part Two

Four

Experiential Influences on Visual Perception: Are Optical Illusions Culture Bound?

Even to someone unsophisticated in psychology, it is obvious that people's social and cultural background shapes certain aspects of their behavior to a marked degree. Beliefs, attitudes, values, and life-styles differ in such striking ways across social classes, ethnic groups, religions, and nations that these differences are taken for granted and hardly seem to require explanation. None of us, for example, considers it surprising that capitalists and socialists place very different values on the multinational corporation.

In contrast, it is not commonly thought that groups of human beings differ in such fundamental ways as in the way they perceive space, size, or distance; in their strategies for remembering and processing information; or even in some of the hopes and aspirations that motivate them. We tend to believe that the world's different languages are merely different ways of expressing underlying thought processes that are fundamentally the same.

While it is obvious that human groups differ in many superficial ways, it is widely assumed that there are basic psychological processes common to all. Thus, there seems little intuitive reason to expect that a sharp, distinct photograph of a woman's face would not immediately be recognized as such by any viewer, regardless of the viewer's class, race, ethnicity, or nationality. Nor would many people expect systematic differences across cultural groups in the detection of length differences in two straight lines. However much various viewers of the photograph might be expected to vary in their *judgments* of the photographed subject's attractiveness or intelligence, they would be expected to agree at least that they were looking at the face of a human being. And however much error might be contained in judgments of the relative lengths of two straight lines, the errors should not differ in degree systematically across cultural groups.

Similarly, redness may call for different color names or may connote different ideas (such as passion or danger) to different people, but all must *recognize* a red object as such when encountering one.

However reasonable this expectation of underlying similarity in basic psychological processes might seem, social psychologists do not hold it unskeptically. Nor have various philosophers and other scholars through the ages. At least from the time of the Greek philosophers, questions have been raised about whether individual human organisms might interact with their own sense impressions and thus participate actively in their perceptions of external objects and events. The result of such interaction would be that any given object or event is perceived uniquely by each person.

This line of reasoning allows for the possibility that any experience a person has is influenced by that person's previous experiences. To the extent that previous experiences are determined by the accident of birth at a particular time in a particular place, it becomes probable that the "same" event will be different events, even in very fundamental ways, to members of different cultural groups.

Not surprisingly, then, cross-cultural psychologists have wondered greatly about both differences *and* uniformities in the behavior of human beings. Much of their research has been designed to find out why readily visible differences across human groups exist. At the same time, in the face of such variety some of the research consists of a search for human universals. Although cross-cultural psychologists are prone to the same prejudices, blind spots, and ethnocentric expectations as other people, they try in their research to keep an open mind. Somewhat paradoxically, as we shall see, their research has led to the tentative conclusion that cultural groups are in some ways *less different* than is popularly believed and in other ways *more different*.

In Part Two of the book we will concentrate on research that has revealed—and sought explanations for—some cross-cultural differences in fundamental behaviors. These behaviors are seemingly so basic that the mere fact that there are differences will probably surprise many people. We will review in the three chapters that make up this section some of what has been learned about the influence of culturally mediated experiences on perception, cognition, and motivation—three very basic classes of psychological process. We will begin with what is perhaps the most basic of all: perception of the physical world.

Within this class we will concentrate on visual perception, because vision is the preeminent sense for humans and the most thoroughly studied. And we will, in the balance of this chapter, deal intensively with a single problem of visual perception: cultural differences in susceptibility to optical illusions.

This problem illustrates the slow, sometimes tortuous, methods scientists must use to understand how culture influences behavior. Several different investigators have worked on the problem for many years. It has been approached in different ways, and findings have been subjected to different, sometimes competing, interpretations.

Concentrating, as we are about to do, on a single issue in visual perception should not be taken to mean that other issues in this domain have been neglected by cross-cultural researchers. There are, for example, extensive bodies of work on color perception and pictorial depth perception, to name only two. These are interesting issues in their own right and, incidentally, are not unrelated to our focal concern in this chapter, illusion susceptibility. So, a few words about them are in order.

Cross-cultural studies of color vocabulary—from which scholars are sometimes able to draw cautious inferences about color perception—have revealed both differences and universals. The best recent analyses of both kinds of findings are provided by Berlin and Kay (1969), Heider (1972), and Osgood, May, and Miron (1975, Chapter 6). Explanations for the systematic differences in color naming vary from the physiological (such as eye pigmentation correlated with race, as in Bornstein, 1973) to the cultural (such as richness of color vocabulary correlated with societal complexity, as in Berlin & Kay, 1969). We will see shortly that this competition between a physiological and a cultural explanation is also characteristic of theorizing about illusion susceptibility.

Research on pictorial depth perception began with Hudson (1960, 1967) and has been extended profitably in an excellent series of studies by Deregowski (1968, 1971, 1972) and by Jahoda and McGurk (1974a, 1974b, 1974c). The central finding from this work was that the perception of depth in drawings and photographs is *not* immediate or unlearned. Rather, the ability to utilize perspective and other depth cues contained in photographs and "realistic" drawings was held to be acquired with certain kinds of experience, especially schooling, the availability of which covaries with other cultural variables.[1] This finding, as will soon become apparent, is of considerable import for our understanding of how visual information conveys meaning differently to members of different cultures.

---

[1]There is recent evidence that 7-month-old U.S. infants display pictorial depth sensitivity (Yonas, Cleaves, & Pettersen, 1978).

The reader should therefore appreciate that concentrating on a single issue is justified for two reasons: (1) because it provides a richer sense of both the difficulties and intellectual rewards of research and (2) because the methods, theories, and controversies on which we will concentrate are similar to those that pertain to other issues. But our decision to specialize also results in a sacrifice of breadth of coverage. Accordingly, the reader is well advised to search out some accounts of color perception and pictorial depth perception in the literature. Good summaries can be found in Triandis, Malpass, and Davidson (1971), Miller (1973), Serpell (1976, Chapter 6), and Ember (1977).

But for now, let's plunge into cross-cultural research on susceptibility to optical illusions. We'll begin by dipping a toe or two into some familiar philosophical concepts.

Perception: Determined by Reality?

The premise that the world is what it appears to be was challenged many centuries ago by Plato (circa 390 B.C.) in his famous parable of the cave (*Republic* 7). People are imprisoned in the cave, able to see only shadows and reflections of what transpires about them. Plato's point was that the prisoners will take these shadows for reality. If the prisoners are released and directly witness the objects and events that are casting the shadows, Plato said, the objects and events will appear less real than their reflections.

Subsequently, Locke in 1690 and Berkeley in 1713 extended Plato's suggestion that the world, rather than appearing to us as it is, appears to us in ways determined by our prior experience. These two philosophers employed a particularly compelling example: a single event generates two opposite impressions in the same observer at the same time! In Berkeley's version, contained in *Three Dialogues between Hylas and Philonous* (1713/1927, p. 18), this seeming paradox is recounted as follows:

> *Philonous*: Is it not an absurdity to think that the same thing should be at the same time both cold and warm?
>
> *Hylas*: It is.
>
> *Philonous*: Suppose now one of your hands was hot, the other cold, and that they are both at once put into the same vessel of water in an intermediate state: will not the water seem cold to one hand, and warm to the other?
>
> *Hylas*: It will.
>
> *Philonous*: Ought we not therefore by your principles to conclude it is really both cold and warm at the same time? That is, according to your own concession, to believe an absurdity?
>
> *Hylas*: I confess it seems so.

In this dramatic experience—which, incidentally, can be repeated by anyone with three basins of water, one hot, one lukewarm, and one cool[2] —Berkeley demonstrates the way the state of the observer helps determine his or her observation. He and many other philosophers have thus warned us against "naive realism." A psychological counterpart to that philosophical concept has been called *phenomenal absolutism* (Segall, Campbell, & Herskovits, 1966). This term calls attention to the widespread tendency of human beings to assume, naively, that the world is exactly as it appears. That tendency is probably reinforced by the phenomenal clarity, constancy, and thing-ness of the content of our perceptions. All I am suggesting by this notion of phenomenal absolutism is that, given the structure of the organism and the way the world is filtered through our sense organs, it does *appear* solid and real and constant.

Perceptual constancy has a long tradition of research in psychology. In such studies, one asks for judgments about a varying stimulus and finds that the judgments are quite constant over a wide range of variation.

For example, there have been many studies in size constancy. An experimenter takes two objects, usually familiar ones such as a beer can or a tomato. Then he varies the distance from which a viewer is permitted to look at the objects. The experimenter asks the viewer to judge how large they are. As he moves the stimulus farther from the viewer, so that its image gets smaller on the retina of the eye, there will be—within a certain range at least—a tendency to see the object as not really changing in size.

Nativism versus Empiricism

One way of interpreting such data is to assume that constancy has something to do with the way the human nervous system is constructed. There are basically two schools of thought in research on perceptual constancy: *nativism* and *empiricism*. On the one hand, the nativists typically assert that all the facts we have discovered about perception, including constancy, can be interpreted as telling us how the human nervous system is constructed. Nativists argue that experience is of relatively minor import for perception.

The empiricists, on the other hand, say that the data we have about the way the organism behaves when it is looking at something reveal the role of experience. Whenever you say the individual is *interpreting* cues you are really taking an empiricist position. Empiricist psychologists suggest that human beings are easily misled about the world because of our tendency to be phenomenal absolutists. Phenomenologically, the world seems to be perceived absolutely. But, the empiricists suggest, there is actually considerable relativity in our perceptions—the nature of any experience is relative to the state of the

[2]Place one hand in the hot water and the other hand in the cold water, keep them there for about three minutes, then plunge both into the lukewarm water. You will be impressed, even though you know what to expect.

perceiver. Perception is not stimulus-determined. It is the product of an organism interacting with a stimulus.

We can now consider in a little detail the nativism/empiricism controversy in psychology. In a history of experimental psychology by E. G. Boring (1942), this controversy was described as one of the oldest in experimental psychology. During the 18th and 19th centuries, arguments flowed back and forth without being settled. The controversy continued into the present century, and there have been recent efforts to resolve it with research.

For example, consider the work of J. J. Gibson (1950), who took a nativist position. Gibson argued that the problem of how an organism perceives a three-dimensional world, even though that world is projected visually on a two-dimensional surface—the retina of the eye—is essentially no problem at all. What happens, according to Gibson, is that the retinal image contains all the information the organism needs for the brain to process the information automatically. Hence, individuals know immediately, intuitively, without really having to process that information, that they are living in a three-dimensional world. In Gibson's view, the brain (at least that part of the brain involved in visual perception) has built into it an innate ability to perceive that the world is three dimensional.

Empiricists, in contrast, say that the key to answering this question lies somewhere in an analysis of experience. In short, people somehow learn something from earlier experiences, and what they learn enables them to perceive a three-dimensional world.

Brunswik's Empiricist Theory: A Base for Research

There are many versions of empiricist theories, one of which was employed by Segall, Campbell, and Herskovits in a cross-cultural study begun in the late 1950s. The particular empiricist theory they used is that of Egon Brunswik (1956). Most of the psychologists who studied during the first third of the 20th century in Europe, known collectively as Gestalt psychologists, were nativists. Brunswik was an exception. He developed a point of view called *transactional functionalism*, which asserted that perception involves certain functional transactions between the organism and the incoming sensory material. By functional, he meant that the end result of a transaction is adaptive, contributing to the ultimate survival of the organism. This result is something that works, something that helps the person get around in the world, something that prevents him or her from walking into walls. Brunswik argued that the actual properties of an object are the outcome of a combined operation of the object and the organism. In the organism's process of perceiving an object, he said, its past experience plays a very important part.

In Brunswik's laboratory, subjects would look through a peephole and report what they saw. In a typical experiment, a subject would say that what she "saw" was a *"chair."* Then Brunswik could say, in effect, "I've got you. What I have done is suspend some strings in an otherwise darkened room, hanging them from the ceiling and tying them up in such a way that they *look like* a chair. But they are not a chair. They are just a bunch of strings."

If you look at a photograph of a chair, it is really nothing more than shades of gray arranged in a particular pattern. And yet you "know" it is a chair. What Brunswik demonstrated was that we conclude that a certain pattern of visual stimulation is "something" because of our previous experiences with things like it. Clearly, Brunswik argued, it is functional to use whatever cues we have learned in the past to be connected with, say, chairness. If those cues reappear, we conclude that we are looking at a chair. That is functional because, in the vast majority of instances when those cues are present, we will indeed be looking at a chair. It is only on occasional instances that chair cues will emanate from something that is not a chair.

The important points in this Brunswikian argument are that (1) people will interpret cues as they have in the past, (2) it is functional to do so because they will usually be right, but (3) under certain circumstances the very same cues can be misleading.

Whenever we look at something, we make an assumption about what we are looking at. These assumptions have been built up over the years on the basis of experience. The assumptions usually lead us to accurate perceptions—but they don't always have to. In Brunswik's view, *all* the cues that we look at are inherently ambiguous. The cues that tell us we are looking at a chair *could* come from something else that is not a chair at all.

The position that Segall, Campbell, and Herskovits (1966) took is essentially Brunswikian. They argued that individual perception of objects distributed in space comes to us with such vivid clarity that it is hard to imagine our visual perception to be affected by learning. But, they said, that is a proposition that deserves further test. Furthermore, if perception *is* influenced by prior experience, then there may well be ecological and cultural differences in fundamental processes of visual perception. This is true because, if people grow up in different environments, they may indeed learn different things about the interpretations of cues.

Brunswik's *transactional functionalism* can be applied in an explanation of optical illusions. This simply requires a hypothesis that any illusion taps a process that is functional in general but misleading in the particular instance. What makes the process misleading is the *ecological unrepresentativeness* of the situation: it is unlike the general run of situations to which the process is functionally adapted and adaptive.

Thus, optical illusions may be thought of as providing atypical settings for visual performance, thereby offering misleading cues.

To extend our concern to culture requires one simple application of this theory: *if human groups differ in their visual inference systems, it is because their environments differ.* It seemed reasonable to assume that neither by learning nor by genetic selection would populations have come to differ on these processes unless the ecological validities of the processes differed. (Note the compatibility of this logic with Berry's formulation, which we discussed in Chapter Two.)

Three Empiricist Hypotheses

Starting from this position, Segall and his colleagues (1966) derived three hypotheses at a more specific level. These are based on three environmental phenomena: (1) the carpentered world, (2) front-horizontal foreshortening, and (3) symbolizing three dimensions in two. We will discuss these briefly.

The Carpentered-World Hypothesis. This hypothesis can best be described by applying it to the Sander parallelogram, an example of which is shown in Figure 4-1.

For this drawing, the well-established tendency (at least of Western or Westernized respondents) is to judge the diagonal on the respondent's left as longer than it really is. This bias is understandable as the result of a tendency to perceive a parallelogram drawn on a flat surface as a representation of a rectangular surface extended in space. Hence, the viewer judges the *distance* covered by the left diagonal as greater than the distance covered by the right diagonal.

This judgment reflects a habit of inference that has ecological validity in highly carpentered Western societies. Such societies provide environments replete with rectangular objects. These objects, when projected on the retina, are represented by nonrectangular images. The tendency to interpret obtuse and acute angles in retinal images as deriving from rectangular objects is likely to be so pervasively reinforced that the tendency becomes automatic and unconscious relatively early in life. For those living where carpentered structures are a small portion of the visual environment, straight lines and precise right angles are a rarity. As a result, the inference habit of interpreting acute and obtuse angles as right angles extended in space would not be learned, at least not so well.

The application of this line of reasoning to the Müller-Lyer illusion shown in Figure 4-2 is somewhat more complicated. We again assume, however, that persons raised in a carpentered world would tend to perceive the Müller-Lyer figure as a representation of three-dimensional objects, extended in space. In

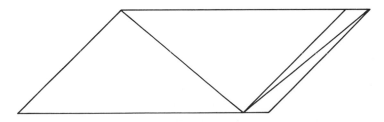

Figure 4-1. The Sander parallelogram

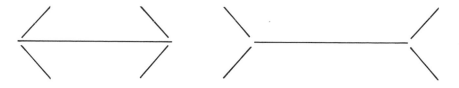

Figure 4-2. The Müller-Lyer illusion

this instance, the two main portions of the drawing represent two objects. For example, for the portion on the left, if the horizontal segment were perceived as the representation of, say, the edge of a box, it would be a *front edge*. For the portion on the right, if the horizontal segment were perceived as the edge of another box, it would be the *back edge* along the inside of the box. Hence, the left-hand horizontal would "have to be" shorter than the drawing makes it out to be, while the right-hand horizontal would "have to be" longer.

Front-Horizontal Foreshortening. Lines in the horizontal plane that extend away from an observer appear to be more foreshortened than lines that cross the viewer's line of vision. Picture a sidewalk one yard wide and marked off in squares one yard long (see Figure 4-3). Consider first the square at your feet, then a square 50 yards away. In terms of retinal images (or extent on the surface of a photograph), whereas all dimensions of the square are reduced in the 50-yard case, the edges parallel to the line of regard are much more foreshortened.

Thus, as Woodworth (1938) observed, "A short vertical line in a drawing may represent a relatively long horizontal line extending away from the observer. The horizontal-vertical illusion can be explained by supposing the vertical to represent such a foreshortened horizontal line" (p. 645). Such an inference habit would have varying validity in varying environments. For people living on flat plains with open vistas, there would be great ecological validity in interpreting vertical lines on the retina as long lines extending into the distance. The opposite should pertain for canyon dwellers or rain-forest dwellers, who should be less susceptible, therefore, to the horizontal/vertical illusion than plains dwellers.

Symbolizing Three Dimensions in Two. Another dominant ecological factor relevant to the line illusions is the pervasive role of symbols on paper in Western civilization. Although most of this symbolization is connected with the representation of language, it has also been used for an iconic representation of space, as in maps and figures of persons, animals, houses, and so on. An increasingly dominant portion of such drawings has involved representing three-dimensional spatial arrays on the two-dimensional surfaces of paper, canvas, or wall.

It is hard for Westerners to realize that this tradition of representing three dimensions in two has the character of an arbitrary linguistic or cultural

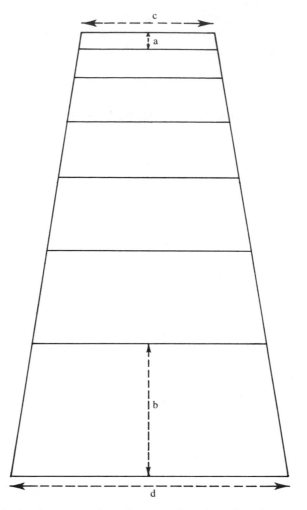

Figure 4-3. A view in perspective of a 50-yard section of roadway, constructed of square sections, extending into space, directly in front of the viewer. Note how the equally long distances *a* and *b* differ in appearance compared to the same distances *c* and *d*. Distance *a* is shortened in relation to *b* far more than *c* is shortened in relation to *d*. In reality, of course, $a = b = c = d$.

convention. This convention may also be expected to relate to illusion susceptibility.

To summarize:

1. So-called optical illusions may result because learned habits of inference are inappropriately applied.

2. In different physical and cultural environments, different habits of inference are likely to be acquired, reflecting differing ecological validities.

3. There is a learned tendency among people in carpentered environments to interpret nonrectangular figures as rectangular, to perceive the figures in perspective, and to interpret them as two-dimensional representations of three-dimensional objects. Such a tendency produces, or at least enhances, the Müller-Lyer illusion and the Sander parallelogram illusion. Since the tendency is assumed to have more ecological validity for peoples in Western, or carpentered, environments, it is predicted that Western peoples will be more susceptible to these illusions than those dwelling in uncarpentered environments.

4. The horizontal/vertical illusion results from a tendency to counteract the foreshortening of lines extended into space away from a viewer. Since the tendency has more ecological validity for peoples living mostly outdoors in open, spacious environments, it is predicted that such peoples will be *more* susceptible than Western peoples in urban environments. But some non-Western people should be *less* susceptible to the illusions—for example, rain-forest or canyon dwellers.

5. Learning to interpret drawings and photographs should enhance these illusions.

Cultural Differences in the Perception of Geometric Illusions

Initial Support for the Empiricist Theory

To test these ideas, stimulus materials based on geometric illusions were prepared in 1956 for standardized administration under varying field conditions. Over a six-year period, anthropologists and psychologists administered these tests to 14 non-European samples of children and adults. The samples ranged in size from 46 to 344 and were taken in 12 locations in Africa and one in the Philippines. There were also three "European" groups: a sample ($N=44$) of South Africans of European descent in Johannesburg, an American undergraduate sample ($N=30$), and a house-to-house sample ($N=208$) in Evanston, Illinois. In all, data were collected from 1878 persons.

Analysis provided evidence of substantial cross-cultural differences. The evidence constituted strong support for the empiricist hypothesis that the perception of space involves the acquisition of habits of perceptual inference.

The stimulus materials consisted of many items, each one a variation of figures constructed of straight lines, generally referred to in the psychological literature as geometric illusions. These included the Müller-Lyer figure, the Sander parallelogram, and two forms of the horizontal/vertical figure. For each illusion the discrepancy in length of the segments to be compared varied from item to item. As each stimulus was shown, the respondent's task was simply to indicate the longer of two linear segments.

To minimize difficulties of communication, the linear segments to be compared were not connected to the other lines and were printed in different colors. Respondents could indicate choice by selecting one of two colors (saying "red" or "black") in response to the horizontal/vertical items and by indicating right or left for the other illusions. Another step taken to enhance the validity of response protocols was the administration of a short comprehension test requiring judgments similar to, but more obvious than, those demanded by the stimulus figures.

On both the Müller-Lyer and Sander illusions the three "European" samples made significantly more illusion-produced responses than did the non-European samples. On the two horizontal/vertical illusions, the European samples had relatively low scores, with many but not all of the non-European samples earning significantly larger mean scores. When the samples were ranked according to mean number of illusion responses, the rank orders varied across two classes of illusion. The Müller-Lyer and Sander parallelogram illusions composed one class; the two horizontal/vertical illusions, another. The overall pattern indicated not only cross-cultural differences in illusion susceptibility but also differences in both directions.

This outcome had been anticipated by the findings of W. H. R. Rivers, a participant in the turn-of-the-century Cambridge expedition to the Torres Straits. Rivers collected quantitative data using two geometrical illusions (the Müller-Lyer figure and the horizontal/vertical figure) among several samples in the Torres Straits and in Southern India. For comparison purposes, data were also collected among English adults and children. In two reports Rivers (1901, 1905) had also found that non-Western groups were *more* subject to the horizontal/vertical figure and *less* subject to the Müller-Lyer illusion than were English groups. Most provocative was the fact that differences between Western and non-Western people existed in both directions: the non-Western people were less subject to one illusion but more subject to another. Obviously, the failure to find differences consistent in direction eliminates any simple explanation of the existing differences. One of those explanations, prevalent during the 19th century, held that—because "primitive" peoples are less well endowed intellectually than "civilized" people—they should be more easily duped by illusions and therefore consistently more subject to them. The suggestion in Rivers's data that for the Müller-Lyer illusion the "primitives" might actually be *less* subject to the illusions was embarrassing to any such hypothesis.

To illustrate the findings of the more recent study, Segall and colleagues (1963, 1966) calculated the proportions of individuals in each sample choosing the typically overestimated line segments. Graphs were constructed from these proportions, and points of subjective equality (or the average discrepancy at which two lines were seen as equal) were determined from these graphs. Figure 4-4 contains four sets of graphs that illustrate (1) the lesser susceptibility of the combined non-European samples to the Müller-Lyer and Sander illusions and (2) the greater susceptibility to the two horizontal/vertical illusions shown by one non-European sample group as compared with one European sample, and the lesser susceptibility of another non-European sample.

So, what we have seen so far is evidence for cross-cultural differences in susceptibility to optical illusions. These differences accorded well with a theory that attributes perceptual tendencies to ecologically valid inference habits.

That the data fit the theory does not mean, however, that the data rule out alternative theories. Nor can it be asserted that the data fit the theory perfectly. In the next sections we will consider an aspect of these data that does not fit the ecological theory very well, and then we will consider a plausible alternative theory.

Age Trends in the Illusion Data:
A Challenge to the Empiricists

One aspect of the Segall et al. cross-cultural findings that does not accord well with empiricist theorizing is the repeated tendency for illusion susceptibility to *decline* with age. This age decline was found for all illusions and in nearly every society. Decline in illusion susceptibility with increasing age is a widely replicated phenomenon. It was first reported by Binet (1895). It was confirmed for the Müller-Lyer by Piaget and von Albertini (1950), by Pollack (1970), and by Armstrong, Rubin, Stewart, and Kuntner (1970). And it was confirmed for several illusions by Stewart (1973) and Weaver (1974).

The empiricist line of thinking has to predict—for carpentered-world dwellers, at least—an increase in Müller-Lyer and Sander illusion susceptibility with age. In an effort to explain the failure of their own data to show any such increase—and, instead, a decline—with age, Segall and his associates suggested that the relevant learning that is assumed to produce susceptibility to illusions appears by early childhood (no later than age 6). They further suggested that, following early childhood, analytical skills are acquired that permit individuals to counteract their tendencies to rectangularize nonorthogonal junctures. This "analytic-sophistication" hypothesis permitted retention of the empiricist theory.

Until recently, the hypothesis was purely "after the fact." But recent studies employing another illusion seem to clarify matters. The problem of age trends in illusion susceptibility is salient in some studies of the Ponzo illusion, a version of which appears in Figure 4-5.

This is an illusion to which ecological factors, such as experience with railroad tracks and with many other perspective cues, are very plausibly thought to contribute. Indeed, that such cues *should* contribute is intuitively obvious. Not surprisingly, this suggestion has been made by many psychologists from the very early days of research on visual perception. (See, for example, Wohlwill, 1962, for a historically oriented discussion of some effects of perspective on pictorial perception. And see Gregory, 1966, for a theory of "misplaced constancy," which explains illusions in much the same manner as does the ecological-cue-validity approach and which applies to the Ponzo illusion more obviously than to any other.)

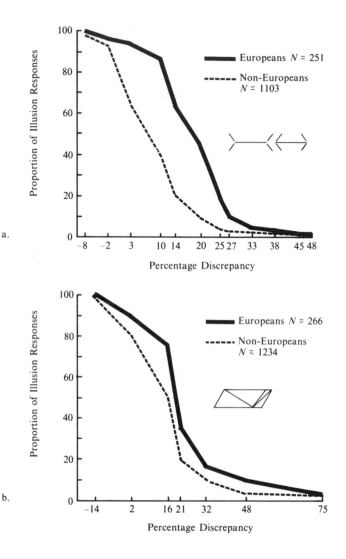

Figure 4-4. Psychophysical ogives based on proportions of illusion responses to item of varying percentage discrepancy. *Upper left*: Müller-Lyer illusion responses plotted for Europeans (three samples combined) and non-Europeans (all other samples combined). *Lower left*: Sander parallelogram illusion responses plotted for same two combined groups. *Upper right*: Horizontal-vertical (⊥) illusion responses by one European and two non-

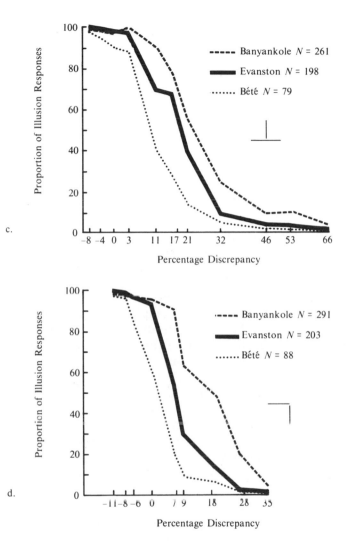

European samples. *Lower right*: Horizontal-vertical (⌐) illusion responses by same three samples. These graphs are all based on internally consistent cases only. (From "Cultural Differences in the Perception of Geometric Illusions," by M. H. Segall, D. T. Campbell, and M. J. Herskovits, *Science*, 1963, *193*, 769–771. Copyright 1963 by the American Association for the Advancement of Science. Reprinted by permission.)

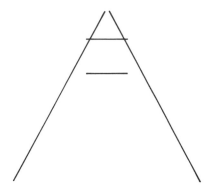

Figure 4-5. The Ponzo illusion

Cross-Environment Differences, Ignoring Ages. Using various versions of this illusion, several investigators have, in fact, found differences across samples that had grown up in different environments (see, for example, Leibowitz, Brislin, Perlmutter, & Hennessey, 1969; Leibowitz & Pick, 1972; Brislin, 1974; Kilbride & Leibowitz, 1975; Brislin & Keating, 1976). The last study, done in Hawaii by Richard Brislin and Caroline Keating, employed wooden boards arranged to form a large Ponzo figure. The figure was displayed horizontally on the ground 13 meters (approximately 40 feet) from three sets of adult respondents, all of whom had recently arrived in Hawaii.

One group was from the mainland United States, another from the Philippines, and a third from various small islands in Micronesia, Melanesia, and Polynesia. The third group had grown up in environments that had very few constructed perspective cues. The other two groups (one Asian, the other U.S.) were from environments rich in such cues. Hence, Brislin and Keating reasoned that, if the ecological hypothesis *did* explain the Ponzo illusion, the Philippine and mainland-U.S. samples should *both* be more susceptible to it than the small-islands sample. This is what they found, confirming earlier cross-cultural results with two-dimensional versions of the illusion. They showed that ecologically valid inferences about perspective are apparently elicited by three-dimensional shapes in a natural environment, a phenomenon that heretofore had been assumed, but not actually demonstrated.

Intraenvironment Differences across Stimulus Variations. In several earlier studies of two-dimensional versions of the Ponzo (see, for example, Leibowitz et al., 1969; Brislin, 1974) it was also shown that, for young-adult subjects, the more depth cues included in the stimulus, the more potent the illusion. The version show above in Figure 4-5, a line drawing, is sparse and abstract. It contains virtually the bare minimum of perspective cues. But they are compelling ones. Thus, the two converging lines could be interpreted as parallel lines extending into space away from the viewer. And the fact that one of the horizontal comparison lines is above the other could lead to the inference that it is farther away. Both factors, according to the ecological hypothesis, contribute to the illusion for persons who have grown up in environments in which such depth cues are prevalent. Of course, the second factor must be present everywhere; the first one is present only in places where parallel lines prevail.

Consider now another version, in which the two horizontal lines are superimposed on a photograph of a field. On such a picture, contextual depth cues have been added. Consider still another, in which the comparison lines are placed against a photograph of a railroad track extending perpendicularly across a field, thereby adding additional contextual cues for depth. These latter two versions of the Ponzo figure are usually more potent than the abstract version, at least for adults—for example, American college students (Leibowitz et al., 1969).

What we have seen so far about the Ponzo illusion is all in accord with the kind of ecological, empiricist theorizing that has been stressed in this chapter. But, as already noted, the age trends that have been discovered in studies employing this illusion present a sticky problem.

Age Trends with the Ponzo Illusion: A Clarification. Some researchers employing one or another version of the Ponzo illusion have found increased susceptibility with age (which is what empiricists would expect). But some have found a decrease, some a decrease followed by an increase, and some no trend at all!

Confronted with these contradictory findings and taking note of the existence of different versions of the illusion as just described (abstract, "field," and "railroad track"), Wagner (1977) attempted to sort it all out in a study done in Morocco.

To allow age trends to reveal themselves, Wagner employed 384 boys in four different age groups (approximately 7, 11, 14, and 19 years of age). To study the possible effects of schooling, Wagner constructed half of his sample with school-going boys and the other half with boys who had never been schooled or had had less than one year of schooling. To allow ecological conditions to influence illusion susceptibility, Wagner selected half of the sample in Marrakesh, an urban, "carpentered" environment, and the other half from a rural setting in the middle Atlas Mountains.

The several versions of the Ponzo illusion were administered to all the subjects, plus a "control" figure composed simply of two horizontal lines. Obviously a complex research design, Wagner's study yielded complex results. These will be described briefly and selectively, in the interest of comprehension.

For the abstract version of the Ponzo illusion, susceptibility *decreased* slightly, but consistently, with increasing age for all subjects—schooled or unschooled, urban or rural. Since this version is structurally simple, Wagner (1977, p. 172) suggests that it might be well to think of it as an example of what the Swiss developmental psychologist Jean Piaget (1969) has called a "primary," or Type I, illusion. Piaget asserts that this kind of illusion decreases with age (or intellectual development) as children become increasingly able to make multiple glances that diminish the "Gestalt" of the compelling illusion.

Whether or not we accept the Piagetian theoretical idea, or even Piaget's terminology, this result of Wagner's (the decline with age in susceptibility to the abstract Ponzo) accords with an empiricist view mentioned earlier. This view holds that whatever produces the illusion in the first place (be it an innate disposition or an early-learned tendency) either decays from middle childhood through adolescence *or* is counteracted by other tendencies acquired as one matures, without necessary help from schooling or urban experience.

But for the two context-rich versions of the Ponzo illusion, the field and track pictures, susceptibility *increased* with increasing age. It increased more for urban dwellers than for rural dwellers, more for schooled than for unschooled boys, and most for boys who were *both* urban and school going. Moreover, although for all groups combined the abstract illusion was more potent on the average than the two context-rich ones, the oldest-schooled subjects were more susceptible to the two complex illusions than to the abstract one. Thus, the findings described in this paragraph provide evidence for the view that susceptibility to the more complex Ponzo figures *grows* as a product of increasing perceptual and cognitive activity of the kinds made more probable by living in an urban environment and going to school.

(This positive age trend may also be explained in Piagetian terms by assuming the complex figures to be "secondary," or Type II, illusions. In this case, the "multiple glances" that Piaget assumes one learns help to produce —rather than diminish—the illusions. However, as with Type I illusions, this theoretical approach appears to add nothing by way of explanation.)

These findings seem quite compatible with an ecological, empiricist argument:

Firstly, for two out of three versions of the Ponzo there is increasing susceptibility with increasing age, a finding that Segall and colleagues (1966) had sought in vain.

Secondly, these positive age trends, as Wagner has put it, seem to require "perceptual development that is not merely 'age-related' or maturational," because they depend on schooling and an urban environment.

Thirdly, because the more context-rich figures are *in general* less potent illusions than the abstract version, it makes sense in the light of the empiricist theory that the complex figures accrue potency, especially for subjects who have opportunities to acquire illusion-enhancing inference habits (older, urban, schooled boys). These relatively weak versions, obviously not yet "at ceiling" for younger boys, can reveal the effects of relevant inference habits as these habits are acquired by older boys. By the same token, the abstract version of the illusion is already so strong for 7-year-olds that age trends will either be flat or, as Wagner found, declining.

All in all, then, this well-designed study from Morocco goes a long way toward clarifying heretofore confusing age-trend data on the Ponzo illusion. It also applies, by implication, to other illusions (for example, the Müller-Lyer figure and Sander parallelogram), susceptibility to which is believed by many cross-cultural psychologists to be explained by the learning of inferences adaptive to life in a carpentered world.

A Plausible Rival Hypothesis

Despite the support now available for the ecological theory, a physiological hypothesis must also be considered.

The ability to detect contours has been shown to be negatively correlated with age. Pollack (1963) found that older subjects have greater difficulty detecting contours. Because several investigators had found decreasing illusion susceptibility with age, Pollack found it compelling to suggest that this susceptibility might be functionally related to contour-detection ability. Moreover, a Chicago study by Pollack and Silvar (1967) showed a correlation between contour-detection ability and susceptibility to the Müller-Lyer illusion. The harder it was for subjects to detect contours, the less susceptible they were to the illusion.

The same two investigators (Silvar & Pollack, 1967) also showed that skin pigmentation is correlated both with retinal pigmentation and with contour-detection threshold. In other words, persons with denser retinal pigmentation have more difficulty detecting contours.

Another physiological/anatomic factor, corneal density, correlates with age and with exposure to sunlight. So Pollack has suggested that either this factor or retinal-pigmentation density—both of which might have varied across the samples employed in Segall and his colleagues' cross-cultural study—could account for what they took to be differences that were ecocultural in origin. Noting that their non-Western samples were all non-Caucasian, Pollack suggested that race might be responsible for what Segall and his associates had accepted as cultural differences.

An early challenge to Pollack's physiological hypothesis was provided by Armstrong, Rubin, Stewart, and Kuntner (1970). They administered the Müller-Lyer and Sander illusions, as well as the Ames Distorted Room, to 65 White and 65 Black children (aged 5 to 19 years) in Evanston, Illinois. The investigators also assessed the retinal pigmentation of their subjects. The pigmentation scores correlated very highly with race, so race was employed as an independent variable, along with age and sex, in analyses of illusion susceptibility. For all three illusions, only age related to susceptibility.

That race showed no relationship to illusion susceptibility seriously challenged, at the least, the generalizability of Pollack and Silvar's (1967) finding. Their own particular experiment had employed an unusual variant of the Müller-Lyer illusion, presented under very special illumination conditions.

Support for the physiological hypothesis soon came from several sources, however. John Berry (1971) administered the Segall-and-colleagues version of the Müller-Lyer illusion to samples of Scottish, Sierra Leonean, Australian aboriginal, Eskimo, and New Guinean groups. Berry ordered his samples along two dimensions—carpenteredness and skin pigmentation—and then calculated the rank-order correlation of illusion susceptibility with each of those two dimensions. His calculations yielded correlation coefficients of .64 between susceptibility and carpenteredness and .82 between susceptibility and skin color. When Berry refined his reanalysis by calculating partial correlations—that is, the correlation of susceptibility and pigmentation with carpenteredness controlled, and vice versa—he obtained support for the view that skin pigmentation accounted for more of the cross-cultural variance in Müller-Lyer susceptibility than did carpenteredness.

The analytic technique employed by Berry may fairly be criticized as somewhat gross, with its numerical outcome dependent on the investigator's own ranking of the five societies along the carpenteredness and pigmentation dimensions. A change of position along either dimension for any two of the societies would very probably have resulted in correlation coefficients of different magnitude. Nevertheless, Berry's 1971 paper showed that pigmentation could account for his cross-cultural differences in illusion susceptibility at least as well as, if not better than, degree of carpenteredness. On the basis of Berry's work, then, Pollack's hypothesis had to be retained as a plausible alternative.

Data collected by Jahoda (1971) from Scottish and Malawian university students (24 in each society) also provided support for Pollack's line of argument. To understand the implications of Jahoda's study, we must consider some facts about wavelengths and how the color of stimuli relates to their visibility. It is in the shortwave region of the spectrum that density of retinal pigmentation is correlated with contour detectability. This was why, incidentally, Pollack and Silvar (1967) presented their Müller-Lyer stimulus under blue lighting. If Pollack were correct, Jahoda reasoned, it should matter whether or not a Müller-Lyer stimulus is presented in red or blue, but only for darkly pigmented subjects. Jahoda summarized this line of reasoning, modified it slightly, and then tested a very interesting cross-cultural prediction. Jahoda's argument went as follows:

> Scottish and African Ss ought to be equally susceptible when the lines are red, but Africans should experience a lesser illusion with blue lines. Such a formulation assumes that retinal pigmentation is the sole determinant of differential suscepti-bility; . . . such an assumption is probably too strong. Hence the hypothesis was cast in the following form: . . . African Ss will show a significantly greater suscepti-bility to a red Müller-Lyer illusion than to a blue one, while there will be no such difference for Scottish Ss [1971, p. 202].

That predicted difference was the only significant difference obtained by Jahoda. As such, it supports the pigmentation hypothesis of Pollack.

More recently, however, Jahoda (1975) attempted to replicate his 1971 study but failed to obtain the same findings. This failure, of course, cast doubt on his 1971 findings.

Still, efforts to test the Pollack position continue. For example, there has been a provocative attempt to link, theoretically, what is known about cross-cultural differences in color naming with parallel facts about illusion susceptibility (Bornstein, 1973). In contrast to most recent writers on the subject of color naming (for example, Berlin & Kay, 1969), Bornstein contended that eye-pigmentation differences cause color-perception differences. He argued that such physiological/perceptual phenomena underlie color-naming variations across cultures.

Bornstein suggested, for example, that people whose environment promotes the development of dense eye pigmentation, as is the case near the Equator or at high altitudes, would suffer from a relative inability to perceive blueness. This differential ability, according to his argument, would explain the relative poverty of color terminology in the blue-green area of the visual spectrum that has been found to be characteristic of (some) societies composed of dark-skinned peoples in tropical climates. To complete the theoretical linkage, Bornstein (1973, p. 71) also argued, like Pollack but in far less detail, that differential pigmentation lies at the root of illusion-susceptibility differences. Differential visual acuity somehow mediates that relationship, he contended.

A Challenge to the Rival Hypothesis. Struck by Bornstein's innovative attempt to integrate color-naming and geometric-illusion phenomena, Bolton, Michelson, Wilde, and Bolton (1975) undertook a well-designed study of illusion susceptibility and color naming in the Central Andes of Peru. One sample lived on a 13,000-foot-high plateau and another in a forested hillside at 4500 feet. Both samples lived between 14 degrees and 15 degrees south of the Equator, and they were equally carpentered. Besides differing in altitude, however, the two samples differed in openness of vistas—great for the high-altitude sample and limited for those living at the lower altitude.

Accordingly, Bolton and his colleagues reasoned that the pigmentation hypothesis of Bornstein would lead to a prediction of lower susceptibility to four different illusions (Müller-Lyer, Sander, and the two versions of the horizontal/vertical) for the high-altitude sample. An ecological hypothesis, they reasoned, would predict intersample differences in the *opposite* direction, but *only* for the horizontal/vertical illusions. Their data showed precisely what the empiricist hypothesis predicted.

The only significant differences obtained were for the two horizontal/vertical illusions. On these, the high-altitude dwellers, who "can see to distant horizons from 30 to more than 100 miles away" (Bolton et al., pp. 412–413), were more susceptible than the sample dwelling on forested hillsides 8500 feet lower. Thus, Bolton et al. found the Bornstein argument as applied to illusion susceptibility unable to account for their Peruvian findings. But these findings are quite in accord with the ecological hypothesis.

With regard to verbal differentiation of colors, they did find a significant relationship between altitude and reduced differentiation between blue and green and between red and green. This particular finding accords with Bornstein's argument. But Bolton and his associates asserted that other findings of theirs on color naming "fail to support Bornstein on this question" (1975, p. 422).

Thus, on both counts (the pigmentation hypothesis applied to color naming and to illusion susceptibility) the Bornstein hypothesis was not supported by the differential-altitude study. The illusion portion of this study certainly provided, as the authors stated, "additional confirmation for the hypothesis presented by Segall, Campbell, and Herskovits" (Bolton et al., 1975, p. 422) and, by implication, another challenge to the nativistic, pigmentation hypothesis of Pollack.

Two More Responses to Pollack's Hypothesis. Stewart (1973) correctly pointed out that Pollack's challenge to ecological theory underlines the need for a dual research strategy. First, one holds environmental carpenteredness constant while varying race. And second, one tests across environments while holding race constant. In short, race and environment have to be unconfounded in order to assess their possible contributions to illusion susceptibility. To test across race with environment held constant, she administered the Müller-Lyer and Sander illusions to 60 Black and 60 White schoolchildren, ranging in age from 6 to 17 and selected randomly from three schools in Evanston, Illinois. She found no significant difference in susceptibility between the two racial groups.

To test across environments with race constant, Stewart administered the same stimulus materials to Zambian school-aged children, again ranging in age from 6 to 17 and again with the sexes equally represented. In Zambia, however, the five levels sampled ranged widely from a group of unschooled Tonga children living in the very uncarpentered Zambezi Valley region to a group of middle-class children living in Zambia's cosmopolitan capital, Lusaka. A total of 432 Zambian subjects, all Blacks, were tested. The major finding was that for both illusions susceptibility rose with increases in the degree of carpenteredness.

Stewart's overall findings are summarized in Table 4-1 (data selected from Stewart, 1973), which combines the Evanston and Zambian phases of her research.

Table 4-1. Mean numbers of illusion-supported responses.

	Zambezi Valley unschooled	Lusaka middle class	Evanston Black	Evanston White
Müller-Lyer	4.63	5.81	6.10	6.10
Sander	4.24	5.33	5.59	5.40

Clearly, susceptibility to both illusions increased with increasing carpenteredness of environment, whereas race mattered not at all. Stewart's research failed to replicate Pollack's research, even though she varied race in the same geographical setting as Pollack had, the Chicago metropolitan area. Her study's support for the ecological hypothesis is quite strong, because she employed more than one illusion and got essentially the same findings with both. Moreover, she actually used a third instrument in Zambia—a miniature version of the Ames Distorted Room—and got similar results. Clearly, Stewart's research findings offer strong support to the empiricist point of view.

Another recent study that bears on the controversy was done by Donald Weaver (1974), who derived another prediction from Pollack's position. Weaver's derivation took into account a combination of some facts we have already covered, plus a new one. The new fact was a demonstration by Pollack (1970) that, although the magnitude of the Müller-Lyer illusion decreases with the age of the viewer when the figure is produced by lightness contrast (or white lines on a black background), there is no such decline with age when the figure is produced by hue contrast. This finding, incidentally, is compatible with Pollack's contour-detection hypothesis, because lightness contrast—but not hue contrast—relates to contour detectability.

Considering this, Weaver deemed it useful to test illusion susceptibility to Müller-Lyer stimuli using both hue contrast and lightness contrast. The cross-cultural samples in such a test would be African and American, and carpenteredness and retinal pigmentation would thus vary in a confounded manner. But Weaver reasoned that the competing hypothesis would be put to test. He argued that, if the physiological hypothesis were singularly valid, the non-Western samples would be less illusion susceptible than the Western samples when the stimulus was produced by lightness contrast, but there would be no difference when the stimulus was produced by hue contrast. If the empiricist hypothesis were singularly valid, he asserted, then the non-Western samples would be less illusion susceptible than the Western samples when the stimulus was produced by lightness contrast *and* when it was produced by hue contrast.

The prediction concerning hue versus lightness contrast that Weaver actually tested was couched in terms of age. As he interpreted the empiricist point of view, it predicted that, if a decline in susceptibility by age were obtained, it should be more marked among carpentered-world subjects. Further, this carpenteredness-by-age interaction should occur regardless of whether the stimuli were produced by hue contrast or lightness contrast.

Weaver, therefore, employed one set of Müller-Lyer figures that were red on gray (red because the effects of retinal pigmentation are least expected at the red end of the visual spectrum) and a set of white on black (for lightness contrast). He sampled widely on age, using two ranges, 8 to 14 and 18 to 21 years. He also employed subjects of both sexes, although he had no theoretical predictions about sex differences. And, most importantly, he employed

Ghanaian subjects who could be individually classified as carpentered or uncarpentered, the latter having spent at least the first two years of life in an uncarpentered environment. Weaver employed a similar research design with the Sander parallelogram, varying lightness versus hue contrast, age levels (this time 10 to 12 and 18 to 19 years), sex, and carpenteredness.

First, we will consider some of his Müller-Lyer results. Among children 8 to 14 years of age, ignoring contrast type of stimulus for the moment, (1) illusion susceptibility was greater among carpentered-world subjects, (2) illusion susceptibility declined steadily with age, but (3) the decline with age was produced mainly by the carpentered sample. These results are in full accord with the empiricist hypothesis.

When the children (8 to 14) and the adults (18 to 21) were compared, age mattered and so did carpenteredness, which confirmed that the carpenteredness variable mattered more for the younger than for the older subsample.

On the Sander parallelogram, Weaver found for the 10-, 11-, and 12-year-olds that (1) the carpentered sample was more susceptible and (2) the hue figures induced greater susceptibility than the lightness figures. The first finding accords with the empiricist hypothesis, but the second contradicts both hypotheses. With regard to the latter finding, Weaver reported another technical difficulty with the hue-contrast Sander parallelogram stimuli. He concluded, therefore, that the second finding was of no theoretical import.

These findings, Weaver concluded, provided striking support for the empiricist hypothesis. They showed, firstly, that differences in illusion susceptibility exist between groups equated for retinal pigmentation but dissimilar in terms of early ecological experience. They also showed that the probability of such differences' occurring depends on age. Weaver in the end interpreted age as an index of perceptual/cognitive development reflecting the extent to which the relevant visual inference habits are employed.

One Final Study

To round out our very intensive examination of the theoretical conflict surrounding visual illusions and the many cross-cultural studies that bear on this conflict, we will consider one more study that tests the "learned-habits-of-inference" position (Pollnac, 1977). In examining a report amusingly subtitled "Is the carpentered world hypothesis seaworthy?" we discover that the author in fact tested not the carpentered-world hypothesis but its companion piece, the frontal-plane-foreshortening hypothesis. Employing a sample of 21 fishermen who work a very broad expanse of ocean along the Pacific coast of Costa Rica, Pollnac demonstrated that susceptibility to the inverted-T form of the horizontal/vertical illusion was significantly related to years of fishing experience and to degree of responsibility for navigation. The correlation between mere chronological age and susceptibility reduced to zero when it was controlled for by those two indexes of experience in making survival-crucial judgments of distance and size.

Thus, Pollnac demonstrated that variance in illusion susceptibility, within such a small sample occupying a single ecological niche, is very well accounted for by relevant experience. This is impressive support indeed for the ecological interpretation of visual illusions that we have so painstakingly examined in this chapter.

Conclusion

Thus, by 1978 it may be stated with increased confidence that people perceive in ways that are shaped by the inferences they have learned to make in order to function most effectively in the particular ecological settings in which they live. The generalization we can derive from the research we have considered in this chapter is that we learn to perceive in the ways that we need to perceive. In that sense, environment and culture shape our perceptual habits.

In the next chapter, we will see whether a similar phenomenon exists with regard to cognition. Might it also be the case that our culture provides guidelines for—and limits to—the way we think?

References

Armstrong, R. E., Rubin, E. V., Stewart, M., & Kuntner, L. *Susceptibility to the Müller-Lyer, Sander Parallelogram, and Ames Distorted Room Illusions as a Function of Age, Sex, and Retinal Pigmentation among Urban Midwestern Children.* Duplicated research report, Department of Psychology, Northwestern University, 1970.

Berkeley, G. *Three Dialogues between Hylas and Philonous.* Chicago: Open Court, 1927. (Originally published, 1713.)

Berlin, B., & Kay, P. *Basic Color Terms: Their Universality and Evolution.* Berkeley: University of California Press, 1969.

Berry, J. W. Müller-Lyer susceptibility: Culture, ecology, or race? *International Journal of Psychology,* 1971, *6,* 193–197.

Binet, A. La mésure des illusions visuelles chez les enfants, 1895. Translation by R. H. Pollack & F. K. Zetland in *Perceptual and Motor Skills,* 1965, *20,* 917–930.

Bolton, R., Michelson, C., Wilde, J., & Bolton, C. The heights of illusion: On the relationship between altitude and perception. *Ethos,* 1975, *3,* 403–424.

Boring, E. G. *Sensation and Perception in the History of Experimental Psychology.* New York: Appleton-Century-Crofts, 1942.

Bornstein, M. The psychophysiological component of cultural differences in color naming and illusion susceptibility. *Behavioral Science Notes,* 1973, *8,* 41–101.

Brislin, R. W. The Ponzo illusion: Additional cues, age, orientation, and culture. *Journal of Cross-Cultural Psychology,* 1974, *5,* 139–161.

Brislin, R., & Keating, C. Cultural differences in the perception of a three-dimensional Ponzo illusion. *Journal of Cross-Cultural Psychology,* 1976, *7,* 397–411.

Brunswik, E. *Perception and the Representative Design of Psychological Experiments.* Berkeley: University of California Press, 1956.

Deregowski, J. B. Difficulties in pictorial depth perception in Africa. *British Journal of Psychology,* 1968, *59,* 195–204.

Deregowski, J. B. Orientation and perception of pictorial depth. *International Journal of Psychology*, 1971, *6*, 111–114.

Deregowski, J. B. Pictorial perception and culture. *Scientific American*, 1972, *227*, 82–88.

Ember, C. R. Cross-cultural cognitive studies. *Annual Review of Anthropology*, 1977, *6*, 33–56.

Gibson, J. J. *The Perception of the Visual World*. Boston: Houghton Mifflin, 1950.

Gregory, R. L. *Eye and Brain: The Psychology of Seeing*. New York: McGraw-Hill, 1966.

Heider, E. R. Universals in color naming and memory. *Journal of Experimental Psychology*, 1972, *93*, 10–20.

Hudson, W. Pictorial depth perception in sub-cultural groups in Africa. *Journal of Social Psychology*, 1960, *52*, 183–208.

Hudson, W. The study of the problem of pictorial perception among unacculturated groups. *International Journal of Psychology*, 1967, *2*, 89–107.

Jahoda, G. Retinal pigmentation, illusion susceptibility and space perception. *International Journal of Psychology*, 1971, *6*, 199–208.

Jahoda, G. Retinal pigmentation and space perception: A failure to replicate. *Journal of Social Psychology*, 1975, *97*, 133–134.

Jahoda, G., & McGurk, H. Development of pictorial depth perception: Cross-cultural replications. *Child Development*, 1974, *45*, 1042–1047. (a)

Jahoda, G., & McGurk, H. Pictorial depth perception: A developmental study. *British Journal of Psychology*, 1974, *65*, 141–150. (b)

Jahoda, G., & McGurk, H. Pictorial depth perception in Scottish and Ghanaian children: A critique of some findings with the Hudson test. *International Journal of Psychology*, 1974, *9*, 255–267. (c)

Kilbride, P., & Leibowitz, H. W. Factors affecting the magnitude of the Ponzo perspective illusion among the Baganda. *Perception and Psychophysics*, 1975, *17*, 543–548.

Leibowitz, H. W., Brislin, R., Perlmutter, L., & Hennessey, R. Ponzo perspective illusion as a manifestation of space perception. *Science*, 1969, *166*, 1174–1176.

Leibowitz, H. W., & Pick, H. A. Cross-cultural and educational aspects of the Ponzo perspective illusion. *Perception and Psychophysics*, 1972, *12*, 430–432.

Locke, J. *An Essay Concerning Human Understanding*. Oxford: Clarendon Press, 1975. (Originally published, 1690.)

Miller, R. J. Cross-cultural research in the perception of pictorial materials. *Psychological Bulletin*, 1973, *80*, 135–150.

Osgood, C. E., May, W. H., & Miron, M. S. *Cross-Cultural Universals of Affective Meaning*. Champaign-Urbana: University of Illinois Press, 1975.

Piaget, J. *Mechanisms of Perception*. London: Routledge, 1969.

Piaget, J., & von Albertini, B. L'illusion de Müller-Lyer. *Archives de Psychologie* (Genève), 1950, *33*, 1–48.

Plato. [Republic.] In W. H. F. Rouse (trans.), *The Great Dialogues of Plato*. New York: Mentor, 1956.

Pollack, R. H. Contour detectability thresholds as a function of chronological age. *Perceptual and Motor Skills*, 1963, *17*, 411–417.

Pollack, R. H. Müller-Lyer illusion: Effect of age, lightness contrast and hue. *Science*, 1970, *170*, 93–94.

Pollack, R. H., & Silvar, S. D. Magnitude of the Müller-Lyer illusion in children as a function of pigmentation of the Fundus oculi. *Psychonomic Science*, 1967, *8*, 83–84.

Pollnac, R. B. Illusion susceptibility and adaptation to the marine environment: Is the carpentered world hypothesis seaworthy? *Journal of Cross-Cultural Psychology*, 1977, *8*, 425–433.

Rivers, W. H. R. Vision. In A. C. Haddon (Ed.), *Reports of the Cambridge Anthropological Expedition to the Torres Straits* (Vol. 2, Part 1). Cambridge: University Press, 1901.

Rivers, W. H. R. Observations on the senses of the Todas. *British Journal of Psychology*, 1905, *1*, 321–396.

Segall, M. H., Campbell, D. T., & Herskovits, M. J. Cultural differences in the perception of geometric illusions. *Science*, 1963, *193*, 769–771.

Segall, M. H., Campbell, D. T., & Herskovits, M. J. *The Influence of Culture on Visual Perception*. Indianapolis: Bobbs-Merrill, 1966.

Serpell, R. *Culture's Influence on Behaviour*. London: Methuen, 1976.

Silvar, S. D., & Pollack, R. H. Racial differences in pigmentation of the Fundus oculi. *Psychonomic Science*, 1967, 7, 159–160.

Stewart, V. M. Tests of the "carpentered world" hypothesis by race and environment in America and Zambia. *International Journal of Psychology*, 1973, *8*, 83–94.

Triandis, H. C., Malpass, R. S., & Davidson, A. R. Cross-cultural psychology. In B. J. Siegel (Ed.), *Biennial Review of Anthropology*. Stanford, Calif.: Stanford University Press, 1971.

Wagner, D. A. Ontogeny of the Ponzo illusion: Effects of age, schooling, and environment. *International Journal of Psychology*, 1977, *12*, 161–176.

Weaver, D. B. *An intra-cultural test of empiricistic vs. physiological explanations for cross-cultural differences in geometric illusion susceptibility using two illusions in Ghana*. Unpublished doctoral dissertation, Northwestern University, 1974.

Wohlwill, J. F. The perspective illusion: Perceived size and distance in fields varying in suggested depth, in children and adults. *Journal of Experimental Psychology*, 1962, *64*, 300–310.

Woodworth, R. S. *Experimental Psychology*. New York: Holt, 1938.

Yonas, A., Cleaves, W. T., & Pettersen, L. Development of sensitivity to pictorial depth. *Science*, 1978, *200*, 77–78.

Five

Cognition:
Information Processing
in Various Cultures

How Culture Influences Thinking

In the previous chapter it was asserted that the most basic of psychological processes are shaped by cultural influences. We also saw in some detail that stimuli impinging on human beings are not passively received but are dealt with in an active way. Our perceptual functioning seemingly involves selective filters derived from culturally shaped experiences.

In analogous fashion, cognitive processes are culturally influenced. As we will see, information is processed by active minds employing rules—or templates, as it were—that are based in culture. Some of the ways in which culture influences thinking will be the subject of this chapter.

To cover this topic, we will consider a number of questions and raise several issues. We will ask, only because the question refuses to go away, whether all groups of people possess approximately similar levels of general ability. We will also consider both universals and differences in the process of cognitive growth and development. To what extent do humans everywhere move through stages of intellectual growth? Do these stages follow in fixed order everywhere, and at the same rate? Or do they emerge in different orders and at different speeds in different social settings?

We will also examine empirical research on classification behavior, concept discovery and formation, memory, problem solving, and more complex behaviors such as the drawing of inferences about causal relationships. In the course of this review we will see that culture indeed provides the context for, and much of the content of, these uniquely human activities known collectively as thinking.

Some Obviously Universal Intellectual Activities

When we use the term *cognition*, we are talking about the processes humans engage in when they plan, when they analyze, when they consider probabilities, and when they solve problems—in short, all those activities we consider to be intellectual.

We all, for example, *categorize*—that most basic of intellectual activities. The mere attaching of a name to more than one object, such as calling several differently shaped and upholstered (or unupholstered) objects "chairs" (or *chaises*) is to classify them, to treat them as exemplars of a particular category. By thus recognizing a common attribute—in this example the communality refers to the shared function of "sit-on-ability"—we are using the single most important cognitive tool available to us. That tool is, of course, language. The substantives (or nouns) of language are, basically, category labels. Because every human being above some minimal age employs at least one language and because every language contains names for things, everyone categorizes.

Everyone must also perform certain logical operations, such as deciding whether two separate things are in any way equivalent or different. These operations are also made possible by language, and in all languages the tools for these operations are apparent.

It must also be obvious that persons everywhere solve problems of various degrees of complexity. A common form of problem solving is *planning*, or the predetermination of a course of action. You may, for example, have to decide when to leave home in order to catch the 8:12 A.M. train to the city or to reach the marketplace early enough to acquire the kidneys and liver before other discriminating buyers reach the butcher's stall. People everywhere, of course, are regularly confronted by practical problems that they must solve. Survival depends on it. Again, language makes it possible. In this case, the availability of future and conditional tenses and subjunctive moods permits the contemplation of both the here and not here and the now and not now.

The final example in our nonexhaustive list of universal cognitive activities is *quantification*. Everyone counts and otherwise uses mathematics. Readers who may consider themselves inept with numbers, but competent "verbally," will probably at first resist the notion that counting is a verbal, or linguistic, activity. But surely it is, albeit a specialized one. Every language includes a number system, composed of words designating quantities, orders, magnitudes, and relationships. Different languages have different number systems, and some are more complex than others. But each has a system, and every speaker of any language employs it with varying degrees of sophistication. Even the basic logical operation of deciding whether X is more than Y is, strictly speaking, an instance of quantification, just as is determining whether you could arrive in Nairobi by airplane earlier than you could arrive in Stamford, Connecticut, by car.

Why Study Cognition Cross-Culturally?

The study of cognitive activity is fundamental to psychology. Students of the learning process, developmental psychologists, and psychometricians have all been concerned with aspects of cognition since the early days of psychology. Learning theorists have sought the general principles of the process of how knowledge and skills are acquired. Developmental psychologists have tried to delineate the growth of understanding that occurs as maturation and experience interact to produce changing views of the world. And psychometricians have developed techniques and instruments for measuring and describing both general and specific aptitudes. For the most part these psychological specialists have worked in European and North American settings, but they have nevertheless had as their goal the discovery of panhuman generalizations about cognition. One reason, then, for cross-cultural research on cognition has been to test the generalizability of earlier established principles of cognitive behavior.

Another reason, rooted in the history of European contact with non-European cultures, has been a long-felt need on the part of Europeans to discover *how* non-Europeans think. From the earliest contacts up to the present, it has been popularly believed that "they" don't think quite as rationally as "we" do, that there is a form of thinking somehow adequately described as "primitive." To put it most bluntly, many Westerners have thought that these so-called primitive peoples are, simply, intellectually inferior. Some early examples of cross-cultural research were motivated by an intent to test this facile and obviously ethnocentric proposition. Later cross-cultural research, usually directed to other ends, has nonetheless served to demonstrate the invalidity of the "superior-us/inferior-them" world view.

As the research grew in sophistication, more valid justifications for it became obvious. Theories emerged that made it plausible to expect that people in different cultural settings vary in the way they learn to solve problems (cognitive-style differences). People might also be expected to differ in the patterns of skills they acquire, with cultures varying in the salience attached to certain skills or in the order in which competencies are acquired.

Thus, while abandoning the ethnocentric expectation of gross differences in the quality of cognitive activity, cross-cultural psychologists have continued to search for performance differences that might help them understand *how* cognitive behavior is influenced by culturally shaped experiences. The ultimate objective of such research is not to understand non-Western peoples per se. (This is an intermediate goal that is, of course, both worthy and elusive in its own right.) The goal is to improve our knowledge of how human beings everywhere come to interpret and cope with the world in which they live.

On Intercultural Differences in Cognitive Ability

Europeans' early interest in the intellectual performance of non-European peoples was, as noted above, based on the ethnocentric premise of inferiority or, at least, significant qualitative deficits.[1] Although this premise dates back to the earliest contacts between Europe and non-Europe, we find its echoes up to the present. In this century, the respected French scholar Lucien Lévy-Bruhl (1923, 1910/1926) characteristically analyzed non-Western thought processes as "pre-logical." In his many contrasts between what he termed "primitive" and "civilized" thinking, he stressed that the difference was truly qualitative. So-called primitives were said to think in a genuinely different manner from so-called civilized persons. Fully 50 years later the eminent British social anthropologist E. E. Evans-Pritchard (1971), although asserting that Lévy-Bruhl's conclusions about primitive mentality could no longer be accepted, still bowed in the direction of a qualitative difference. He asserted that "much of the thought of primitive people [sic] is difficult, if not impossible, for us to understand" (p. 283).[2]

The tenacity of this kind of ethnocentrism may in part reflect an evolutionary bias common to much social-science theory, at least that part of it most strongly influenced by late-19th- and early-20th-century biology. There has long been a tendency for social theorists to think of development, both individual and social, as a kind of linear unfolding process, or maturation. Thus, the development from childhood through adulthood is viewed as analogous to a development from primitive society through sophisticated or civilized. The basic idea as applied to an individual organism has obvious merit. But the validity of the analogy concerning human groups is extremely dubious. Yet developmental psychologists (see, for example, Werner, 1948, and Werner & Kaplan, 1956) occasionally assign the "mental development" of non-Western peoples to a category that includes children and mental patients.

The clear implication of this point of view is that non-Western peoples suffer from arrested development. If this idea were not so dangerous and not so

---

[1]See Berry and Dasen (1974), especially pages 2–12, for an excellent summary of early cross-cultural work on intellectual performance.

[2]See also two papers by the anthropologist Robin Horton (1967a, 1967b), who found abstract, theoretical thinking—albeit different in content—present in all societies. But he also found somewhat more rigidity and reliance on traditionally accepted beliefs in societies not oriented toward science or technology.

recurrently fashionable and if it were not reasserted by otherwise competent and respected scholars, it could be dismissed as ludicrous.

But it is a tenacious idea that is reinforced by, and in turn reinforces, racism. If millions of brown- and black- and yellow-skinned people all over the world respect and envy us ("and surely they must"), how could it be otherwise than that we are superior to them? Hence, our inability to understand them is facilely attributed to their qualitatively different, primitive way of thinking.

Unfortunately for that self-serving line of argument, the vast bulk of contemporary cross-cultural studies on intellectual performance contradicts it. In an article written after the modern era of cross-cultural research had begun, Scribner and Cole (1973) could confidently state "All cultural groups thus far studied have demonstrated the capacity to remember, generalize, form concepts, operate with abstractions, and reason logically" (p. 553).

This is not to say, of course, that there are no cross-cultural differences in cognition or good reasons for studying them. There certainly are both.

The nature of cultural differences in cognition is still not clear. Theories and expectations about such differences are varied. In a recent review of cross-cultural work on cognitive development, Serpell (1976, Chapter 5) noted that some students of cognition postulate differences in very general and very basic intellectual processes, whereas others expect differences in specific skills only. Another difference of opinion among theorists highlighted in Serpell's review is their expectation regarding the magnitude of difference. Some take a quantitative, "matter-of-degree," or retardation view. Others have a qualitative, "different-in-kind" expectation (Serpell, 1976, pp. 69–71).

Whatever different expectations exist among theorists, there is a growing body of empirical research showing that patterns of skills vary, classification schemes vary, and cognitive development follows somewhat different timetables in different cultures. These differences (and the similarities that are also found) are worth studying for numerous reasons, among them the following:

1. It is obviously desirable to document variations in human cognitive behavior, because they are interesting in their own right.

2. Knowing the range of variations permits us to test and, when necessary, amend our purportedly general theories of cognitive behavior.

3. Learning intensively about the cognitive behaviors of specific cultural groups—along with other facts, ecological and social, that make up the settings for those behaviors—can ultimately lead to a clearer understanding of the forces that produce or at least influence human cognition generally.

Berry's Framework. The third reason listed above is probably the most important, for it induces psychologists to formulate their research in a way that yields the maximum number of theories. A leading exponent of this approach, as we first learned in Chapter Three, is John Berry. His ecological framework forces attention to the physical and social environments in which behavior develops in individuals. A recent application of this framework to cognitive development, accompanied by examples of empirical work by several psychologists, appears in Berry and Dasen (1974); an even fuller treatment appears in Berry (1976).

What makes this framework so promising is that it encourages psychologists to look first at the setting of behaviors to find possible reasons for their development. From Berry's framework one can derive testable predictions about cross-cultural differences in cognitive-task performance, particularly with tests that measure skills subsumed by Witkin's concept of *differentiation* (Witkin, 1967; Witkin & Berry, 1975). In its generic sense, this concept refers to a manifest ability to discriminate parts from the whole field in which they are embedded, as in isolating a relatively simple figure from a more complex one that includes it.

Since 1966, when Berry first reported a comparison made in 1964 and 1965 between Eskimo samples and samples drawn from the Temne people of Sierra Leone, Berry has been judiciously applying Witkins's concept and his own framework to predict and account for cross-cultural differences in differentiation skills. Berry's Eskimo/Temne comparison revealed, for example, significantly superior performance by Eskimos on the Embedded-Figures Test, Raven's Progressive Matrices, and Kohs Blocks (Berry, 1966). In a subsequent study, Australian-aboriginal and New Guinean samples—as well as two Scottish samples, one rural and one urban—were added. These provided a range of societies varying along an ecocultural continuum of degree of food accumulation. Systematic, predictable differences were found, both for traditional samples and for somewhat more acculturated samples (Berry, 1971).

The differences were quite consistently in the direction of superior performance on these spatial-abilities tests by people from low-food-accumulating societies. Such people typically engage in hunting and fishing for their food, and these activities obviously require a high degree of spatial skills. The Eskimo samples, both traditional and transitional, exceeded all others on all three measures. The Temne, an agricultural (high-food-accumulating) people, earned scores nearest to the "undifferentiated" end of the psychological-differentiation continuum. Also, performances on all three tests were highly intercorrelated, with each sample's rank on any one test being the same on the other two. Moreover, performance on the three tests correlated with a measure of independence versus conformity. Groups that were highly differentiated on the spatial-cognitive tasks were also highly independent; those that were undifferentiated tended to be more susceptible to social influence.

This last fact also enhances the validity of the construct "differentiation." This is true because that construct is meant to include not only the ability to isolate figures from grounds (as in the Embedded-Figures Test) or to switch readily to new problem-solving strategies but also the ability to resist suggestion and get along with minimal help from others. So, in Berry's 1966 and 1971 studies, it was found that two aspects of psychological differentiation were both manifested more readily by low-food-accumulating groups of people.

Subsequently, Berry administered two of the spatiocognitive tasks (Kohs

Blocks and Raven's Matrices) and the independence/conformity measure, as well as some other tests, to a new set of samples. These subjects represented a more restricted range of ecological settings within a single cultural area—all of them Amerindians living in various regions of Canada. His aim in this study was to determine whether the earlier findings (Berry, 1971) of a systematic relationship between ecology and differentiation could be replicated under the rather stringent conditions of a restricted ecological range. In this case there was no possibility of extraneous differences due to vastly different cultures, as pertained in the earlier research.

This later work (Berry & Annis, 1974) employed semitraditional and acculturated samples—and in one case a clearly traditional one as well—from three ecological settings: high food accumulating (Tsimshian), medium (Carrier), and low (Cree). The Cree are the most involved in hunting and fishing. In a clearly traditional Cree community, some 80% of the food is derived from hunting and fishing. Their more acculturated Cree brethren derive from 15% to 60% in this manner. Among the Carrier, hunting is present, but it plays a much smaller role in their subsistence. The Tsimshian people do not hunt at all. Although they fish, their livelihood from the waters is in fact described as marine agriculture, so they may accurately be described as high food accumulating.

Berry expected the Cree to demonstrate high levels of performance on the Kohs and Raven's tests, thereby displaying psychological differentiation as a reflection of the ecological requirements of a hunting way of life. The Carrier were expected to have slightly less differentiated scores, influenced positively by their hunting background but depressed by their rather strict socialization practices. The Tsimshian were expected to perform in a less differentiated way than either the Cree or the Carrier but better than other nonhunting, high-food-accumulation peoples previously studied. This was because they frequently made sea voyages that required considerable spatiocognitive ability and because they had highly developed art forms.

In fact, the Kohs Blocks data approximated these predictions nicely, but the Raven's Matrices differences were essentially in the wrong direction. Thus, the evidence is equivocal on whether the earlier demonstrated link between degree of food accumulation and spatiocognitive performance is general and replicable within a single culture area. Moreover, no trends were apparent in the independence/conformity scores either, so the later study also failed to replicate the earlier one with respect to this other aspect of psychological differentiation. It is difficult to know which to weigh more heavily, the failures to replicate or the reoccurrence of systematic differences on the Kohs Blocks.

Berry himself has said "Depending on one's orientation, we could marvel at the persistence of differential Kohs scores . . . and conclude some support for the model over this restricted ecological range" (1974, pp. 219–220). Certainly, if we consider the whole set of studies—begun in 1966 and embracing samples from West Africa, Australia, New Guinea, and Canada—there is reason to believe that the ecological model provides a sound basis for designing and pursuing research on spatiocognitive functioning, if not on other aspects of psychological differentiation. Berry's work stands as an excellent example of theory-guided research that seeks meaningful differences in performance across cultures. Additional research employing this framework and methodology is clearly worth doing.

LeVine's Approach. There are, of course, other approaches to the study of culture and cognition. Robert LeVine, a psychological anthropologist who has made many important contributions to our understanding of child development in non-Western—especially African—societies, has advocated an alternative research strategy. He proposes beginning with reliably demonstrated performance differences and *then* searching for their causes. LeVine (1970) has argued that using the dependent variable as a starting point assures scientists that their efforts are directed toward explaining a phenomenon that is already considered to be important or interesting. Were they to initiate research with the independent variable (for example, an aspect of culture that they think might produce a behavioral difference), they could arrive at merely trivial or irrelevant effects or—worse—no differences at all.

This is a persuasive and valid argument. But, as LeVine himself properly notes, this "etiological approach" exposes some major weaknesses of cross-cultural research in its actuality—most especially the paucity of well-established differences! As LeVine (1970) has said with regard to cognitive performances of children in non-Western cultures, "We do not have comparable developmental data for children the world over or even for a diverse sample of societies, and much of the cross-cultural data we do have is of dubious quality because of questions concerning the validity and/or comparability of the data collection procedures" (p. 22).

What *are* available are numerous studies that report performances on certain tasks in one or more cultural settings. But these studies usually ought not be read as their authors intended them to be read—that is, as demonstrations of the probable validity of their authors' own etiological hypotheses. There are three reasons why this is so: (1) Many of the studies are two-group-only comparisons (recall the discussion in Chapter Three of Campbell's [1961] warning that all studies consisting solely of single-pair comparisons are uninterpretable). (2) They rely on a single instrument. (3) They present a statistically significant difference and fallaciously assume it to mean that the author's preferred view of the cause of that difference has been empirically supported.

Instead, we can read these studies for whatever empirical facts they may provide about performance differences on certain tasks. Then, following LeVine's argument, we can engage in preliminary etiological speculations. In any case, whenever we are confronted by empirical evidence that people in different parts of the world respond differently to some test, then such a finding at least offers a puzzle that can stimulate subsequent hypothesis-testing research. Let us look, therefore, at some studies that present us with such puzzles.

Some Puzzles: Cross-Cultural Performance Differences

Sensorimotor Development among the Very Young

Among the most provocative puzzles provided by cross-cultural research are consistently superior performances by non-Western infants (from birth to approximately 2 years of age) on various tests of psychomotor development, such as holding up the head, sitting up unsupported, and grasping. A recent review of approximately 50 studies done in non-Western societies (Werner, 1972) confirmed that non-Western infants nearly always perform well above Euro-American norms. This finding has most consistently occurred in sub-Saharan Africa (see Warren, 1972, for a discussion of African precocity, about which he raises some doubts).[3] But it has also been found that Latin American and Indian infants, although falling short of most African scores, exceed Euro-American norms.

The infant performances in question have been studied intensively by developmental psychologists since the time of Gesell and his colleagues at Yale, beginning in the 1930s, mostly among White-American infants. The Gesell team and other psychologists (see, for example, Bayley, 1969) have produced age scales of infant development that permit assessment within cultures of individual developmental rates in relation to norms, or average scores of large samples. Individual differences have long been noted within Euro-American groups. And there is evidence that performances on these infant-behavior scales correlate positively, although not very highly, with performances on "intelligence" tests later in childhood.

Of concern to us here is that, when these infant tests (sometimes termed, not very accurately, "infant IQ tests") are administered to African and other non-Western infants, *average* scores obtained usually exceed the American norms very markedly. Sometimes nearly every baby tested exceeds the American average, so the phenomenon we are discussing is a very robust one indeed.

The Baganda. Consider, for example, what we know about the Baganda, one of several ethnic groups in Uganda. The Baganda (singular, Muganda) live in that part of Uganda that includes its capital city, Kampala, but many are rural-dwelling farmers. A significant minority are quite cosmopolitan and

---

[3]Warren's doubts are based on the fact that many of the pertinent studies employed inadequate sampling methods and presented results in ways that made their reanalysis by other interested scholars impossible. Also, most of the studies did not employ European control groups, tested by the same person who administered the tests to the African groups, but instead relied on published European performance standards. In a recent review of psychological research done in Africa, Hoorweg (1976) endorsed Warren's cautions.

engage in a European-influenced, modern life-style. In the late 1950s Geber, a pediatrician, studied Baganda babies as young as a few hours, using Gesell tests and other standard infant-performance scales. Geber found very striking precocity vis-à-vis American norms, from birth up to 2 years of age (Geber, 1956, 1958b, 1960; Geber & Dean, 1957, 1958). The degree of precocity was greatest for the Baganda neonates, and it declined steadily from birth to age 2.

A newly born Muganda, if placed on its stomach, could press down with its hands, lift up its head, and follow a light with its eyes. This behavior is typical of a several-*weeks*-old Western infant. In terms of Bayley scores, some of the Baganda neonates earned a developmental quotient of 180 (with 100 being the U.S. norm). In general, the typical Muganda infant in its first day of life behaved like the typical 6-week-old U.S. baby.

Geber's striking findings have been replicated by others working in Uganda. Ainsworth (1967) intensively studied a rural sample of 28 Baganda babies ranging in age from a few weeks to two years. Using the Griffiths Infant IQ Test, she found precocity until the babies approached 2 years of age. Later, Kilbride, Robbins, and Kilbride (1970), working with 163 rural Baganda infants, found that 75% of their entire sample scored at least one standard deviation above average on the Bayley scales. Further 23% were within one *SD* of the American norms. The researchers were using recently revised norms (Bayley, 1969), which reflected a general improvement in the performance of U.S. children as compared with that of the original normative sample collected in the United States in the 1930s. Had Kilbride and his associates used the earlier U.S. norms, they would have found that every child in their sample from Uganda was above average.

This African precocity is not peculiar to Ugandans. Similar abilities have been found thousands of miles away in Senegal, among different ethnic groups living near Dakar (Falade, 1955). In Werner's (1972) review article, still other examples may be found.

Interpretations of African Infants' Precocity. The first puzzle raised by these and similar findings concerns the reason for this initial precocity. Since it exists virtually from birth, one must entertain the possibility that it reflects genetic factors. In support of this possibility are several studies done in the United States (see Bayley, 1969; Knobloch, 1958; Knobloch & Pasamanick, 1960). All of these have shown superior performance by Black-American as compared with White-American babies. Since the former probably do not enjoy more stimulation during infancy than do the latter, the superior performance of the Black babies may very well reflect a genetic predisposition. Black-American babies have some African ancestry, of course, but some of them have European ancestry as well. So the fact that their precocity falls short of African precocity[4] is consistent with a genetic hypothesis.

[4]Kilbride, Robbins, and Kilbride (1970) found their Baganda babies to be superior to both White and Black Americans in Bayley's (1969) U.S. sample.

Despite this, and despite the fact that the African precocity is manifest at birth, environmental influences must also be considered. Geber herself (1958b) and nearly everyone else who has studied psychomotor development in Africa has been struck by certain experiential factors. Some of these have been succinctly discussed by Munroe and Munroe (1975), who cited the high level of physical activity typical of African women during pregnancy and the low level of psychological stress they enjoy. Both of these factors would operate prenatally. After birth, non-Western infants, especially those in Africa, are carried about a lot. They experience very high levels of stimulation—visual, auditory, and kinesthetic. They are in nearly constant contact with their mother, often held on her back in a sling throughout the day, while she carries on her arduous daily tasks of cooking, weeding the garden, fetching and carrying firewood or water, and the like. Babies are usually handled in ways that may well contribute positively to their development of psychomotor skills. During the first 18 months or so typical African babies are breast fed, and as a result their diet is probably adequate. Thus, it is the widely held opinon of those who have studied child development in Africa that the experiential forces impinging on African babies during the first year or two of life are conducive to development that at least matches that found in technologically more developed nations.

Janet Kilbride, reporting in 1978 a longitudinal study of mother/infant interaction *and* infant sensorimotor development among the Baganda, found that precocity was not as general as had earlier been reported. Instead, she found it to be specific to those aspects of behavior that are valued by the Baganda and encouraged and reinforced by parents in their interaction with their babies (J. E. Kilbride, 1978).

Philip Kilbride provided further evidence for this selective socioenvironmental explanation of African precocity by comparing Baganda socialization with Wasamia (a Kenyan group) socialization and noting correlated differences in infant behavior. Baganda babies receive more intensive training in behaviors that cluster into a "sociability" syndrome and are, in fact, more precocious with regard to those behaviors than are Wasamia babies (P. L. Kilbride, 1978). These two reports, then, provide both support and clarification for a social-learning explanation of sensorimotor development.

Consistent with this environmentalistic interpretation of African precocity during infancy are two facts about the subsequent period of life. The first is that the precocity disappears by about age 2. The second is that conditions of life change very dramatically for African babies at about the same time. Typically, they have been weaned by then and shifted to a diet that is nutritionally inadequate. They are likely to have been replaced in their mother's attention by a younger sibling and relegated to the care of an older sibling.

Thus, there is a discontinuity in experience that corresponds with a relative decline in performance. This correlation adds force to the argument that the performance is influenced by experience, positively up to about age 2 but negatively thereafter. Munroe and Munroe (1975) summarize this argument as follows: "Either favorable prenatal conditions or a high level of early stimulation apparently results in first-year psychomotor developmental precocity, which in the second year erodes and dissolves as the stimulation level is reduced, as the social expectations change, and as the nutritional situation deteriorates" (p. 75).

Before we leave this topic, a word of caution must be interjected. It is possible that both the precocity and its decline are to some extent artifactual. It may be that the kinds of performances measured by the infant-development tests, although the tests were developed in the West, just happen to be encouraged by African parents to a greater extent than they are by European parents (who, presumably, would be encouraging *other* skills). And, with regard to the measured decline in precocity, it is very likely—indeed almost certain —that the tests used to measure performance from age 2 onward are composed of items that favor Western children.

In short, both kinds of instruments may be culturally biased, with the early tests making the non-Western children appear precocious and the later tests making them appear slower. As of this writing, the possibility of such artifacts cannot be dismissed.

Performance Differences among Older Children

We have just seen that cultural influences, possibly working in conjunction with genetic and dietary factors, appear to impinge on cognitive development from very early in life. We have also noted that a necessary lack of confidence in the cross-cultural applicability of our measuring instruments causes us to be wary of possible exaggerations in the magnitude of the cross-cultural differences that have been reported.

This fear of test-produced artifact is enhanced when older groups are compared, because our cognitive-performance tests are increasingly culture bound as their intended age range rises. Cognitive development at later ages is measured largely by verbal-content test items. As a result, what is measured probably reflects little more than the degree of Western influence—by urbanization, education, participation in a cash economy, and so on—to which the test respondents have been exposed. If this is true, we must expect the average scores of non-Western samples to deviate from Western norms to roughly the same degree that their populations deviate from the West in various socioeconomic characteristics.

For this reason alone, psychologists are not very interested in intercultural comparisons of mean performance scores of a global, or summary, nature. This is not to say that such studies have not been reported. The literature, in fact, abounds with such studies. Their findings usually reveal, to no one's surprise, that in terms of overall "intelligence" scores relatively un-Westernized samples of children perform less well than Western children.

Patterns of Performance. Of real interest are studies that examine different *patterns* of performance across groups and among various types of test items.

Such studies try to relate aspects of performance by members of a particular cultural group to aspects of their own culture. And they focus not on whether an answer is correct or not but on the actual content of answers and the processes by which the answers are arrived at. Some examples of such studies follow.

In a paper read at the 1967 meetings of the American Psychological Association (a version of which subsequently appeared in a volume of readings edited by Lambert & Weisbrod, 1971), Goodnow reported research designed to reveal differential patterns of performance across cultural groups. To accomplish this, of course, she had to employ a number of different tasks as tests. Before undertaking her own study, Goodnow reviewed the literature and found sufficient reason for expecting that on some tasks non-Western, unschooled children would perform less well than "average" children of comparable age in the United States. She also expected that on other tasks the non-Western children would perform even better than children from the United States. And she predicted that on still other tasks no differences in performance would occur.

With data collected in Hong Kong and the United States (Goodnow & Bethon, 1966), she derived a very interesting differential performance across groups. Three groups of 11-year-old boys were tested. One of these comprised unschooled Chinese. The other two groups were American, one with a median IQ of 80 and the other with a median IQ of 111.

Four tasks were employed. Three of these were Piagetian conservation tasks—conservation of surface, volume, and amount. The fourth, called combinatorial reasoning, required the child to discover a systematic approach to composing all possible pairs—repeating none and omitting none—from a set containing six colors. Only on this last task did the Chinese sample not perform at the same level as the average-IQ American sample. On the combinatorial-reasoning task the Chinese boys dropped to the level of performance of the lower-IQ American group. Furthermore, average scores for both American groups on the combinatorial-reasoning tasks were not lower than their average scores on the other three tasks. But for the Chinese children the combinatorial-reasoning scores were clearly lower than their scores on the other tasks. Here, then, the major cross-cultural difference was a difference in *pattern* of performance across tasks.

This led Goodnow to consider the nature of the tasks, especially the features of the combinatorial-reasoning tasks that were not present in the conservation tasks. One feature to which she attached considerable importance was termed "the need to make transformations in the head," a skill that, she supected, is acquired with formal schooling. Lacking formal schooling, the Chinese boys did relatively poorly on the combinatorial-reasoning task; despite the lack of schooling, they did well on the conservation tasks. If Goodnow's interpretation is correct, then she has demonstrated an interesting link between manifest skill and culturally mediated experience.

The Importance of Schooling. It is probably impossible to exaggerate the influence of formal schooling, as practiced in the Western world and emulated elsewhere, on both the content and the style of cognitive behavior. Certain cognitive activities are valued in technological societies, regularly measured by psychologists interested in cognition, and taught—directly or otherwise—in classrooms. The combinatorial reasoning measured by Goodnow in the research reviewed above is probably such an ability.

Many psychologists have noted the role that formal schooling plays in shaping cognitive development, but few have discussed it as thoroughly as Jerome Bruner (Greenfield & Bruner, 1966; Bruner, Olver, & Greenfield, 1966). In his view the single most important aspect of formal (Western) schooling is that it is removed from the real world, or separated from immediate contexts of socially relevant action. For children who are being schooled, learning becomes an act in itself, permitting what is learned to be imbedded in the context of language (symbolic activity). Essentially, then, schooled children receive much practice in dealing with the world symbolically, and they learn to process experience in the symbolic mode.

According to Bruner, there are three modes of representation of reality available to human organisms, and these three form a developmental hierarchy. The first, or *enactive*, mode is characteristic of very young babies, to whom the world is known primarily in terms of the actions performed in it. Subsequently, children become more perceptual in their orientation to the world, processing it through images of experiences. Bruner calls this mode of representation *iconic*. Eventually, children improve their linguistic skills to the point at which they can translate their actions and their images into symbols. Presumably, all children in all societies reach this *symbolic* mode of reality representation. But unless children receive certain special training in symbolic (linguistic) representation, they may—even as adults—continue to employ the far less flexible enactive and iconic modes to a considerable extent. And it is precisely schooling of the formal, Western-influenced variety that provides that special training.

Frequent classroom events include "telling out of context" (as contrasted with "showing in context"), separating self from experience (stating why "I think X is so" and not merely why "X is so"), and considering the *not* here and the *not* now. Perhaps a simpler way of stating this is that schoolchildren become practiced in dealing with the world abstractly rather than concretely. In school, children and their teachers spend much time talking, in effect, in the subjunctive mood. They consider what might be, what might have been, and what is possible, not merely what is obvious to the senses. An essential result of schooling, then, besides the acquisition of specific curricular content, is learning to free oneself from more perceptual (iconic) or direct-action (enactive) modes of processing reality.

This Brunerian line of argument should lead us to expect that schooled children, in whatever society, will perform certain tasks better than unschooled children. We have already seen an example of an empirical study (Goodnow & Bethon, 1966) in which this was the case. Let us look at another.

A Demonstration of the Importance of Schooling. Earlier in this chapter I said that classification, or categorization, occurs universally. All intact organisms can classify objects and experiences on the basis of shared attributes. Considerable research has shown, in addition, that there are developmental trends in classificatory behavior. Younger children tend to judge objects as equivalent primarily on the basis of striking, superficial, or even incidental perceptual properties, such as form or color. Older children are likely to classify on the basis of such attributes as shared functions—"These are all items of clothing." Such age trends in societies with formal schooling have led developmental psychologists to speak of stages in conceptual behavior (see, for example, Inhelder & Piaget, 1964; Bruner et al., 1966).

In studies done in some non-Western societies, especially in Africa, it has been common to find that sorting by color is most often employed, followed by sorting by form and, finally, sorting by function. These results have emerged when children, and sometimes adults, are administered free-sorting tasks—that is, permitted to sort objects any way they like (Suchman, 1966; Price-Williams, 1962; Greenfield, Reich, & Olver, 1966). In general, the African subjects in such research have lagged behind Western subjects in their employment of form and functional sorting. But, significantly, it was found in a study done by Greenfield and her colleagues in Senegal that children with schooling tended more than unschooled children to ignore color and employ other features, especially form. The schooled children were thus seemingly performing at a developmentally superior stage. Still, the overriding impression left by the earlier studies done in Africa was that children were hardly able to sort by function.

After considering these findings, Evans and Segall (1969), working in Uganda, decided to employ a learning-to-classify task rather than a free-sorting task. They suspected that free-sorting tests, as employed in the earlier studies, revealed only habits and not abilities. And they believed that a learning task could reveal differential ease of learning to sort in various ways.

In other words a particular child might be able to sort by function but might never do so if merely asked to sort. But that same child, if instructed to find the way the experimenter wanted her to sort (and rewarded for doing so), might reveal some difficulty in discovering how to do it but might nevertheless come to do it. In short, a learning paradigm—or, more properly, a concept-discovery paradigm—provides a basis for inferring differential ease of sorting by various means, whereas a free-sorting task does not permit such inferences.

Evans and Segall designed their study to answer several questions:

1. Even with a concept-discovery task, would sorting by color be generally easier than sorting by function?

2. Are there similar or different developmental trends for both types of sorting? That is, might age matter differentially in the ease of learning the two manners of sorting?

3. How does the factor of schooling interact with the tasks?

These three questions applied to children, and the third is the one of most substantive interest. A fourth question concerned adults: If schooling were found to be a factor in the performance of children, how would adults —schooled or unschooled—perform the same tasks?

The subjects in the main experiment were children from three different places in the Baganda region of Uganda (urban, semiurban, and rural). They were unschooled or schooled; those in school were in one of three primary grades—one, three, or five. In an ancillary experiment, subjects were adults, rural and urban, with either none to three years of primary education or four to seven years.

All subjects were given two sorting tasks to perform. In one they were to find things alike on the basis of physical appearance. In the other they were to find things alike on the basis of function. Half the subjects had to discover first that color was the appropriate basis for alikeness; and, after 20 trials with that rule in effect, they had to discover that the same materials were to be sorted on the basis of shared functions. The other half of the subjects performed the same two tasks in reverse order.

On any given trial, subjects were shown a set of four pictured objects, two of which were the same color and one of which was functionally related to a third. For example, one set included two blue objects and two objects of two other colors; of the four objects, two were containers and the other two quite unrelated, such as a book and a hat. Subjects were told only to put together two that were alike. Subjects in the color-first sequence were told during their first 20 trials that they were correct if they selected the two objects of the same color; during their second 20 trials they were rewarded for sorting by function. For subjects in the other sequence this was, of course, reversed.

Between the two sets of 20 trials the experimenter said merely "You have done very well. Now I am going to show you the same pictures again, and this time we want you to put them together in another way." It should be clear that the subjects had to discover for themselves the basis for sorting and that they had to discover both bases, color and function.

The first finding to emerge from the experiment with children was that color was in general an easier concept for schoolchildren to discover than was form. Using four correct trials in a row as a criterion of learning, Evans and Segall found that 84 children never reached that criterion when the rule was function. But only 35 failed to reach the criterion for color. Also, with all nine groups of school-going children combined, the average trial on which the criterion was reached for color was 7.5, while for function it was 11.3. Thus the study replicated earlier work to the extent that it showed, even with a different method (concept discovery rather than free sorting) that color is in general an easier basis for sorting than function.

The next finding concerns the nine school-going groups compared with two groups of non-school-going rural children, one with no education at all and one with up to three years of primary school. The unschooled children performed as well as the school-going ones on the color task but much more poorly on the function task. They reached the criterion for color in about 7 trials but took all 20 trials (on the average) to reach the criterion for function. Indeed, many of them never solved the function problem.

Children in grade one also had great difficulty with the function problem. But learning to sort by function was progressively easier with increasing grade level. Most strikingly, sorting by function was just as easy as sorting by color for fifth-graders (except in the most rural of schools). But sorting by color was generally no easier in higher grades than in grade one.

As for adults, none of them who had had less than four years of primary school learned to sort by function, but nearly all of them solved the color-sorting problem. Adults who had had at least four years of education performed as well as schooled children on the function task and considerably better than the non-school-going children.

Clearly, then, the number of years in school was the critical factor relating to manifest ability to classify objects on the basis of shared function. The experiences inherent in schooling enabled subjects to entertain more complicated hypotheses than color and to comprehend the function-sorting task more readily than the lesser educated children or the adults for whom schooling had been minimal and remote in time. In support of the authors' emphasis on the importance of schooling was the intriguing fact that the children in grade five, unlike any other group in the study, tended to sort by function on their very first trial. This suggests that the tendency to search for less obvious attributes of a stimulus is a very well-practiced response in children who have had that much schooling.

Taking into account their own findings and those of the earlier studies done elsewhere in Africa, Evans and Segall (1969) suggested with regard to the oft-found preference for sorting by color that "unless *S*s are induced by the *E* to look for some less obvious characteristic, and unless they have some countertendency established by prior experience of the kind gained in school, they will employ the most obvious one available as the basis for sorting" (p. 51).

The view of developmental trends in classification behavior that emerged from the Evans and Segall project is that sorting by the perceptual, or iconic, mode appears early and is easy because of the salience of color. Sorting by function (when color is simultaneously available) requires being taught—as children in school *are* taught—to consider less obvious stimulus attributes. This conclusion was further substantiated by findings that emerged from a later study done in Colombia. In this study (Evans, 1975), learning to sort on the basis of abstract qualities was shown to be dependent on grade level in school. Thus, functional sorting is not merely maturationally induced. It is a product of experience, and a requisite kind of experience is clearly schooling.

Other Influences on Classification Behavior. The late Michael Okonji (1971), a

Nigerian psychologist, compared school-going children in a rural town in midwestern Nigeria with an age-comparable group of schoolchildren in Glasgow, Scotland. He was able to demonstrate that the Nigerian children employed more accurate, inclusive, and superordinate bases for grouping and classifying objects than their Scottish counterparts (significantly so for those aged 11 to 12) when the objects to be sorted were more familiar to the Nigerian children than to the Scottish children. This occurred even though his younger Nigerian subjects (mostly between 6 and 8 years) often used color as a sorting basis, whereas none of the Scottish children did. Despite this tendency to employ a perceptual basis for sorting on some trials, the Nigerian children performed overall at a level of conceptualization that at least equaled that of the Scottish sample.

Okonji expressed confidence that the high performance of the Nigerian subjects was attributable to their familiarity with the objects. A similar point had been made by Price-Williams (1962) in a study that demonstrated European-like performance by non-Europeans when the testing materials were not strange to the subjects. In a similar study by Irwin, Schafer, and Feiden (1974) subjects showed difficulties in sorting unfamiliar materials.

Working in Australia, de Lacey (1970, 1971, 1972) studied the ability to classify as manifested by aboriginal children in the age range 6 to 10 years. One group of such children had had high contact with Euro-Australians; another had not. The former group performed significantly better than the latter on several different classification tests. In the same project Euro-Australian children were also found to perform either well or not so well depending on their socioeconomic status. And the high-contact aborigines performed similarly to the Euro-Australians low in socioeconomic status.

These findings led de Lacey to conclude that classification performance relates to the degree of enrichment in children's environment. This was the case for both Euro-Australians and aborigines. His project also showed that the correlation between ability to classify and performance on a test of verbal skills among aborigines varied in magnitude with the degree of environmental enrichment.

It thus seems that the process of classifying experience occurs in much the same fashion among a wide variety of ethnic groups. Qualitative differences are found primarily among people who are not educated, who are tested with unfamiliar materials, who are drawn from culturally deprived backgrounds, or who are otherwise disadvantaged. What was once thought to be a difference across ethnic groups in the *ability* to process information—a difference often characterized as revealing inherent inferiority—is better thought of as a reflection of the experiences people have and of the cultural appropriateness of the way their skills are assessed. To put it bluntly, given the right opportunities to learn to play the Euro-American psychologists' sorting games, people anywhere can come to play them well.

A Methodological Dilemma: How Can One Study a Classification Scheme in Another Culture?

Along with other psychologists who have issued similar warnings, Price-Williams (1975) recently admonished us: "Our own categories of explanation and definition, embedded in our psychological theories, may not be appropriate when projected on some other culture" (p. 23).

This admonition is epitomized by the *emic/etic* distinction, a term first employed in anthropology by Pike (1954). He made an analogy with the usage of the term's components in linguistics, where phon*etics* involves application of a universal coding system for sounds employed in any language and phon*emics* involves study of meaning-bearing units in a particular language. Pike urged that we try to penetrate a culture and see it as its own members do. Thus, psychological research designed to show how a particular people classifies experience, yielding the classification system they habitually employ, would be emic research and has come to be known as ethnopsychology.

For example, Valentine (1963) studied personality theories of the Lakalai people of New Britain. He discovered that they assigned persons to several contrasting types of pairs, as in men of anger/men of shame. Such research is clearly worth doing, for we surely want to know how persons in different cultures slice up the experienced world. But we also want to compare the classification systems of various cultural groups. And we often find it useful, or at least tempting, to apply our own culture's scheme as a springboard, or baseline, for understanding another's.

Berry (1969) has addressed himself to the problem of how an alien psychologist, armed initially with his or her own culture's category system (emic within that culture but etic as soon as it is applied elsewhere), can avoid invalid comparisons of two or more cultural classification schemes:

> An emic description can be made by progressively altering the imposed etic until it matches a purely emic point of view; if this can be done without entirely destroying or losing all of the etic character of the entry categories, then we can proceed to the next step. If some of the etic is left, we can note the categories or concepts which are shared by the behavior system we knew previously and the one we have just come to understand emically. We can now set up a derived etic which is valid for making comparisons between two behavior settings and we have essentially resolved the problem of obtaining a descriptive framework valid for comparing behavior across behavioral settings [p. 124].

Thus, Berry advocates deriving an etic scheme for cross-cultural comparisons of emic schemes employed in each culture that is entered into comparison. This seems a simple and adequate technique for making meaningful comparisons. What needs emphasizing, however, is that any single culture's classification system should first be expressed in the terms employed indigenously. It is that system, after all, that makes up the cognitive map of persons in that culture. And it is that system, expressed in its own terms, that is of paramount interest to the psychologist who would seek reasons, embedded in other facts about the behavioral setting, for the presence of such a system. To understand *why* a people think the way they do, we must first appreciate *how* they think. And for that we must discover each people's emic system.

Working among the Kpelle in Liberia, the psychologist Michael Cole and his colleagues (see, for example, Cole, Gay, & Glick, 1968) have exemplified this approach. They provided their respondents with very open-ended tasks, in which they could indicate what an object was called and what it was not, what was an example of something like it and not like it, and so on. This permitted the alien psychologists gradually to construct an indigenously labeled system of categories. A subsequent objective of Cole and his associates has been to compare systems within the culture, seeking their interrelationships and thereby approaching a picture of the overall cognitive system of a single people. All this is done before venturing to make cross-cultural comparisons.[5]

The Emic/Etic Distinction and Subjective Culture. In a manner analogous to the search for indigenous classification systems, Triandis has attempted to ascertain, in different societies, what he terms *subjective culture*. This concept was first employed in a work done during the late 1960s with colleagues from and in various societies (Triandis, Vassiliou, Vassiliou, Tanaka, & Shanmugam, 1972). In most of his empirical work (see, for example, Triandis, Davis, & Takezawa, 1965; Triandis, Vassiliou, & Nassiakou, 1968), Triandis has sought the respondents' own models of the social rules governing some complex aspects of social behavior, such as interpersonal and intergroup relations.

From his various findings, Triandis (1975) has generalized that information processing is essentially the same everywhere. But, he says, cultural differences occur "(a) in how basic processes are combined into 'functional cognitive systems' and (b) in the *weights* humans (in different cultures) give to the information" (p. 4). It is thus apparent that Triandis's subjective-culture approach is concerned more with culturally influenced norms and values than with classification behavior.[6] But his approach is clearly compatible with the emic emphasis of Cole and his associates. And it also seeks to result in a view of the world as held by the respondents themselves.

However difficult it may be for an alien psychologist to discover an indigenous cognitive map of the world, the effort is clearly worth making. Ultimately, however, whatever is discovered will somehow have to be compared

---

[5]The manner in which a people classifies experience probably relates to the way they remember. This notion was investigated by Cole and his colleagues. See this chapter's later section on memory.

[6]An example of Triandis's subjective-culture approach is presented in Chapter Eight where cultural differences in beliefs relating to intergroup relations are discussed.

with, and related to, the psychologist's own conceptual tools. It is this ultimate objective toward which those who have wrestled with the emic/etic distinction are pointing.

Memory

If people in different cultures classify objects and events differently, do they remember differently? Do different classification schemes assist memory? Is it possible that certain groups, especially people in nonliterate societies, have quantitatively *better* memories than people in Western societies?

Anecdotal evidence abounds that people in technologically simpler societies have phenomenal memories compared with people from more complex societies. Many observers, in tales of their travels to exotic lands, have reported remarkable feats of memory. But the scientific evidence is not at all clear.

Some serious students of behavior in various cultures, perhaps influenced by these anecdotes, have found good reason to expect that memory skills in preliterate societies develop differently from, if not better than, those in literate societies. They have noted that daily life in nonliterate societies places a premium on remembering details of the sort that in literate societies are a matter of bookkeeping or other forms of written record. Thus, Cole and Gay (1972) theorized that memory skills may be reinforced in some traditional societies both by the lack of a written language and by the emphasis placed on learning tribal histories and traditions.

Research with the Kpelle. Cole and his colleagues (see, for example, Cole, Gay, Glick, & Sharp, 1971; Cole & Scribner, 1974) reported a complex series of experiments with schooled and unschooled Kpelle in Liberia, the results of which are also complex. In one early experiment ten adult Kpelle subjects, non-English-speaking, heard and were then asked to recall the names of 20 common items, five each in four categories—food, clothing, tools, and utensils. They were given several trials. Compared with American college students, the Kpelle subjects remembered less, improved less over trials, and clustered the names into their appropriate categories less.

This surprising result prompted the psychologists to consider the possibility that the categories employed (imposed etically) were inappropriate for the Kpelle. But three different eliciting studies, in which the Kpelle were allowed to display an indigenous classification scheme showed that the groupings employed in the memory experiment *were* culturally appropriate.

The researchers subsequently did a number of other widely varied experiments. They tested both educated (in Western style) and uneducated Kpelle. They employed both clusterable and nonclusterable names. They varied the order of names. They used real objects, not merely their names. And they varied the conditions of presentation, among which was an ingenious procedure known as *concrete cueing*, in which objects were held over chairs. Among the diverse findings that emerged were the following:

1. Clusterable lists were more easily learned than nonclusterable lists, and even more so by educated subjects.

2. Whereas American subjects showed serial position effects—that is, they recalled items late in a list best, those at the beginning next best, and those in the middle least well—Kpelle recall was unrelated to serial position.

3. Concrete objects were recalled better than a list of their names, but only among educated Kpelle.

4. The concrete-cueing procedure enhanced recall, especially when clustered objects were each held over a particular chair.

5. The employment of an explicit verbal instruction such as "Tell me all the tools you remember" also enhanced recall. This was true both for Kpelle and American subjects.

What can be made of all this? The results may fairly be summarized as showing that, with the employment of certain aids to clustering the material to be remembered, the Kpelle subjects, particularly those with some schooling, were able to recall in a manner and to a degree comparable with American subjects. The experiments did not reveal any superior memory skills among the Kpelle. But they did allow specification of circumstances under which Kpelle memory would function like that of Americans—who, it may be suspected, were more practiced in employing aids to memory. Signaling categories latent in clusterable lists was the technique that aided the Kpelle most.

A major implication of the research program conducted among the Kpelle is that schooling heavily influences the performance of tasks requiring memorization. Poor recall was characteristic of unschooled subjects—who could, nevertheless, benefit from techniques imposed by Cole and his colleagues. The use of conceptual organization as a means to remembering was more likely to be characteristic of schooled persons.

In a comprehensive review of the Kpelle research (Cole & Scribner, 1974) the point is made that schooling teaches people that they must often remember aggregates of material that are not at first perceived as interrelated. Thus, people become practiced in learning new organizing principles, the acquisition of which then facilitates the remembering of instances that relate to the principle.

In any event, it must be repeated that in this research program no evidence was found for superior memory skill among the unschooled Kpelle. This series of studies certainly did not support the view that memory processes are inherently better in preliterate societies.

Other studies, however, do show some superiority in memory among persons reared in societies with a strong oral tradition.

Other Studies. Ross and Millsom (1970) suspected that the reliance on oral tradition characteristic of African societies might make Africans more likely to remember details in orally presented stories than a comparable group of Americans. Both groups were university students, one in Ghana and the other in New York. The researchers read several stories and tested retention of the several themes contained in each story. They found that, in general, the Ghanaian students recalled the stories better than the New York students. The sole departure from this finding was with regard to one story that was told in 17th-century English. Still, the Ghanaian performance was impressive, especially if one keeps in mind that the Ghanaian students both heard and reproduced the stories in English, which to most of them was a second language.

Putting aside words for the moment, it may also be that people in preliterate settings exceed those in literate societies in the memory of objects and pictures. In literate societies people are practiced in coding experience into words, which may enable them to recall large quantities of coded information. At the same time, individuals in literate societies, because they can rely on memory banks such as telephone directories and history books, may have lost memory skills through lack of practice. By contrast, individuals in preliterate settings may employ modes of memory that involve less encoding. And, because there are few alternatives to storing experience "in their own heads," they may be well practiced in storing images of concrete experiences.

A phenomenon rather like this was reported by Doob (1964). He tested the incidence of eidetic imagery (photographic memory) in a sample of Ibo people of Nigeria, a haphazardly selected group of 45 persons, male and female, children and adults, urban and rural. Doob found the Ibo performance to be "dramatically higher than that normally found in the West." In that same study, he found significantly more use of eidetic imagery among rural Ibo than among urban Ibo. Suspecting that eidetic imagery may correlate negatively with the Western character of a community, Doob continued his search for high levels of eidetic imagery in other non-Western settings. He did not find it, so the 1964 study remains unreplicated and its findings unexplained.

Deregowski, Ellis, and Shepherd (1973) predicted that Rhodesian subjects would remember faces better than they did common objects, such as cups, but that Western subjects would not differentially remember faces and objects. This complex prediction was based on the notion that, because of the high value placed in African cultures on social matters, the memorizing of faces would be a more relevant and practiced skill among Africans than among Westerners. The prediction was *not* supported by the data. In fact, the Western subjects performed better than the African subjects on memory for faces *and* on memory for cups. The authors could not explain these findings.

There are other studies in the literature pertaining to culture and memory. But the few reviewed here suffice to illustrate how little is really known or understood about possible cultural differences in what, how, and how well things are remembered.

But classification is a process that probably assists memory. And, as we saw in a preceding section of this chapter, there are probably no marked differences in the quality of classification *abilities* across ethnic groups. Therefore, it is probably safe to assume that there are no serious intergroup differences in *ability* to remember, either.

Neither should we be surprised by future research that may show more intriguing differences in memory as a function of what is to be remembered, how it is tested, and the particular mode of remembering that is encouraged.

Cognitive Development

The Piagetian Perspective: Cultural Influences on "Stages" of Development

The famous Swiss psychologist Jean Piaget has for decades tried to ascertain what he calls the "structures" of thought as they appear developmentally from early childhood. Basic to Piaget's theories of the process by which individuals come to interact intelligently with their worlds are the notions of adaptation to the environment and a hierarchical set of stages of development. (See Flavell, 1963, for an excellent summary in English of Piaget's ideas.) Although Piaget's theoretical contributions were originally based on research done in Western settings, most notably in his home city of Geneva, much cross-cultural research has been done more recently to test the generality of his "structures" and of his hypothesized stages of development.

Pierre Dasen, also a Geneva psychologist, has provided a thorough and comprehensive summary of cross-cultural Piagetian research (Dasen, 1972; reprinted in Berry & Dasen, 1974). Although the present account relies heavily on Dasen's work, that work should be read in its entirety by the serious student of cross-cultural psychology.

As Dasen (1972) notes, cross-cultural research done in a Piagetian conceptual framework seeks to determine whether the same sequential succession of stages as described by Piaget for Western cognitive development occurs elsewhere in the world and, if so, whether at the same or different ages.

From among Piaget's stages, the ones of most interest to cross-cultural researchers have been the "concrete-operational stage" and the "preoperational stage." Passage to the concrete-operational stage is usually indexed by an individual's demonstrating *conservation*, or the recognition that something (weight, volume, and the like) cannot possibly have changed, even though it may superficially have appeared to.

In two studies already mentioned in the present chapter, conservation was found among non-Western children at the same ages as is normal for Western children. Price-Williams (1961) found this for Tiv children in Nigeria with regard to conservation of quantity and number. And Goodnow & Bethon (1966) found it among Hong Kong Chinese children for conservation of amount, weight, and volume.

Piaget himself, in a 1966 paper calling for cross-cultural research in genetic psychology, cited research by Mohseni (an unpublished thesis) done in Iran. Mohseni found that children living in the city of Tehran performed similarly to Genevan children (aged 5 to 10 years) with regard to conservation of substance, weight, and volume. Mohseni also found that rural Iranian children showed the same stage-like development, but with a 2- to 3-year delay.

Although the few studies just mentioned found both the same sequence of development *and* similar timing in non-Western groups (except for the rural Iranians in Mohseni's study), time lags have been found in the majority of studies done in non-Western settings.

Several studies have shown relatively late ages for the acquisition of conservation concepts—or relatively small proportions of children at a given age displaying conservation. To mention only a few, studies have been done in Senegal on conservation of quantity (Greenfield, 1966), in Algeria on conservation of length (Bovet, 1971; English translation in Berry & Dasen, 1974), and in Uganda on many different conservation tasks (Vernon, 1969).

There are also several studies in which a majority of children tested failed to display conservation at ages when nearly all European children typically display it. These studies raise the possibility that not all people, even adults, in all societies reach the concrete-operational stage. On the other hand, the studies in which nonconservers dominate may not have extended the age range sufficiently, so this question cannot yet be answered.

What the cross-cultural studies on conservation do clearly suggest, as Dasen (1972) has put it, is "that, among the factors influencing cognitive development, cultural ones might be more important than had previously been hypothesized" (reprinted in Berry & Dasen, 1974, p. 418). A generalization that Dasen has offered is that progress toward the concrete-operational stage is probably accelerated among subjects in non-Western settings who have a high degree of contact with agents and agencies of Western culture. He has also suggested that other variables that affect rate of cognitive development include malnutrition, early physical and social stimulation, and linguistic structures. But he notes that such variables have not yet been investigated systematically with Piagetian tasks.

The list of published cross-cultural studies of conservation and other Piagetian intellectual tasks is very large and rapidly growing. The few studies cited in this account are a very small portion of this literature.[7] There is certainly no other approach to the analysis of cognitive development that exceeds the Piagetian approach in its appeal to cross-cultural psychologists. But an approach that may soon equal it is concerned with cognitive style, based on the theoretical work of Witkin.

---

[7]An excellent survey of recent cross-cultural contributions to Piagetian psychology can be found in a volume edited by Dasen (1977a) and a chapter by the same author (1977b) in Warren (1977).

The Witkinian Perspective: Cultural Influences on Cognitive Style

Earlier in this chapter, the work of John Berry was cited (Berry, 1966, 1971; Berry & Annis, 1974). These cross-cultural studies are just a few of the many that have tested the generality of Witkin's psychological-differentiation theory. Simultaneously, these studies have used that theory and related testing procedures as a guide to understanding cultural influences on cognitive development.

The concept of *cognitive style* has been articulated in great detail by Witkin in several different papers (see, for example, Witkin, 1967). Briefly, in Witkin's own words, " 'Cognitive styles' are the characteristic self-consistent modes of functioning found pervasively throughout an individual's cognitive, that is, perceptual and intellectual, activities" (Witkin, 1967, p. 233). These modes are thought to lie along a dimension from global to articulated—or, as it is more often termed, undifferentiated to differentiated. An individual's style, or position along this dimension, is hypothesized to be influenced socially, most notably by socialization practices that encourage either dependent or independent functioning.[8]

Witkin also expects the nature of the environment in which a child grows up to influence his or her developing cognitive style, especially if ecological forces relate systematically to socialization practices, including mother/child interactions. This expectation has invited much cross-cultural research.

Working in Sierra Leone in the 1960s, Dawson (1963, 1967) found greater field dependence among the Temne than among the Mende. He could cite a number of differences in socialization practices that might plausibly account for the difference in cognitive style. Indeed, the same cluster of socialization practices that earlier research by Witkin and his colleagues in the United States had found to be related to cognitive style was apparent in the Temne/Mende contrast. Among the characteristics of Temne socialization were stress on conformity to adult authority, severe discipline, physical punishment, and maternal dominance in child rearing.

Working in New York City, Dershowitz (1971) tested three groups of 10-year-old boys, two Jewish and one White Anglo-Saxon. He found Jews who were more assimilationist to be generally more field independent than more traditional Orthodox Jews of an Eastern European background. Both Jewish groups were somewhat less field independent than the White Anglo-Saxon comparison group. With regard to the Orthodox group, Dershowitz viewed the values and patterns of traditional living as likely to inhibit the development of a sense of separate identity. These values stressed conformity, limited criticism

---

[8]Field dependence/independence is another terminology that is frequently employed to refer to cognitive style. A field-independent person is typically autonomous, not easily influenced, and "psychologically differentiated."

of elders, encouraged a sense of indebtedness to parents, suppressed the assumption of a male aggressive role, limited the child's personal and material responsibility, indulged the child's will, and denigrated the body and its physical expression. All of the foregoing (cited here in Dershowitz's own language) were seen by him as inhibiting the development of psychological differentiation among the Orthodox boys.

His results were consistent with this argument, particularly those that showed the Orthodox sample as less differentiated than the assimilationist Jewish sample, with the latter group less differentiated than the non-Jewish sample. On some tests the assimilationist sample did not score as less differentiated than the non-Jewish sample, though the Orthodox sample did. Clearly, then, the Orthodox group was less differentiated than both non-Jews and assimilationist Jews on all measures, whereas the assimilationist Jews were as differentiated as non-Jews on some measures. Whether or not the particular characteristics cited by Dershowitz in his argument are the relevant factors, it is clearly some set of cultural factors that underlies this pattern of intergroup differences.

The two studies just cited are, once again, a small sample of existing cross-cultural studies that suggest that cultural forces influence cognitive style.

Sex and Culture as They Relate to Cognitive Style

In research on cognitive style in the United States, many hundreds of studies have revealed sex differences in degree of psychological differentiation. Males are more field independent, although this sex difference is not so reliable until adolescence. Recently, cross-cultural studies have partly confirmed the American findings. But they have also resulted in some other findings that throw light on the mechanisms that might possibly have produced the sex differences first noted in the United States.

By 1978, Mary Stewart Van Leeuwen, a Canadian cross-cultural psychologist, could review 30 studies[9] done outside the United States, employing various measures of psychological differentiation. In not all of these were significant sex differences found. But when differences were found, they were nearly always in the direction of males' earning scores closer to the differentiated end of the scale (Van Leeuwen, 1978). Although Van Leeuwen acknowledged that this clear trend is consistent with a hypothesis of the universality of sex differences, she properly noted that a more intriguing characteristic of the findings is the variation in the magnitude of the sex differences revealed. She reasoned quite rightly that an effort to explain this variation—from minimal to large—might result in a better understanding of the social and cultural forces that impinge on

[9]The 30 studies, published between 1955 and 1975, were conducted in the Netherlands, Japan, Sierra Leone, Canada, Nigeria, India, Mexico, Israel, New Guinea, Australia, Zambia, and Jamaica and with a variety of non-White U.S. samples.

psychological differentiation generally—that is, for individuals regardless of sex—as well as an understanding of the sex differences themselves.

Van Leeuwen's efforts resulted in one theory, called an ecological model, that seems admirably to encompass the findings from a number of the studies reviewed, including all of them done in non-Western societies engaged primarily in subsistence-level economic activities. (Two ancillary models, consistent with the ecological model and easily subsumed by it, produced a set of three "theories" that together account for the findings in all of the societies. But here we will concentrate on the ecological model.)

The Ecological Model. This model points to economic conditions in subsistence-level societies that can produce either minimal or large sex differences in psychological differentiation through socialization practices that may or may not differentially influence the two sexes.

Key features of the ecological model are based on John Berry's ecological conceptual framework, with which readers of this book are already familiar. As will be recalled, Berry's (1966, 1971) notion includes the view that the degree of food accumulation in a subsistence-level society will, among other things, influence its level of psychological differentiation. It is in low-food-accumulating societies like the Eskimos' that the environment demands very sharp perceptual articulation for survival. Berry's framework and Van Leeuwen's employment of it are both consistent with earlier work done by Herbert Barry and colleagues (see, for example, Barry, Child, & Bacon, 1959). These studies showed that socialization for obedience and responsibility was stressed in high-food-accumulating societies, while socialization for achievement, self-reliance, and general independence was more likely to be stressed in low-food-accumulating societies.

Taking into account the findings of Barry and his associates, Berry's ecological hypothesis, and some additional information (to be described below at appropriate points in the argument), Van Leeuwen formulated the essence of her ecological model. That is, "The relatively greater freedom of women in more nomadic hunting-gathering societies will result in lesser sex differences in performance on differentiation tasks, whereas the restrictiveness of agricultural groups will produce greater sex differences in performance" (Van Leeuwen, 1978, p. 96).

The first point to be made about this statement is that it is perfectly consistent with the available cross-cultural data. It is low-food-accumulating groups—for example, Eskimos, aborigines, and some Canadian-Indian groups—that show minimal or even no sex differences in psychological differentiation. And high-food-accumulating groups—for example, the Temne, Ibo, Zulu, and New Zealand indigenes—show significant sex differences.

Van Leeuwen's formula is also consistent with a second aspect of the findings of Barry and his colleagues (1959). Those researchers found that in cultures where nurturance, obedience, and responsibility training are stressed (high-food-accumulating societies), they are stressed more strongly for girls. Also, a study by Barry, Bacon, and Child (1957) found that factors that enhanced the compliance training of girls included the cultivation of grain crops and the domestication of large animals, both characteristic of high-food-accumulating societies.

Thus, Van Leeuwen's ecological model begins with and is consistent with reliable correlations between degree of food accumulation and strength of sex differences in psychological differentiation. The balance of her model is more theoretical and is concerned with possible mechanisms for these empirical relationships. Among them are the following:

1. A perceived differential in physical strength and the biological facts of child bearing lead to a specialization of labor by sex in large-grain-crop or large-animal-subsistence societies. Family-maintenance tasks are relegated to women, and, hence, compliance, dutifulness, and nurturance are stressed for girls.

2. Greater role specialization in sedentary groups leads to a more exclusively female preoccupation with child-related activities. Hence, girls receive more training in social sensitivity (a characteristic of the so-called undifferentiated cognitive style).

3. The low role diversity in non-sedentary groups leads to a higher valuation of women's activities. In sedentary, agricultural groups, however, the role of women is more apt to be regarded with contempt (possibly feigned). Male activities are accorded inflated prestige, and male adults scorn participation in child-rearing activities. All of these contribute to maternal dominance of children, considerable paternal absence, and measures to keep women "under control." Maternal dominance and father absence contribute to an undifferentiated cognitive style in general, and the control of women contributes to the even less differentiated cognitive style characteristic of women in such societies.

It is Van Leeuwen's opinion that any or all of these mechanisms can account for variations in degree of sex differences in psychological differentiation in essentially subsistence-level societies.

For essentially Western or Westernized societies, Van Leeuwen notes, variations in sex differences can be accounted for by such variables as degree of obedience, conformity, family and religious loyalty, and mother salience in early childhood. Once again, those societies that stress such socialization practices stress them more for girls than for boys. Hence, she postulates a "social-conformity model" to encompass the pattern of sex differences found in studies done in more Westernized societies. It should be noted that this second model is consistent with and incorporable within the ecological model.

Whether one is considering subsistence-level societies or societies in which food getting is less of a preoccupation, it appears that the socialization practices that tend toward compliance and conformity—and that contribute to greater field dependence—are inflicted more on females than on males.

Thus, we can now understand the variations across societies in the degree of sex differences in cognitive style as a likely product of differential socialization with regard to compliance. So, too, we can now interpret cross-cultural differences (regardless of sex) in cognitive style as a likely product of varying degrees of compliance training. And, finally, Van Leeuwen's theoretical efforts have helped us to perceive how cognitive style is shaped by culture, via socialization, with socialization in turn at least partly shaped by ecological and economic factors.[10]

Cultural Influences on Prediction, Inference, and the Perception of Causality

The drawing of inferences and the predicting of future events based on an analysis of past events—processes that often require making causal hypotheses —are forms of cognitive behavior characteristic of science. In the Western view of the world such behavior is considered by many to represent the ultimate in intelligence. To the degree that an individual behaves "scientifically," he or she is perceived as intelligent, competent, and capable of perceiving the world as it really is.

In Piaget's model of the development of modes of acquiring knowledge, the ultimate level toward which development tends is the formal stage. At this stage one becomes capable of performing formal, logical operations. It emerges, according to Piaget, only after the concrete-operational stage has been attained, and it may not be reached by everyone. Indeed, Piaget suggested (1966, p. 30) that few individuals in so-called primitive societies could attain the stage of formal operations.

Drawing inferences, particularly causal inferences, and discovering general principles on which valid predictions can be based are, of course, highly intellectual activities. They are extremely difficult to perform well in many instances, even for highly trained persons. The complex methodologies and theories that characterize modern science, the complex statistical techniques that have been devised to guard against perceiving a relationship when none in fact exists, and the frequency with which such errors are nevertheless made all testify to the difficulty of scientific thinking. Yet, even in everyday life as lived by persons who are not professional scientists, scientific thinking, logical analysis, the making of predictions, and similar activities must occur. And for centuries in the West, scholars have struggled to provide all of us with guidelines for such scientific thinking.

Not surprisingly, people who have been reared in the West value such cognitive functioning and are probably well practiced in it. Only a minority of

[10]Accordingly, Witkin and Berry (1975) could conclude "The concepts derived from differentiation theory can be meaningfully applied across cultures, due largely to the structural nature of differentiation and to its base in a cultural universal socialization. . . . Factors such as general pressure toward conformity, the structure of authority, and role diversity and evaluation . . . have been implicated" (pp. 72–73).

thoughtful persons argues that any other mode of knowing—for example, intuition, mysticism, or some other form of direct, just plain knowing—is a superior way of understanding reality. This is not to say that there are none who argue the case for other forms of knowing. Western culture has its share of poets, mystics, and others who insist that there are mysteries that cannot be penetrated by scientific inquiry. Still, it is the scientific mode of knowledge seeking that dominates and is accorded supreme status.

What is the case in non-Western societies? Is Piaget correct, for example, in assuming that all people tend toward formal-operational (scientific) thinking but that non-Western people fall short of its achievement? Might it be that such thinking is absent from non-Western societies? Is there some other mode so highly valued and practiced that it takes the place of science and serves as well or even better to reveal "knowledge"? It is questions like these that may have prompted a number of cross-cultural studies. We will now consider a few of these studies.

Cross-Cultural Studies. Some studies have employed Piagetian tests of formal reasoning and have found relatively small proportions of nonurban, essentially subsistence-level, individuals performing these operations. For example, Peluffo (1967) found that only 25% of 11-year-olds and 20% of adults living in technologically undeveloped Sardinia were successful on such tests. But a majority of the sons of urban workers in Genoa, Italy, and a majority of the sons of clerks and professionals in Sardinia were successful. Working in New Guinea, Were (1968) found no success among 14- to 16-year-olds on these tests.

In neither of these studies, however, is there any information that permits us to guess why the performance of logical operations was so poor. We cannot rule out, for example, an artifact due to testing itself, which elicited performances from which inferences on capability ought not be drawn. Still, data such as these are consistent with the view that, in cultural settings in which science and the formal schooling that science may require are absent, individuals will not be able—at least not readily—to perform logical operations.

In a study done with schoolchildren in Ghana (Mundy-Castle, 1967), it was found that the ability to make correct predictions about gradually emerging patterns of visual stimuli improved between the ages of 5 and 7 years but not between 7 and 9. In one task employed in Mundy-Castle's study, a straight line of dots was shown, and the child was instructed to predict how the series would continue, or where the next dot would be. Using similar procedures with White American schoolchildren in a suburb of Philadelphia, Snelbecker, Fullard, and Gallagher (1971) found similar shifts in performance. But for the Americans, the improvement occurred at a *later* age (between the second and fourth grades). The authors of the American study concluded only that the developmental shift in prediction-making skill found by Mundy-Castle was not unique to Ghanaians. They offered no explanation for the fact that this shift occurred at an earlier age in Ghana than in Philadelphia.

Unlike the two studies just described, most cross-cultural comparisons involving American schoolchildren show them to be advanced in the development of causal thinking relative to non-American schoolchildren. For example, Walker, Torrance, and Walker (1971), working with third- and sixth-graders in New Delhi and Minneapolis, showed a picture of a scene from the nursery rhyme "Little Boy Blue" and elicited reasons for the action depicted in it. They found an increase in the perception of situational causality from the third to the sixth grade only for the Americans. And they found a higher incidence of situational causality in the responses of the Americans at both the third- and sixth-grade levels.

Langgulung and Torrance (1972) compared the causal thinking of both advantaged and disadvantaged fourth- and sixth-graders in Mexico and the urban United States, employing the Torrance tests of "creative thinking." They found more causal thinking by Americans than by Mexicans, by sixth-graders than by fourth-graders, and by advantaged children than by disadvantaged children. The same authors (Langgulung & Torrance, 1973) used part of the same test with similar samples in India and Samoa. They replicated their earlier findings concerning grade and economic differences in each culture. But in addition they found that the Indian children were similar to the American children in their superiority vis-à-vis both the Mexican and Samoan schoolchildren. Also, they reported a number of statistically significant grade-by-culture interactions in performance. They interpreted these as indicating that the developmental trends in causal thinking are modified by cultural forces but that the nature of these forces cannot be specified.

The differences in age—or better, perhaps, in year of schooling—at which logical behavior appears in different cultures are difficult, if not impossible, to interpret. Perhaps the more significant aspect of the findings of the several studies just reviewed is that school-going subjects in the societies visited by the cross-cultural psychologists sooner or later displayed logical behavior. In this regard Cole, Gay, Glick, and Sharp (1971), noting that Liberian high-school students performed logical operations very much as American high-school students did, suggested that "education shifts dramatically the mode of response to . . . verbal problems so that the particular content no longer determines the answer" (pp. 193–194).

The significance of this performance among secondary-schooled Liberian Kpelle is underscored by comparing it with the typical performance of Kpelle village elders. An example of this comparison was recently extracted from the study above and published in a review of research on cognition done in Africa (McLaughlin, 1976). Because it illustrates so well the manner in which traditional thought does not contradict or violate logic but instead may simply ignore it and substitute some other form of "knowing," we can close this section on cultural influences on causal thinking by reproducing it, with no further comment.

Experimenter: At one time, spider went to a feast. He was told to answer this question before he could eat any of the food. The question is: Spider and black deer always eat together. Spider is eating. Is black deer eating?

Subject: Were they in the bush?

Experimenter: Yes.

Subject: They were eating together?

Eperimenter: Spider and black deer always eat together. Spider is eating. Is black deer eating?

Subject: But I was not there. How can I answer such a question?

Experimenter: Can't you answer it? Even if you were not there, you can answer it (repeats the question).

Subject: Oh, oh, black deer is eating.

Experimenter: What is your reason for saying that black deer was eating?

Subject: The reason is that black deer always walks about all day eating green leaves in the bush. Then he rests for a while and gets up again to eat [McLaughlin, 1976, p. 91].

Summary and Conclusions

In this chapter we have discussed numerous studies conducted in many different parts of the world. They were done with children and, to a lesser extent, with adults. They have dealt with a variety of cognitive activities —classification, concept discovery, memory, logical analysis, and problem solving. In the bulk of the studies reviewed, we found evidence of *differences* across cultural groups, *differences* in habitual strategies for classifying and for solving problems, *differences* in cognitive style, and *differences* in rates of progression through developmental stages of modes of knowing. Variation across groups in the way individuals interact with the world around them appear from the very earliest days of life. And contrasting performances are also found in cross-cultural comparisons involving adults.

The picture is, clearly, one of differences, to repeat the word once more! For the most part, these differences are puzzling. There exist few good reasons for choosing from among several competing explanations for particular differences reported in individual studies.

Theories, or conceptual frameworks, have appeared that provide promising guidelines in our search for an understanding of these puzzling differences. First, there are models of cognitive development such as Bruner's enactive/iconic/symbolic progression and Piaget's stages. Both of these purport to describe a universal, invariant sequence of modes of knowing, against which the cognitive behaviors of real children anywhere can be measured and classified. It is probably fair to say that such models describe growth in the science-oriented Western world and that they constitute a picture of an ideal Western individual-becoming-scientist. Their value outside the West may prove to be primarily heuristic, permitting psychologists working anywhere to compare what is discovered about cognitive behavior with these idealized models. The models, of course, also serve to suggest the kinds of tasks and problems that might most usefully be employed to discover *how* people anywhere resemble human *qua* scientist or otherwise function cognitively.

And the idealized picture provided by such models may, in broad outline, at least, reflect the reality of cognitive growth throughout the world. As Jahoda (1970) said, after reviewing cross-cultural studies that could be taken as tests of Piaget's framework, "The core of Piagetian theory—an invariant sequence of identifiable stages—survives intact. At the same time it has undergone very substantial modifications as a result of cross-cultural work" (p. 61).

For example, Posner and Baroody (1978) administered a standard Piagetian number-conservation task to schooled and unschooled 9- to 10-year-olds, both rural and urban, in the Ivory Coast. They found that the urban Dioula were far better at it than the rural Baoule, with only the latter displaying a positive effect of schooling. The authors also measured simple counting performances and found that knowing how to count, whether it was learned in school among the Baoule or in everyday activities by the merchant-oriented Dioula, was the key to differences in performance on the conservation task. They consider their study a challenge to the Piagetian view that faulty performance of a number-conservation task reflects an inferior (pre-concrete-operational) intellectual level. Instead, they prefer the Scribner and Cole (1973) view that intellectual capacities are similar the world over but that these capacities are integrated into different "functional learning systems," revealed by particular skills that make up the specialized adaptations selected by a culture.

Perhaps then, stage "theories" of cognitive development are better thought of as models, rather than as theories. For the most part they describe, rather than explain. It is true that the writings of both Bruner and Piaget contain some concern for the kinds of experiences that influence progression through the stages—for example, Bruner's emphasis on the role of schooling. But it is to concepts of "functional learning systems" and to theories of ecological, cultural, and socialization forces that we must turn for the most promising insights into why different peoples develop different cognitive skills or develop the same skills at different rates.

In the work of several psychologists, notably John Berry, Herman Witkin, and Mary Stewart Van Leeuwen, we found a mutually compatible set of ideas that can go a long way toward solving the puzzles presented by cross-cultural differences in cognitive performance. The essence of this set of ideas is that the modes of knowing toward which development tends in any setting are those produced by the socialization practices that happen to be emphasized in that setting. The socialization emphases in turn are influenced by ecological facts and reflect the social and economic adaptations to those facts. Thus, each individual in any culture is viewed as the heir to a way of conceptualizing his or her world and his or her relation to it. What is thus inherited will tend to conserve the modes of knowing that have, over generations, permitted the society to survive in its particular habitat.

But this model does not predict a static adherence to traditional cognitive styles. On the contrary, the model is inherently dynamic and serves to underscore the fundamental flexibility of the human organism. Implicit in the model is the notion that, as ecological or cultural forces change, so will cognitive processes. Rather than treating cognitive styles as superior or inferior, the model sees any prevalent style as adaptive, or tending toward maximal suitability for the *prevailing* ecological and cultural context. Inevitably, according to this view, as the context changes, so will cognition.

An implication of this line of argument is that any test of ability constructed in one cultural setting will, most probably, elicit relatively "poor" performances in some other culture. In general, we know this to be the case for Western intelligence tests applied to non-core-cultural Americans. But, armed with the emphasis on learning that is at the core of the ecology-cognition model, we need no longer accept the characterization of different performances by such persons as "poor."

We will probably soon come to recognize that the Western world's concept of intelligence is culturally bound, as are the tests that measure it. This recognition will probably induce cross-cultural psychologists to investigate other cultures' definitions of intelligence, as Wober (1974) has done for the Baganda people of Uganda. Within any culture for which the concept of intelligence had been *appropriately* defined, it would then be possible to assess individual differences. Such an assessment will probably illustrate that there is a distribution of abilities that resembles, in shape and spread, the distribution found in our own.

We saw earlier in this chapter that our own definition of intelligence, and the tests that reflect it, relates primarily to academic performance. In other societies, the key concept will be whatever is *valued*, just as academic performance is valued in ours. But whatever kinds of behavior are seen as intelligent, those behaviors are likely to be found in as good supply anywhere as they are in the West.

Furthermore, to the extent that any society resembles ours or is coming to resemble ours through the introduction of a cash economy, formal schooling, and related values such as individual initiative and autonomy, the cognitive processes and skills of individuals will also come to resemble ours. Thus, the numerous puzzling differences in cognitive performance may gradually diminish or disappear if, and as, technology and its trappings spread throughout the world.

What we have seen in this chapter to *be* the case, then, may not *always* be the case. Cross-cultural research on cognition has resulted in a complex picture of different performances by various people in different parts of the world, as the world happens to be constituted *now*.

We can leave this topic of cultural influences on cognition with what I hope is an enlightened perception of human thinking as an active process dynamically influenced by cultural forces. All of us everywhere, cross-cultural research seems to have revealed, adapt to the world around us in ways that our cultural ancestors have found to be functional. Within any cultural setting, some of us may be better equipped than others to apply the skills and strategies bequeathed to us. And across cultures, the preferred skills and strategies will vary. But everywhere, humans have found ways that work. The optimistic prediction that we will continue to find ways, as the old ways may prove less functional, is at least consistent with what we have seen in this chapter.

References

Ainsworth, M. D. S. *Infancy in Uganda*. Baltimore: Johns Hopkins University Press, 1967.

Barry, H., Bacon, M. K., & Child, I. L. A cross-cultural survey of some sex differences in socialization. *Journal of Abnormal and Social Psychology*, 1957, *55*, 327–332.

Barry, H., Child, I. L., & Bacon, M. K. Relation of child training to subsistence economy. *American Anthropologist*, 1959, *61*, 51–63.

Bayley, N. *Manual for the Bayley Scales of Infant Development*. New York: Psychological Corporation, 1969.

Berry, J. W. Temne and Eskimo perceptual skills. *International Journal of Psychology*, 1966, *1*, 207–229.

Berry, J. W. On cross-cultural comparability. *International Journal of Psychology*, 1969, *4*, 119–128.

Berry, J. W. Ecological and cultural factors in spatial perceptual development. *Canadian Journal of Behavioural Science*, 1971, *3*, 324–336.

Berry, J. W. Ecology, cultural adaptation, and psychological differentiation: Traditional patterning and acculturative stress. In R. W. Brislin, S. Bockner, & W. J. Lonner (Eds.), *Cross-Cultural Perspectives on Learning*. Beverly Hills, Calif.: Sage, 1974.

Berry, J. W. *Human Ecology and Cognitive Style: Comparative Studies in Cultural and Psychological Adaptation*. Beverly Hills, Calif.: Sage, 1976.

Berry, J. W., & Annis, R. C. Ecology, culture and psychological differentiation. *International Journal of Psychology*, 1974, *3*, 173–193.

Berry, J. W., & Dasen, P. R. (Eds.). *Culture and Cognition: Readings in Cross-Cultural Psychology*. London: Methuen, 1974.

Bovet, M. C. *Étude interculturelle des processus du raisonnement. Notions de quantités physiques et relations spatio-temporelles chez des enfants et des adultes non-scolarisés*. Doctoral dissertation, University of Geneva, 1971. (See also Chapter 19 in J. W. Berry & P. R. Dasen (Eds.), *Culture and Cognition: Readings in Cross-Cultural Psychology*. London: Methuen, 1974.)

Bruner, J. S., Olver, R. R., & Greenfield, P. M. *Studies in Cognitive Growth*. New York: Wiley, 1966.

Campbell, D. T. The mutual methodological relevance of anthropology and psychology. In F. L. K. Hsu (Ed.), *Psychological Anthropology*. Homewood, Ill.: Dorsey, 1961. Pp. 333–352.

Cole, M., & Gay, J. Culture and memory. *American Anthropologist*, 1972, *74*, 1066–1084.

Cole, M., Gay, J., & Glick, J. Reversal and nonreversal shifts among a West African tribal people. *Journal of Experimental Psychology*, 1968, *76*, 323–324.

Cole, M., Gay, J., Glick, J. A., & Sharp, D. W. *The Cultural Context of Learning and Thinking.* New York: Basic Books, 1971.

Cole, M., & Scribner, S. *Culture and Thought.* New York: Wiley, 1974.

Dasen, P. R. Cross-cultural Piagetian research: A summary. *Journal of Cross-Cultural Psychology*, 1972, *3*, 23–39.

Dasen, P. R. (Ed.). *Piagetian Psychology: Cross-cultural contributions.* New York: Gardner, 1977. (a)

Dasen, P. R. Are cognitive processes universal? A contribution to cross-cultural Piagetian psychology. In N. Warren (Ed.), *Studies in Cross-Cultural Psychology.* London: Academic Press, 1977. Pp. 155–201. (b)

Dawson, J. L. M. *Psychological effects of social change in a West African community.* Unpublished doctoral dissertation, Oxford University, 1963.

Dawson, J. L. M. Cultural and physiological influences upon spatial-perceptual processes in West Africa (Pts. 1 & 2). *International Journal of Psychology*, 1967, *2*, 115–128 and 171–185.

de Lacey, P. R. A cross-cultural study of classificatory ability in Australia. *Journal of Cross-Cultural Psychology*, 1970, *1*, 293–304.

de Lacey, P. R. Classificatory ability and verbal intelligence among high-contact Aboriginal and low socio-economic white Australian children. *Journal of Cross-Cultural Psychology*, 1971, *2*, 393–396.

de Lacey, P. R. A relationship between classificatory ability and verbal intelligence. *International Journal of Psychology*, 1972, *7*, 243–246.

Deregowski, J. B., Ellis, H. D., & Shepherd, J. W. A cross-cultural study of recognition of pictures of faces and cups. *International Journal of Psychology*, 1973, *8*, 269–273.

Dershowitz, Z. Jewish subcultural patterns and psychological differentiation. *International Journal of Psychology*, 1971, *6*, 223–231.

Doob, L. W. Eidetic images among the Ibo. *Ethnology*, 1964, *3*, 357–363.

Evans, J. L. Learning to classify by color and by class: A study of concept discovery within Colombia, South America. *Journal of Social Psychology*, 1975, *97*, 3–14.

Evans, J. L., & Segall, M. H. Learning to classify by color and by function: A study of concept-discovery by Ganda children. *Journal of Social Psychology*, 1969, *77*, 35–53.

Evans-Pritchard, E. E. Introduction. In L. Lévy-Bruhl, *The Soul of the Primitive.* Chicago: Regnery, 1971.

Falade, S. *Le Développement Psychomoteur du Jeune Africain Originaire du Sénégal au Cours de sa Première Année.* Paris: Foulon, 1955.

Flavell, J. H. *The Developmental Psychology of Jean Piaget.* Princeton, N.J.: Van Nostrand, 1963.

Geber, M. Le développement psychomoteur de l'enfant Africain. *Courrier*, 1956, *6*, 17–28.

Geber, M. L'enfant Africain occidentalisé et de niveau social superieur en Uganda. *Courrier*, 1958, *8*, 517–523. (a)

Geber, M. The psycho-motor development of African children in the first year and the influence of maternal behavior. *Journal of Social Psychology*, 1958, *48*, 185–195. (b)

Geber, M. Problèmes posés par le développement du jeune enfant Africain en fonction de son milieu social. *Travail Humain*, 1960, *23*, 97–111.

Geber, M., & Dean, R. F. A. The state of development of newborn African children. *Lancet*, 1957, *272*, 1216–1219.

Geber, M., & Dean, R. F. A. Psychomotor development in African children: The effects of social class and the need for improved tests. *World Health Organization Bulletin*, 1958, *18*, 471–476.

Goodnow, J. J. Comparative studies of cognition: Categorizing and communicating. In W. W. Lambert & R. Weisbrod (Eds.), *Comparative Perspectives on Social Psychology*. Boston: Little, Brown, 1971. Pp. 105–120.

Goodnow, J. J., & Bethon, G. Piaget's tasks: The effects of schooling and intelligence. *Child Development*, 1966, *37*, 573–582.

Greenfield, P. M. On culture and conservation. In J. S. Bruner, R. R. Olver, & P. M. Greenfield (Eds.), *Studies in Cognitive Growth*. New York: Wiley, 1966. Pp. 225–256.

Greenfield, P. M., & Bruner, J. S. Culture and cognitive growth. *International Journal of Psychology*, 1966, *1*, 89–107.

Greenfield, P. M., Reich, L. C., & Olver, R. R. On culture and equivalence II. In J. S. Bruner, R. R. Olver, & P. M. Greenfield (Eds.), *Studies in Cognitive Growth*. New York: Wiley, 1966. Pp. 283–318.

Hoorweg, J. Africa (South of the Sahara). In V. S. Sexton & H. Misiak (Eds.), *Psychology around the World*. Monterey, Calif.: Brooks/Cole, 1976, Pp. 8–28.

Horton, R. African traditional thought and Western science. Part 1: From tradition to science. *Africa*, 1967, *37*, 50–71. (a)

Horton, R. African traditional thought and Western science. Part 2: The "closed" and "open" predicaments. *Africa*, 1967, *37*, 155–187. (b)

Inhelder, B., & Piaget, J. [*The early growth of logic in the child*] (E. A. Lunzer & D. Papert, trans.). New York: Harper & Row, 1964.

Irwin, H. M., Schafer, G. N., & Feiden, C. P. Emic and unfamiliar category sorting of Mano farmers and U.S. undergraduates. *Journal of Cross-Cultural Psychology*, 1974, *5*, 407–423.

Jahoda, G. A cross-cultural perspective in psychology. *The Advancement of Science*, 1970, *27*, 57–70.

Kilbride, J. E. *The African precocity issue: Recent findings from Uganda*. Paper presented at the 1978 annual meeting of the Society for Cross-Cultural Research. (Abstract in *SCCR Newsletter*, 1978, *6*(1), 10.)

Kilbride, J. E., Robbins, M. C., & Kilbride, P. L. The comparative motor development of Baganda, American White, and American Black infants. *American Anthropologist*, 1970, *72*, 1422–1429.

Kilbride, P. L. *Social organization and infant development in two East African societies: The Baganda and Samia*. Paper presented at the 1978 annual meeting of the Society for Cross-Cultural Research. (Abstract in *SCCR Newsletter*, 1978, *6*(1), 13.)

Knobloch, H. Precocity of African children. *Pediatrics*, 1958, *22*, 601–604.

Knobloch, H., & Pasamanick, B. Environmental factors affecting human development before and after birth. *Pediatrics*, 1960, *26*, 210–218.

Lambert, W. W., & Weisbrod, R. (Eds.). *Comparative Perspectives on Social Psychology*. Boston: Little, Brown, 1971.

Langgulung, H., & Torrance, E. P. The development of causal thinking of children in Mexico and the United States. *Journal of Cross-Cultural Psychology*, 1972, *3*, 315–320.

Langgulung, H., & Torrance, E. P. A cross-cultural study of children's conceptions of situational causality in India, Western Samoa, Mexico, and the United States. *Journal of Social Psychology*, 1973, *89*, 175–183.

LeVine, R. A. Cross-cultural study in child psychology. In P. H. Mussen (Ed.), *Carmichael's Manual of Child Psychology* (Vol. 2). New York: Wiley, 1970. Pp. 559–612.

Lévy-Bruhl, L. *Primitive Mentality*. London: Allen & Unwin, 1923.

Lévy-Bruhl, L. [*How Natives Think*] (L. A. Clare, trans.). London: Allen & Unwin, 1926. (Originally published, 1910.)

McLaughlin, S. D. Cognitive processes and school learning: A review of research on cognition in Africa. *African Studies Review*, 1976, *19*, 75–92.

Mundy-Castle, A. C. An experimental study of prediction among Ghanaian children. *Journal of Social Psychology*, 1967, *73*, 161–168.

Munroe, R. L., & Munroe, R. H. *Cross-Cultural Human Development*. Monterey, Calif.: Brooks/Cole, 1975.

Okonji, O. M. The effects of familiarity on classification. *Journal of Cross-Cultural Psychology*, 1971, *2*, 39–49.

Peluffo, N. Culture and cognitive problems. *International Journal of Psychology*, 1967, *2*, 187–198.

Piaget, J. Necessité et signification des récherches comparatives en psychologie génétique. *International Journal of Psychology*, 1966, *1*, 3–13. (Translation by C. Dasen in J. W. Berry & P. R. Dasen (Eds.), *Culture and Cognition: Readings in Cross-Cultural Psychology*. London: Methuen, 1974.)

Pike, K. *Language in relation to a unified theory of the structure of human behavior* (Pt. 1). Glendale, Calif.: Summer Institute of Linguistics, 1954.

Posner, J., & Baroody, A. *The counting hypothesis: A tentative explanation for the number conservation phenomenon in cross-cultural settings*. Paper presented at the 1978 annual meeting of the Society for Cross-Cultural Research. (Abstract in the *SCCR Newsletter*, 1978, *6*(1), 13–14.)

Price-Williams, D. R. A study concerning concepts of conservation of quantities among primitive children. *Acta Psychologia*, 1961, *19*, 669–670.

Price-Williams, D. R. Abstract and concrete modes of classification in a primitive society. *British Journal of Educational Psychology*, 1962, *32*, 50–61.

Price-Williams, D. R. *Explorations in Cross-Cultural Psychology*. San Francisco: Chandler & Sharp, 1975.

Ross, B. M., & Millsom, C. Repeated memory of oral prose in Ghana and New York. *International Journal of Psychology*, 1970, *5*, 173–181.

Scribner, S., & Cole, M. Cognitive consequences of formal and informal education. *Science*, 1973, *182*, 553–559.

Serpell, R. *Culture's Influence on Behaviour*. London: Methuen, 1976.

Snelbecker, G. E., Fullard, W., & Gallagher, J. M. Age related changes in pattern prediction: A cross-cultural comparison. *Journal of Social Psychology*, 1971, *84*, 191–196.

Suchman, R. G. Cultural differences in children's color and form perception. *Journal of Social Psychology*, 1966, *70*, 3–10.

Triandis, H. C. Social psychology and cultural analysis. *Journal of the Theory of Social Behavior*, 1975, *5*, 82–106.

Triandis, H. C., Davis, E. E., & Takezawa, S. I. Some determinants of social distance among American, German, and Japanese students. *Journal of Personality and Social Psychology*, 1965, *2*, 540–551.

Triandis, H. C., Vassiliou, V., & Nassiakou, M. Three cross-cultural studies of subjective culture. *Journal of Personality and Social Psychology Monograph*, 1968, *8*(4), 1–42.

Triandis, H. C., Vassiliou, V., Vassiliou, G., Tanaka, Y., & Shanmugam, A. *The Analysis of Subjective Culture.* New York: Wiley, 1972.

Valentine, C. A. Men of anger and men of shame: Lakolai ethnopsychology and its implications for sociopsychological theory. *Ethnology,* 1963, *2,* 441–477.

Van Leeuwen, M. S. A cross-cultural examination of psychological differentiation in males and females. *International Journal of Psychology,* 1978, *13,* 87–122.

Vernon, P. E. *Intelligence and Cultural Environment.* London: Methuen, 1969.

Walker, C., Torrance, E. P., & Walker, T. S. A cross-cultural study of the perception of situational causality. *Journal of Cross-Cultural Psychology,* 1971, *2,* 401–404.

Warren, N. African infant precocity. *Psychological Bulletin,* 1972, *78,* 353–367.

Warren, N. (Ed.). *Studies in Cross-Cultural Psychology* (Vol. 1). London: Academic Press, 1977.

Were, K. *A survey of the thought processes of New Guinean secondary students.* Unpublished master's thesis, University of Adelaide, 1968. (See also Dasen, 1972.)

Werner, E. E. Infants around the world: Cross-cultural studies of psychomotor development from birth to two years. *Journal of Cross-Cultural Psychology,* 1972, *3,* 111–134.

Werner, H. *Comparative Psychology of Mental Development* (Rev. ed.). Chicago: Follett, 1948.

Werner, H., & Kaplan, B. The developmental approach to cognition: Its relevance to the psychological interpretation of anthropological and ethnolinguistic data. *American Anthropologist,* 1956, *58,* 866–880.

Witkin, H. A. A cognitive style approach to cross-cultural research. *International Journal of Psychology,* 1967, *2,* 233–250.

Witkin, H. A., & Berry, J. W. Psychological differentiation in cross-cultural perspective. *Journal of Cross-Cultural Psychology,* 1975, *6,* 4–87.

Wober, M. Towards an understanding of the Kiganda concept of intelligence. In J. W. Berry & P. R. Dasen (Eds.), *Culture and Cognition: Readings in Cross-Cultural Psychology.* London: Methuen, 1974. Pp. 119–128.

Six

Cultural Differences in Motives, Beliefs, and Values

Introduction

The most obvious differences among peoples of different societies are life-style differences. Travelers to a foreign land are likely on their first stroll down an unfamiliar street to notice new sights, sounds, and smells and to remark on the clothing, the babbling of a foreign tongue, and the aromas of exotic foods.

Soon after, they will become aware that something more profound separates them from their hosts. That something, not easy to put into words, includes a difference in priorities, a departure from the importance that they would attach to events and experiences. Such differences are not directly observable. But they become obvious through numerous behaviors that reflect values, goals, and aspirations that are central to one social group but that may be merely peripheral to another. It is common for visitors to sense that those visited have not only different life-styles but also different attitudes toward life itself.

Sometimes, of course, the visitor exaggerates or otherwise misperceives values inherent in another culture because novel patterns of behavior mask an underlying similarity of values. In like fashion, true value differences may be missed; similar behaviors may be taken as indicative of similar values when, in fact, they express different ones. Both errors are possible because the assessment of values requires inferences from observed behavior, and overt acts can have diverse meanings. Still, the prevailing impression a foreign observer usually forms is that "they" don't believe in ———— the way "we" do, or "they" don't care about ———— to the degree "we" do. And, as we shall see, such impressions are, in some respects, likely to be essentially correct.

It is virtually intrinsic to the concept of culture that different peoples will possess different values, beliefs, and motives. To delineate such differences as they are manifest in behavior is one of the enterprises that engages cross-cultural psychologists. In this chapter we will consider that enterprise in some detail.

The work of cross-cultural psychologists in the domain of values and other shared behavioral dispositions has several objectives. One is simply to discover and describe them. This is a difficult task in its own right, if only because values are never directly observable—they are dispositions inferred from repeated behaviors.

Another objective is to find the ecological and cultural forces with which the values may be correlated. Still another is to make sense out of such links. This effort is usually guided by an assumption that is itself a reflection of a value held high by cross-cultural psychologists. They assume that the behavioral dispositions of the members of any cultural group will be consistent with, reflective of, and supportive of the culture's social economic-political system. A final objective may be an effort to describe the mechanisms that produce these links—usually in the socialization emphases of the society. Such an effort would resemble that of Van Leeuwen, whose theorizing in the context of an analysis of cognitive-style differences across cultures and across the sexes was considered in the last chapter. In the studies that will be reviewed in this chapter, we will see all of these objectives being approached with varying degrees of success.

Why Study Values Cross-Culturally?

As usual when we pose this somewhat rhetorical question, our initial answer is simply "because they are interesting." Like Mount Everest, the values that underlie the behavior of various human groups are *there*, inviting the curious to explore them. A second reason for studying the values of others is to search for universal values, motives that transcend cultural differences in behavior settings. The discovery of such universals would expand our understanding of characteristics shared by all humans and thereby enhance our knowledge of ourselves. A related, albeit opposite, reason is that an examination of the values of others may reveal attractive *alternatives* to our own. It is this reason among the three we have mentioned that may well be the most important. Some of our own prevalent motives may badly need reexamination and refinement, if not abandonment and replacement.

This last point is worth expanding. I will do so in the course of some initial reflections on the value system that characterizes contemporary Western culture.

A Brief Exposé of Western Values

Before considering what cross-cultural psychologists have learned about the values that seem to be inherent in the behaviors of non-Western peoples, it is well to mention some of the more salient aspects of Western values as these have been discerned by a variety of observers, professional psychologists or not. Numerous scholarly analyses of Western values have been made, but none is more thought provoking than that done recently by the eminent American economist Robert Heilbroner (1975). His *An Inquiry Into the Human Prospect* startled a good many readers with its grim predictions and Malthusian warnings.

The Heilbroner Thesis. As Heilbroner sees the prospect facing humankind, there are concrete threats that add up to a great danger: (1) the accelerating population overload, particularly in the poor, so-called less-developed nations; (2) an ominous spread of nuclear weaponry and other forms of potentially coercive power to heretofore exploited nations, a spread that increases the likelihood of both economic blackmail and "wars of redistribution"; and (3) the technologically developed world's continuing, excessive demands on environmental resources. All of these threats, when combined with traditional response dispositions ingrained in Western life-styles (and subject to emulation by non-Western societies striving for "growth" and "development"), make the survival of mankind a dubious proposition. Those response tendencies, if they persist, cannot meet the threats that confront us, Heilbroner says.

The behavioral dispositions, or response tendencies, that give Heilbroner (and his readers) great cause for alarm include some of the most basic, cherished values of Western culture. These are present in both of "the two great socio-economic systems that influence human behavior in our time: capitalism and socialism" (Heilbroner, 1975, p. 63). His characterization of these two fundamentally Western social systems is cogently stated in two stark sentences. "Each has been marked with serious operational difficulties; each has overcome these difficulties with economic growth. Each has succeeded in raising its level of material consumption; each has been unable to produce a climate of social satisfaction" (p. 75).

Common to capitalist and socialist societies is an *industrial civilization*, built on scientific technology and stressing such values as *hard work, efficiency, production, management, the taming and exploitation of the environment*, and *material* (as opposed to spiritual) *achievement*. Although the two systems differ from each other in some values pertaining to the individual and the society, it is this common industrial civilization that Heilbroner labels a "root cause" of the dangers to humanity. Our shared industrial civilization clearly dominates the world as it approaches the 21st century, and it stresses, above all else, growth. It is this dominant orientation of economic growth that must give way, because such strategies are no longer feasible, given dwindling reserves of economic resources. "In place of prodigalities of consumption must now come new frugal attitudes" (p. 94).

Whether or how these values of industrial civilization, epitomized by the growth orientation, will be changed—and mankind thereby deterred from self-destruction—is the subject of much provocative speculation in the latter half of Heilbroner's remarkable book. No attempt will be made here to summarize his wide-ranging speculations, for they must be read in the author's own words to be fully appreciated. But a single aspect of those speculations must be highlighted, for it is so obviously germane to cross-cultural research in values.

To save ourselves, Heilbroner argues, we *must* transform our industrial civilization into a postindustrial society that no longer emphasizes growth. To do so, we may have to turn toward preindustrial societies for guidance. Thus, he suggests:

> Some human societies have existed for millenia, and . . . others can probably exist for future millenia, in a continuous rhythm of birth and coming of age and death, without pressing toward those dangerous ecological limits, or engendering those dangerous social tensions that threaten present-day "advanced" societies. In our discovery of "primitive" cultures, living out their timeless histories, we may have found the single most important object lesson for future man [Heilbroner, 1975, p. 141].

Humans—whom Heilbroner, like Becker (1973),[1] recognizes as the only animals that contemplate their own death—have constructed a variety of life-styles in an attempt to distract themselves from such contemplation. In the Western world their distractions consist of work, achievement, striving after efficiency, and acquisition and consumption of material goods as rewards. As we shall see in detail later in this book, much of the non-Western world is adopting these same distractions. But the whole world had better, in Heilbroner's view, find solace elsewhere, such as in "the exploration of inner states of experience, rather than the outer world of fact and material accomplishment" (p. 140). This means abandoning the work ethic and all the ancillary values that sustain it.

In this brief exposition of the Heilbroner thesis we were confronted by several provocative thoughts that we should keep in sight as we begin our review of cross-cultural research on values. The first is that the core values of Western civilization reflect science, technology, and industry. The second is that these values, however much they have contributed to material well-being, seem not to have produced comparable psychic well-being and, worse, are now propelling us toward our own doom. In terms of Berry's (1976) ecological framework employed in the present text, it is obvious that the changing ecological

---

[1]See the discussion in Chapter One of this book of cultural myths as inventions that permit humankind to cope with the consciousness of its own mortality.

circumstances confronting industrial society have made less functional those cultural and behavioral patterns that must once have been adaptive. It is ecological changes that have produced the need for new coping strategies. Thirdly, and perhaps most important for our present efforts in this chapter, there is something to be learned from a study of the values of existing, nontechnologically oriented societies.

Those values may include the very ones needed to enhance the adaptiveness of our future behavior patterns.

The Plan of This Chapter

Consistent with the objectives mentioned earlier in this Introduction, I will (1) describe variations in values, motives, and other behavioral dispositions that have been recorded systematically by cross-cultural psychologists; (2) relate such variations to ecological and cultural differences or other features of the behavioral settings in which the variations have been noted; and (3) explain the mechanisms by which the behavioral dispositions that seem to "fit" with certain cultural factors come to be learned by the individuals who possess them.

This chapter will try to describe, relate, and explain, in that order, although we will find few facts that go beyond description and few relationships for which a particular explanation *must* be favored. For explanation, we will frequently have to rely on theory. The theories will be, for the most part, familiar. They will be essentially social-learning theories within which socialization is seen as the mediating link between ecocultural forces and individual behavioral dispositions.

The dispositions that we will cover are many and varied. Some will be most readily thought of as beliefs or values, others as motives, still others as personality traits. But they will be alike in that, while none is directly observable, all are "knowable" through inferences from overt behavior. The dispositions to be considered will include conformity, aggressiveness, achievement orientation, morality, and other aspects of "ways to live" that are among humankind's diverse inventions for coping.

Autonomy and Conformity in Different Cultures

Every society, regardless of its size or complexity, instills in its members respect for authority, acceptance of standards, and tendencies to behave in accord with established norms. Every society also permits some deviation from norms and standards, thereby encouraging, within certain limits, individual autonomy. Some degree of tension between the competing values of conformity and autonomy must therefore exist in every society. And it is likely that the equilibrium point of optimal balance between the two tendencies varies across societies and over time within societies.

Within two industrial societies, the United States and Italy, parents were found to have differential preference for training their children to conform or to be independent, depending on their social class (Kohn, 1969). In both societies, upper-middle-class parents stressed independence, whereas working-class parents focused their training on respect for externally imposed rules.

College Students and Conformity. In a large, cross-national study 13 different value-orientations, or individual life-styles, were evaluated by hundreds of college students in the United States, India, Japan, China, and Norway (Morris & Jones, 1955). The authors factor-analyzed the 13 "ways to live" and emerged with a five-factor scale. One of the factors, composed of four of the original 13 life-styles, could be described as a "social restraint and self-control" factor. On it, all five samples scored positively. That is, the average tendency of college students in each of these complex societies was to approve of the ways to live that related positively to this factor and to disapprove of the one way (characterized in part by abandonment and sensuality) that related negatively to the factor. On another factor, called "withdrawal and self-sufficiency," all five samples scored negatively.

In general, students in all samples tended to approve more of life-styles that expressed values consonant with the continuation and smooth functioning of society. They approved less of ways to live that expressed individualistic values. Of course, the materials and procedure employed in this study necessarily resulted in expressions by the respondents of what they believed to be desirable; thus, the results may bear little relationship to the "ways of life" actually pursued. But what is striking about the results of this study is the general tendency of college students in these five large countries to express the desirability of what are, essentially, conformist tendencies.

The two studies just reviewed show simply that adherence to norms is a widespread tendency. We must turn to other kinds of studies to get answers to the more interesting question of the cultural correlates of conformity and autonomy.

Cultural Bases

Basing his predictions on the ecocultural model, Berry (1967) studied conformity in the Asch situation, in which subjects are exposed to false judgments of others in the course of making their own. He found differences between Eskimo and Temne samples. The Eskimos, whose food-getting practices should result in training for independence, were much less conformist on the Asch judgment task than the agricultural Temne, whose subsistence activities demand cooperative activities and whose socialization practices, therefore, should stress conformity.

Working with another African group, the Mashona, which also has a strong conformity emphasis in socialization, Whittaker and Meade (1967) found very high conformity scores, even higher than those typically reported for the United States and other industrial societies.

Studies in different parts of the world on socialization emphases have tended to confirm that compliance training is emphasized in those settings in which cooperative social action is required for subsistence. Pressures toward conformity have consistently been found to be greater in agricultural societies than in hunting and fishing societies, for example.

Thus, Dawson (1972) documented greater emphasis on compliance training among the agricultural Temne than among the hunting Arunta. (He also found a higher incidence of left-handedness among the Arunta, which he interpreted as an index of their higher tolerance of deviance.) The most comprehensive study of cultural differences in child-training emphases yet reported (Barry, Child, & Bacon, 1959) employed data in the Human Relations Area Files on over 100 societies, mostly nonliterate and distributed widely around the world. High-food-accumulating societies were found to exert relatively high pressure toward responsibility and obedience and relatively low pressure toward achievement, self-reliance, and independence training. A very strong correlation between food accumulation and compliance defined in this manner was obtained.

This study by Barry and his associates, it should be stressed, dealt with socialization emphases as the dependent variable, not with the behavior the socialization practices were presumably designed to encourage. But the findings with regard to socialization were so impressive that they clearly inspired later investigators, such as Berry (1967) and Dawson (1972), to extend the empirical investigations to adult behavior. The outcome, as we have seen, was confirmation of the ecological paradigm of the etiology of conformity.

Such studies suggest that, whereas conformity is essential in every society, the degree to which individuals actually conform will vary markedly across societies as a function of adaptiveness. Where the fundamental economic activities require social, as opposed to individual, action, conformity will be emphasized in socialization and displayed in individual behavior. Where individual initiative is required, autonomy will be stressed in socialization and displayed in individual behavior.

It seems very likely that future research on cultural differences in conformity tendencies will yield results consistent with this paradigm.

Cooperativeness and Competitiveness in Different Cultures

Whether one person strives *with* or *against* another in circumstances where limited resources are being sought is probably determined by a complex of factors. Those factors include the nature and degree of scarcity of the resources in question, the kind of affiliation that prevails between one person and the other, and—growing out of these elements, perhaps—the prevailing cultural norms that govern such potentially competitive situations.

When in Doubt, Compete. Much research on cooperation and competition has been conducted in the United States employing one or another variation of the so-called Prisoner's Dilemma game (Luce & Raiffa, 1957). In this game each of two players must choose one of two moves, with the rewards to each player on every trial contingent on the four possible joint choices. If one player chooses the move that offers the maximum possible personal payoff, the payoff will occur only if the other player simultaneously chooses the move with the lesser payoff. If both players simultaneously choose the maximum possible payoff move, they will both, in effect, be penalized by gaining less (or losing more) than they would have if both had chosen the lesser-payoff move (in which case they would each have received a moderate reward).

Obviously, then, in such a game it would be to both players' advantage consistently to make the lesser-payoff move. Any rational player would do so, provided he or she expected the other player to do the same, rather than expecting the other player to take advantage of his or her good will. If players tend to make the lesser-payoff move, it would constitute evidence of mutual trust, mutual expectation of cooperation, and a shared predisposition to cooperate. The general finding in U.S. studies, however, has been that competitive responses (choosing the maximum possible payoff move) predominate.

Gallo and McClintock (1965) reviewed many of these U.S. studies. Their review makes it clear that the typical U.S. player of this game tends to compete. This tendency is found over a wide variety of payoff arrangements. It is found with players of diverse personality profiles (and of both sexes). And it is found over a wide variety of experimental manipulations—for example, even with an experimenter's confederate making a high proportion of cooperative responses. Ways to enhance cooperative playing have been found. For example, having one player (a confederate of the experimenter) cooperate consistently may shame the real player into doing the same. Nevertheless, the prevalent tendency among U.S. players of Prisoner's Dilemma is to attempt to win as much as possible by taking advantage of the other player.

It seems likely, then, that there are widely shared values in our culture that influence behavior in situations that are epitomized by this game. Some of the values, such as being "fair" and kind and reluctant to "take advantage" of another human being, would induce cooperative responding. Other values, such as exerting oneself to the maximum and trying as hard as one can to achieve, would manifest themselves in competitive moves.

When Values Conflict. A study by Oskamp and Perlman (1966) illustrates the possible operation of both of these kinds of conflicting values, interacting in a most intriguing manner. In their study, American male college students played a 30-trial game with cash payoffs. The players were paired on the basis of degree of friendship: pairs were either best friends, acquaintances, nonacquaintances, or mutually disliked persons, as determined earlier by sociometric questioning. The study was done in both a liberal-arts college and a business-training school.

In the former setting, best-friend pairs made an average of 22 cooperative responses; acquaintances, 20; nonacquaintances, 14; and mutually disliked pairs, 11. Clearly, liberal-arts students' cooperativeness was enhanced by the closeness of their relationship. By contrast, best-friend pairs in the business school averaged only 6 cooperative responses, while all other kinds of pairs made about 14! Thus, while friendship encouraged cooperation among the liberal-arts students, it had just the opposite effect among the business-school students.

A reasonable interpretation of these findings is that the values governing behavior toward friends and the values governing individual assertiveness interacted in very different ways in the two settings. In an atmosphere like that of a business school, competitiveness may be so highly valued (and justified as leading to some greater good such as economic progress) that competitive behavior will emerge *especially* when a player is interacting with a person whose approval he or she seeks and respects. A good businessman, like a good poker player, may actually enhance the bond that exists between himself and a good friend by taking advantage of him!

Cultural Roots of Difference

Whether or not that is so, it certainly appears that competitiveness is such a strong value in the United States that it will override other values, at least in some settings. From findings like those of Oskamp and Perlman, it is thus tempting to hypothesize that, in societies in which the socioeconomic system encourages individual initiative, competitiveness will emerge as a dominant life-style.

In any society there are likely to be individual differences, of course. Thus, Albert Pepitone, an American psychologist working with colleagues in France and Italy (Pepitone, Faucheux, Moscovi, Cesa-Bianchi, Magistretti, Iacono, Asprea, & Villone, 1967), found some consistent evidence, at least in the United States and France, that individuals high in self-esteem compete more than persons low in self-esteem in a version of the Prisoner's Dilemma game. (For some unexplained reason, the reverse was true for a sample of Italian university students.) But overriding whatever individual differences might exist within societies, we can probably with good reason expect to find intersocietal differences that correspond to prevailing cultural values that are consistent with the socioeconomic characteristics of the societies.

Picking Up the Marbles. And so we do. Madsen employed a mechanical gadget that is functionally similar to the Prisoner's Dilemma game. Marbles are spilled, rather than won, if the two players pull strings simultaneously. But both players can gain marbles if they take turns pulling. Madsen (1971) found American 8-year-olds from Los Angeles averaging only .3 marbles won on an initial ten-trial exposure to the game. But 8-year-old Mexicans from a small town averaged 6.9 marbles in the same situation. Training in cooperation, which was introduced by the experimenter before a second ten-trial round, led to perfect cooperation among the Mexican children but to about 50% cooperation among the Los Angeles children. With 12-year-old children, cooperation was less in both societies, but the intersocietal difference that had been found for 8-year-olds recurred. Hence, it does appear that different behavioral dispositions regarding competitiveness exist in different societies.

In the Madsen (1971) study, society was confounded with the rural/urban dichotomy. (Recall that the U.S. sample was from a major urban center and the Mexican sample from a small town.) This rural/urban dimension may have been crucial for the behavioral differences noted in the study, for Madsen himself (1967) had found relatively high competitiveness in a sample of urban Mexicans. In other studies that involved rural/urban comparisons (see, for example, Shapira & Madsen, 1969, in Israel; Miller & Thomas, 1972, in Canada) the findings have indicated more competitiveness among urbanites. Since urban settings anywhere are places in which the values of industrial society are likely to prevail, it seems reasonable to attribute the motive power of competitiveness to the values of industrial society.

Munroe and Munroe (1975) have suggested that urban-industrial societies such as the United States, the Soviet Union, Germany, and Japan, all of which are economically forceful and successful, are often stereotyped as—and may actually be—"driven" by individual competitiveness. They note that these four societies even dominate in the Olympic Games, winning gold medals to a degree that is highly disproportionate to their numbers. "East Germany had less than half the population of France (in 1972) but won ten times as many gold medals" (Munroe & Munroe, 1975, p. 137).

So, it does appear that modern, urban, industrial societies—whether capitalist or socialist—encourage more individual competitiveness than do traditional, rural, subsistence-level societies. But within the latter category of societies, if we consider the range of types of subsistence activities (varying along the familiar dimension of degree of food accumulation), what should we expect to find?

Some Sketchy Evidence. Because low-food-accumulating societies (hunting, fishing, or gathering groups that are nomadic rather than sedentary) stress training for achievement, self-reliance, and independence, such societies should value individual competitiveness. But on this point direct evidence is, unfortunately, scarce. The literature does not yet contain studies in which competition versus cooperation has been examined systematically across samples representative of different points along the food-accumulation dimension.

Some indirect evidence that involvement in high-food-accumulation activities leads to lowered individual initiative (a possible correlate of competitiveness) does exist, however. Whiting and Whiting (1971) compared herd-boys of between 5 and 11 years of age in the Kisii district of Kenya (and in some other societies in which herding is an important subsistence activity) with nonherding Gusii schoolboys. They found that the herd-boys (1) were more frequently told what to do by their mothers, (2) were more frequently punished for disobedience, (3) more frequently issued commands and "responsible suggestions" to their peers, and (4) were less often boastful or otherwise likely to call attention to themselves. In short, prosocial behavior was more prevalent among boys assigned the traditional task of caring for the valuable accumulated food that meat on the hoof constitutes in Kisii society than among boys who spent their days in Western-style schools where, according to Whiting and Whiting, "each individual is out for himself and his goal is individual achievement" (1971, p. 36).

It seems to follow that individual self-assertiveness, including overt competitiveness, should be relatively low in high-food-accumulating societies (indeed, lowest in animal-husbandry societies, slightly less low in farming societies, and so on). In the same way, competitiveness should be maximal in urban industrial societies. And it should be *increasing* in nonindustrial societies among those who are departing from the traditional life-styles as a result of exposure to various influences deriving from industrial society, such as formal schooling, urbanization, and participation in a cash economy. Consistent with this argument would be evidence that more Westernized, high-food-accumulating groups (for example, the Kikuyu of Kenya, the Chagga of Tanzania, and the Ibo of Nigeria, to mention only a few oft-cited examples of modernizing groups) display more individual competitiveness than their less Westernized neighbors.[2] But whereas casual observation (and popular stereotypes) suggests this to be the case, there are fewer systematic research findings than we would like in order to be able to assert that the hypothesis has been empirically confirmed.

If we shift our attention slightly from competitiveness per se to individual-achievement orientation, however, we are confronted with a fairly rich picture that is consistent with the speculations with which we have just concluded our consideration of competitiveness.

Achievement Motivation

The class of motives that has been most intensively studied, both within and outside the United States, comprises tendencies toward individual achievement. Before examining some of the findings produced by studies of achievement

[2]Such modernizing societies are, however, less competitive than industrial societies. Munroe and Munroe (1977) found 5- to 10-year-old Kikuyu children in a peri-urban semitraditional community in Kenya to be considerably more cooperative on a Madsen-type task than a comparison group of suburban American children. Munroe and Munroe attributed the Kikuyus' cooperative behavior to the compliance training that is still characteristic of their socialization.

motivation, let us recall that motives of any kind are not accessible to direct observation. Indeed, in a very real sense there is no such thing as a motive, except as a construct used by psychologists to characterize differences in behavior.

When working with nonhumans, for example, a psychologist might observe that some animals will tolerate high levels of electric shock while crossing the grid to reach a sexual partner, whereas others will cross the grid only at lower levels of shock. To summarize this observed behavioral difference, the psychologist might very well speak of differences in level of sexual motivation. The psychologist would be particularly likely to do so if she had differentially deprived her laboratory animals of the opportunity to engage in sexual intercourse and had found that those who tolerated high shock levels to reach a sexual partner were the very animals that had been most deprived.

At the human level there are many other ways to collect behavioral data that might reasonably be employed as bases of inferences about motivation. One obvious way is simply to ask people what they want. One can, for example, offer people choices and determine their preferences. From the choices made, one can then infer differences in needs, wants, and motives. But there are equally obvious problems with such a direct approach. Ever since Freud, psychologists have tended not to trust self-reports on the grounds that individuals may themselves not be aware of their own motives or may be inhibited from revealing them directly.

The Indirect Approach. Not surprisingly, then, psychologists have invented a number of indirect verbal techniques for eliciting behavior from individuals whose motives they want to study. These techniques, known collectively as projective tests, are exemplified by the Thematic Apperception Test, known popularly as the TAT. In this test relatively ambiguous pictures are displayed to respondents, who are instructed to tell aloud the stories that the pictures suggest to them.

Suppose one shows a person a TAT picture that contains a shadowy figure holding aloft a misty object shaped somewhat like a figure eight. Let's say the person tells a story about a young man who practices the violin six hours a day in anticipation of his Carnegie Hall debut before a wildly cheering audience and enthralled music critics. One might then infer that this person attaches high importance to individual achievement, particularly if most other people who are shown the same picture tell stories that lack such individual-achievement themes.

Research on achievement motivation undoubtedly began with the common observation that individuals vary in the degree to which they strive. To summarize such observations and to take into account the fact that these differences in striving levels applied to different circumstances, psychologists postulated (that is, invented) the more general concept of differences in the desire to compete with standards of excellence. Once having postulated such a motive, psychologists had to construct an instrument for assessing it in its general form. The TAT format, using pictures that potentially elicit stories about striving to meet standards of excellence, was a promising candidate.

Before settling on the instrument, however, psychologists had to establish its reliability—that is, the tendency of individuals to respond consistently over separate parts of the instrument and consistently over separate administrations of it. It was also necessary to establish its validity, or the tendency for individuals who score high on the instrument to engage, in real-world settings, in behavior that was indeed achievement oriented.

In the early stages of research on achievement motivation these kinds of steps were taken. The fantasy productions elicited by TAT cards were found to be reliable and correlated with achievement-oriented behavior in the real world (Atkinson, 1958).

Frequent studies, primarily with U.S. males as subjects, have used TAT-elicited stories that are scored according to an achievement-theme manual (McClelland, 1958). These stories have been found to predict performance on a variety of other tasks that can reasonably be taken as indexes of persistence, the willingness to take risks, and the pursuit of difficult-to-attain goals. Accordingly, the employment of fantasy-eliciting instruments like the TAT as a measure of achievement motivation has become standard practice.

What Produces the Need to Achieve? Once armed with an accepted measure of this presumed-to-exist motive to compete with standards of excellence (which we shall henceforth refer to as a "need to achieve," or *n* Ach, as it is popularly known), McClelland and his students and colleagues next postulated and searched for experiential antecedents of different levels of this motive. Still working within U.S. culture, they focused on differences in childhood experience. The findings that emerged from this phase of the research program tended to show that males who scored high on *n* Ach were products of homes in which mothers had been warm and encouraging and fathers nonauthoritarian. Males who scored low had, during childhood, been dominated by respect-demanding, authoritarian fathers (Rosen & D'Andrade, 1959).

Findings pertaining to the psychological antecedents of *n* Ach in U.S. culture soon served as an inducement to expand the research program to other societies. In the first instance the aim was simply to determine whether similar patterns of antecedents could be found in non-American settings. Working in Brazil, Rosen (1962) found that families with highly authoritarian fathers tended to produce sons with relatively low levels of *n* Ach. In Turkey, a society in which the typical father tends to be very authoritarian, even with adult sons, Bradburn (1963) found that individuals who had grown up relatively independent of their fathers scored relatively high on *n* Ach. Rosen's and Bradburn's findings confirmed the existence of similar patterns of antecedents to *n* Ach in at least three different societies.

Bradburn's study addressed itself also to the question of cross-cultural differences in average level of *n* Ach. Given the characteristically high level of authoritarianism among Turkish fathers as compared with American fathers, Bradburn predicted—and found—lower mean scores on *n* Ach for his Turkish sample than for a sample of American graduate students. (The Turkish sample was composed of individuals participating in a management-training program.) Rosen's (1962) Brazilian study also showed lower levels of *n* Ach to be characteristic of that relatively father-dominated society.

Differences like these cross-cultural variations in modal levels of *n* Ach will be a major concern as we continue our examination of achievement motivation. But we will not be primarily interested in modal differences per se. Rather, we will be concerned with a search for both the societal antecedents and the societal consequences of such differences. What ecocultural forces are likely to produce the kinds of socialization practices that instill varying levels of *n* Ach? And what economic consequences may flow from a society's particular level of *n* Ach?

Economic Results of the Need to Achieve

Let us first consider one possible consequence. McClelland (1961) has argued that a society must have a sufficiently high level of *n* Ach before economic development like that characteristic of modern industrial society can take place. His argument has stimulated a remarkably inventive program of research, employing numerous, diverse measures of both *n* Ach and economic development. The result has been considerable support for his contention. Early findings had shown successful entrepreneurs to have been high scorers on *n* Ach measures administered years before their business success was noted (see, for example, McClelland, 1965). McClelland then predicted that any society should experience economic development to the degree that it possesses persons with high *n* Ach.

Folktales as an Indicator. To test this, McClelland first turned to fantasy productions (popular stories) of various societies in order to assess their collective levels of *n* Ach. He could then report "Of the twenty-two cultures whose stories were high in *n* achievement, 74 percent were observed to have at least some men engaged as full-time entrepreneurs, whereas for the twenty-three tribes below average in *n* achievement, only 35 percent contained any full-time entrepreneurs, a difference that could rarely have arisen by chance" (McClelland, 1971, p. 8).* McClelland considered this finding to have at least established the fact that collective fantasies, as in folktales, could be employed as a measure of *n* Ach. The folktale scores related to societal-level entrepreneurial activity just as TAT scores had predicted individual entrepreneurial behavior.

Analysis of the content of textbooks, folktales, and other literary products as an assessment of prevailing motivational structures in various societies has

*This and all other quotations from this source are from *Motivational Trends in Society*, by D. C. McClelland. Copyright 1971 by General Learning Press. Reprinted by permission of Silver Burdett Company.

become a popular and sometimes fruitful enterprise. Child, Storm, and Veroff (1958) related achievement themes in folktales of various societies to socialization practices in those societies. Zimet, Wiberg, and Blom (1971) did a multitheme content analysis of primers employed contemporaneously in 13 (mostly industrialized) nations in an attempt to gain insight into some of the values that are stressed in socialization. They found numerous differences and similarities among these nations' first-grade-textbook themes.

Beshai (1972), working in Egypt, assessed the magnitude of themes relating to n Ach in stories produced during three recent historical periods—the 1920s, the mid-1950s, and the late 1960s. He found a significant increase in n Ach imagery from the earliest to the latest period. He also discovered the overall incidence of n Ach imagery in Egypt to be lower than that reported for the United States and some developing nations, a fact he attributed to the traditional Moslem ethic of egalitarianism and success within the confines of group sanctions. The increase from 1920 to 1970, however, he attributed to the Western-influenced industrial development now under way in Egypt. These and similar studies illustrate the potential usefulness of written materials as a source of inference about shared motives and values relating to achievement.

Berlew (cited in McClelland, 1961, 1971) followed McClelland's lead and analyzed Greek literary documents from three distinct historical periods, one of growth, one of climax, and one of decline economically. Scoring them for achievement themes, without knowing from which period they had originated, Berlew found such themes to have peaked well before the economic growth peaked and to have declined in advance of the economic decline. A similar finding for 15th- through 19th-century England, based on street ballads and other literary products and relating the times at which achievement themes were high to temporal fluctuations in coal imports, was reported by Bradburn and Berlew (1961). These two studies lent support to the proposition that some sufficiently high level of n Ach needs to exist in a society as a *pre*requisite for economic growth.

In what was perhaps the most fanciful set of studies to test this proposition, ceramic designs were used as the source of inferences about n Ach. Inspired by a finding that male U.S. college students with high n Ach doodled in more orderly fashion than those with low n Ach scores (Aronson, 1958), the McClelland team turned to designs on ancient Greek pots. They found that on that basis they could also predict the waxing and waning of Greek economic activity (McClelland, 1971, p. 9). Davies (1969) found the same for the Minoan civilization.

For contemporary nations, McClelland (1961) used children's readers from about 1925 as the source of collective fantasy from which n Ach was assessed. And he used gain in electric-power consumption from about 1925 to 1950 as indicative of economic growth. McClelland found that the former predicted the latter.

However, Finison (1976), who focused on industrialized nations, found no correlation between n Ach in 1950 and growth in electrical production between then and 1971. Finison also reported a negative correlation between n Ach and national-income growth. This failure to replicate McClelland's earlier work casts doubt on his model of development, on its applicability to the time period studied by Finison, or on the measures employed. (As usual, negative results are ambiguous.)

In general, however, McClelland has been able to find historical and contemporary support for his proposition that a shared high level of achievement motivation precedes economic growth. The data, derived from analyses of such diverse collective products as literature and ceramics, at least suggest that the production of achievement themes *does* precede economic growth, in some places at some times.

The next step in the McClelland saga has to do with societal-level antecedents of n Ach.

Sources of Achievement Motivation

Weber's (1904/1930) thesis attributed to Protestantism the sociopsychological impetus for the capitalist spirit that arose in some European countries from the 17th through the 19th centuries. From this thesis McClelland (1971) fashioned a consistent, but more general, argument. He asserted that the key factor in instilling achievement motivation in significant members of a population is the existence of a religious, or ideological, belief. This belief holds, according to McClelland, that one's own group is superior to groups that invest more authority in institutions rather than individuals. Many analyses of groups differing in characteristic levels of n Ach have resulted in findings that are consistent with this argument. Let us examine one of the most thorough of these analyses.

LeVine (1966) collected dream reports from secondary-school boys in Nigeria. The boys were either Hausa (the predominantly Moslem tribe from northern Nigeria), Yoruba (the politically dominant, relatively Westernized tribe from western Nigeria), or Ibo (the economically dominant, also relatively Westernized tribe from eastern Nigeria, the part of the country that temporarily seceded from Nigeria just a few years after LeVine's study to form the short-lived nation of Biafra).

Before considering his results, let us note that LeVine's method for obtaining n Ach scores was to ask individuals for a report of a recent or recurring dream and to score the obtained reports just as if they were stories told after viewing a TAT card. The stimulus employed—the request to tell a story—is far more likely to be culture free than a TAT card, which, however ambiguous, contains some content that is potentially misinterpretable. So LeVine's data-collection method is certainly worthy of note—and of emulation—in future cross-cultural studies of achievement motivation (or other behavioral dispositions, for that matter). And, of course, the fact that a given dream report may be fictional would matter not at all. In any case, a fantasy production would have been elicited, with a minimum of stimulus direction.

With blind scoring of the dream reports, the Ibo sample very decidedly outscored both the Yoruba and the Hausa (especially the latter) on achievement motivation. Ibo performance in this regard fit well their actual achievements as an ethnic group in this large, developing nation. Their reputation as hard working, money-saving individuals, who wandered over all parts of Nigeria, earning the envy and enmity of local people who competed too little or too late for the same jobs, has spread well beyond Nigeria. That Ibo schoolboys should outscore their Hausa and Yoruba peers on *n* Ach corresponds to much of what is known about the three ethnic groups. The really interesting question posed by LeVine's study concerns the reasons, both social and psychological, for the apparent acquisition of different levels of *n* Ach by the three groups of boys.

Analysis of the anthropological and historical facts pertaining to the Hausa, Yoruba, and Ibo societies led LeVine to formulate a "status-mobility" hypothesis. By that term, LeVine was referring to differences among the three societies in their traditional socioeconomic, and related political, practices. At one extreme was the Hausas' centralized and hierarchical system, within which authority trickled down through subservient layers. Power tended to be inherited, although it might shift as the result of warfare. Class status was relatively unchanging, so that a young man not well born might hope to improve his lot only by choosing to serve a powerful leader. At the other extreme, Ibo society was quite decentralized, with a variety of activities leading to wealth and, hence, local power, provided they were well performed and recognized. Such contrasting possibilities for status mobility, LeVine argued, would result in differences in values held by parents. These differences, in turn, would lead to differing child-rearing practices and, finally, to personality differences, probably along several dimensions but certainly including achievement motivation.

LeVine's study stands on its own as a demonstration of how interdisciplinary (psychological/anthropological) research can produce impressive, cohesive findings. It serves also to support McClelland's notion that an individualistic, high-self-esteem ideology can provide the psychological underpinnings for high levels of achievement motivation.

Efforts to Enhance Achievement Motivation

In the preceding sections of this chapter we have considered studies bearing on two of McClelland's ideas about the level of achievement motivation in a society. One of these ideas has to do with the need to have a sufficient number of achievement-oriented individuals if economic development is to occur. The other concerns the need for an individualistic ideology as the stimulus for persons' acquiring achievement motivation. Appropriate ideologies, as we saw in LeVine's Nigerian study, seem to require a whole complex of socioeconomic and political circumstances, exerting their influence through the expression of values that are reflected in historically rooted child-rearing practices. If so, this would mean that nations left to their own devices would experience economic development only to the extent that their traditional values were appropriate to the inducement of achievement motivation in some critical number of individuals who could serve as agents of development.

And what about those nations whose traditional structures—and hence their traditional values—are antithetical to the emergence of *n* Ach? Are they not, according to these arguments and the research findings that are consistent with them, doomed to economic stagnation? McClelland, perhaps reflecting a characteristically American optimism and a faith in the ability of the expert to intervene effectively to influence human events, apparently thinks not. In recent years he has become involved in an effort to assist developing nations that presumably want to experience economic growth by enhancing achievement motivation in some numbers of key individuals.

Evangelism in India. McClelland's own account (1971) of some of these efforts is interesting.

> McClelland reasoned that if ideology was important in raising achievement motivation levels, one could perhaps start up economic development in a society by directly increasing the achievement motivation of a number of its key business leaders. So he arranged to have courses, designed to develop achievement motivation, given to a number of men in two small cities in the south central part of India. Their business activity records before and after the courses were compared to similar records of men who were just like them but who had not been trained in achievement motivation. McClelland and Winter (1969) reported that the trained men were considerably more active: 51% of them had definitely improved their businesses in the two year period after the course, contrasted with only 25% of the untrained men. Furthermore, trained men had invested, on the average, about twice as much money in expanding their businesses and had added twice as many new employees as the untrained men. Two or three years later, there was, however, no evidence that the city as a whole from which the trained men came was markedly more economically advanced than a comparison city. Perhaps the time period was too short for a general economic improvement to be observed or the number of people affected too small. Or perhaps ideological change by itself, without institutional or structural change, is insufficient [pp. 16–17].

This account reveals some success in enhancing the entrepreneurial efforts of persons already oriented toward such activities. But it reveals little else. Moreover, a question must be raised concerning the validity of that small "success." Did the enhanced activity of the trainees stem from the content of the training they received (instruction and encouragement in the production of achievement-oriented fantasies) or merely from the fact that they had been singled out for attention? Ever since the classic industrial-psychology studies conducted in the Hawthorne, Illinois, plant of the Western Electric Company— which showed enhanced production among workers selected for various programs, *regardless* of the content of the programs—psychologists have had to be wary of what has come to be known as the Hawthorne effect. One must suspect such a phenomenon among the Indian trainees. Whatever else may have occurred, the program constituted a marked break in their routine, mundane activities that may have been—in and of itself—a stimulus to increased entrepreneurial activity.

An even more serious criticism of McClelland's flirtation with achievement-motivation evangelism has to do with the ethics of the enterprise. In this regard one is prompted to ask "What if his efforts succeed?" The program is obviously designed to accelerate economic growth in societies that have long survived without it. Would growth be good for these societies? Would their growth, and all that such growth entails, be good for the world generally? Undoubtedly there are many people (perhaps McClelland and the sponsors of his applied research among them) who would unhesitatingly answer these questions affirmatively. But in the light of recent analyses of the costs and dangers of "growth," as in the Heilbroner (1975) thesis summarized earlier in this chapter, the better answer might be "maybe not."

Possible Negative Consequences. McClelland is not insensitive to the possibly negative consequences of economic development. In his own recent summary of research on achievement motivation (McClelland, 1971) he cited Southwood's (1969) cross-national analysis. That study found that economic development (and achievement motivation) was correlated with various indexes of domestic disorder and authoritarian, undemocratic politics, at least among poorer nations with relatively low proportions of school-aged individuals actually in school. Hence, McClelland expressed wariness about circumstances in which numbers of achievement-motivated individuals are confronted with a "low opportunity structure," circumstances that are likely to produce domestic turmoil. But his solution would *not* be to rest content with a low societal level of n Ach. He would attempt simultaneously to enhance it and to provide greater opportunity through increased openings in education and employment. "The moral is not that achievement motivation should remain low, if one wants to avoid violence. Rather, high *n* Achievement and greater opportunity to achieve must go together" (McClelland, 1971, p. 13).

This prescription surely has a positive ring to it, at least to readers reared in industrial societies and to those others who have adopted that ethos. It is a good generalization of the American Dream and of the dreams of many others to acquire the material comforts that an environment that richly rewards hard work can provide. It is the kind of principle that inspires and justifies technical-assistance programs mounted by wealthy industrial nations to spur the economic growth of poorer nations (whatever self-interests might also underlie such programs). It is also a philosophy that leads to a disparagement of whole groups of people (for example, the pastoral Masai of Kenya) within nations whose official policy is oriented toward growth and development on the model of the industrial societies. What of those whose traditional way of life stresses coexistence with nature, rather than its exploitation? Ironically, their way of life may be, as Heilbroner suggests, the one that holds promise for the future existence of the human species.

So, the exportation of ideologies that seem to underlie high levels of achievement motivation and the consequent economic growth may not, after all, be such a good thing. Nevertheless, the findings of the research that McClelland's ideas has spawned are very valuable for the understanding they provide of both the antecedents and consequences of achievement motivation. Confronted with the issue of whether it is good to encourage economic growth, it is certainly well to know what produces it and the social and psychological conditions that must prevail before it can come about. That knowledge could be applied to enhance *n* Ach, to discourage it, or to leave it alone to respond to prevailing sociocultural forces.

What we have learned from our review of cross-cultural research on achievement motivation is that modal levels of *n* Ach vary considerably and relate in systematic ways to variations in values and in child-rearing practices that reflect those values. As we confront a difficult time of choice in human history, the existence of such differences is probably a good thing. Just who will choose to learn from—and emulate—whom, and with what consequences to all, remains to be seen. But at least we can still go either way.

Values, Attitudes, and Behavior Relating to the Sexes

Nearly all of the research on achievement motivation, both in the United States and in other societies, has been done with males. What little has been done with females yielded either inconsistent findings or some provocative facts about females' achievement motivation that makes them appear strikingly different from males in that regard. And the psychological literature contains much about additional differences in motivational patterns, life-styles, and other behavioral dispositions. In this section we will inquire into those sex differences and consider possible explanations, rooted in cultural forces, for them.

Differences in Attitudes toward Success

Not much had been learned about women's achievement motivation until Horner undertook a research program with U.S. university students in the late 1960s. The outcome was striking. Horner interpreted her findings to mean that these women—of above-average intelligence and education, reared and living in one of the most achievement-oriented societies in the world—were typically burdened by strong fears of success.

Horner (1969) administered a standard stimulus, analogous to a TAT picture but in the form of a sentence to be taken as the beginning of a story, to be completed by 90 women as each saw fit. The stimulus sentence read "After

first-term finals, Anne found herself at the top of her medical school class."
Stories were scored[3] as expressing a success/fear disposition if they contained
any references to negative consequences of doing well. Of the 90 stories obtained
from the women, 59 contained such references. For example, the completion of
one such story was as follows: "Anne starts proclaiming her surprise and joy. Her
fellow classmates are so disgusted with her behavior that they jump on her in a
body and beat her. She is maimed for life."

The fears expressed in the 59 stories were varied in content. They included
expectations of social rejection: "She will be a proud and successful, but alas a
very lonely doctor." They also included doubts about femininity: "Anne no
longer feels so certain that she wants to be a doctor. She is worried about herself
and wonders if perhaps she isn't normal." Some of the stories revealed what
appears to be an attempt at denying the very possibility of success: "It was luck
that Anne came out on top because she didn't want to go to medical school
anyway" (Horner, 1969, pp. 36, 38). Such responses are certainly consistent with
Horner's interpretation that women in her study were very much plagued by a
fear of success.

Her findings are all the more striking when contrasted with the behavior of
a control group of 88 male university students who responded to an identical
sentence stimulus—except that the subject was "John." Among these 88 stories,
only eight could be scored as containing fear-of-success themes.

There is, however, some ambiguity in Horner's findings. It is not clear
whether the women were expressing (by negative-consequence stories) an
internalized fear of success or merely a cultural stereotype that surrounds
feminine achievement. In other words, were Horner's female subjects projecting
their own motives on Anne or reacting to Anne in the way their culture had
taught them to respond to a woman occupying a heretofore male-dominated
role? These are, of course, closely related phenomena, but it is worth the effort
to distinguish them, if possible.

Cultural Stereotype at Work. A study by Monahan, Kuhn, and Shaver (1974)
made such an effort. They modified Horner's research design by assigning the
"Anne" story to both male and female respondents. Similarly, they gave the
"John" story to two additional groups of respondents, one male and the other
female. Monahan and colleagues reasoned that, if negative-consequence responses occurred only—or predominantly—among female respondents and
to either the John or Anne cue sentence, this would be strong evidence for an
internalized motive among females. But if only the Anne cue sentence elicited
negative-consequence responses from both males and females, this would be
evidence that the stereotypes surrounding women's achievements are negative
and are learned and accepted by both sexes.

---

[3]As is true for the scoring of achievement-motivation themes in TAT stories, fear of success was scored according to rules explicated in a scoring manual (Horner, Tresman, Berans, &
Watson, 1973).

The researchers also used younger subjects than Horner had studied. They employed 120 sixth- through eleventh-grade students in a middle-class urban school, of whom 52 were boys and 68 girls.

The Monahan team's first finding was a replication of Horner's. They found that a majority of the female respondents confronted by the *Anne* cue told stories with negative content, but only 21% of the male respondents who were given the *John* cue did so. Their most important finding, however, was that for *both sexes* of respondents, the *Anne* cue elicited a higher proportion of negative stories. Coupling that finding with the fact that boys responded to the *Anne* cue even more negatively than the girls did, the authors properly concluded that the sex of the actor in the cue was a more critical variable than the sex of the respondent. The cultural-stereotype hypothesis had to be favored as an interpretation of the reaction-to-success phenomenon.

These two studies (Horner, 1969; Monahan et al., 1974) showed that U.S. values toward success are contaminated by attitudes toward the sexes. Whereas success for males is generally viewed as a positive goal, success for females is not an unqualified good. Female success in a traditionally male role is viewed negatively, by males and females alike. It would be worth determining in future research whether people who have adopted a less sex-linked sense of role demands (who do not perceive one sex or another as more qualified for a particular occupation) would depart from the tendency displayed by the subjects in these two studies.

Competing Values in Kenya. Another study comes from Kenya, which by the 1970s had clearly chosen a path of development of its modern sector in the manner of the Western, free-enterprise model. In addition, a small but visible group of career women had begun to emerge. The study includes observations about negative reactions to success by females that may be manifestations of role conflict to which successful, "modern" Kenyan women are subjected. Beatrice Whiting (1973) observed that Kenyan career women, who are encouraged and expected to be independent and competent in their work roles outside the home, behave very submissively in their relations to their husbands. Whiting also noted that Kenyan men, with considerable regularity, express outspoken criticisms of successful women. In the Kenyan case the ambivalence surrounding success for women probably reflects conflicting values—one set traditional, the other modern—that apply to the female role.

Evidence that these competing values impinge on Kenyan women has been obtained by Fleming (1975). She had 123 University of Nairobi students (44 females and 79 males) and 143 secondary-school students (87 females and 56 males) write stories to Horner's cue sentence concerning success in medical school. The sex of the actor and the sex of the respondent were the same. Although the frequency with which both sexes cited negative consequences for success was lower than in the U.S. studies, it was substantially higher for females than for males, especially among the secondary-school students. In the university-student sample, 36% of the stories about females contained negative imagery, whereas 20% of the male stories did. In the secondary-school sample, 41% of the female stories did, but only 9% of the male stories. Fleming also administered a female-success cue to 51 male university students; of these, 31% produced negative stories. This latter finding was similar to that of Monahan and associates (1974), which had shown that both males and females in the United States react negatively to success by a female.

Ambivalence and conflict, such as we have seen in the U.S. and Kenyan studies, are likely consequences of the coexistence of competing values and of differing definitions of success. The competing values in both these cases are probably a positive evaluation of individual success for people in general and a negative evaluation of female self-assertiveness in situations where it is traditionally unrewarded or punished. To varying degrees in both of these societies, the traditional role definition for females includes submissiveness, subservience, and deference toward males. In that setting a "successful" female would be one who strove, effectively, to meet that role expectation.

A Striking Cultural Difference. That the critical values are cultural (or at least not universal) is most directly demonstrated by studies that assess individual attitudes toward certain values held by both males and females in different cultures. One such study was conducted in the United States and Mexico. Peck (1967) presented male and female students at the University of Mexico and the University of Texas with a list of 15 value terms—for example, love, career success, freedom, and wealth. These terms were to be rank-ordered according to the importance the students would personally attach to them.

For the most part, Peck found the two sexes in each culture agreeing with each other in the rankings assigned to particular terms. For *career success*, however, a striking departure from this general finding occurred. Among the Mexican respondents, career success was ranked first by males and second by females. Among Texas respondents, it was ranked fourth by males but 12th by females! Thus, although Peck's findings showed that both sexes within a given culture acquire similar value orientations—presumably because they are exposed to similar teachings about values—the concept of career success is an exception in at least one culture (the United States) but not in all.

Success for women in the United States and in other societies as well is, as we have now seen in several studies, obviously a mixed blessing. It is not valued in the same way that success for males is valued. Conflict surrounds it[4] and the stereotype of the successful female is hardly flattering. Stereotypes often function as self-fulfilling prophecies. So we should not be surprised to discover that, in cultures where this negative stereotype exists, females react quite

---

[4]In American culture, at least, where competent females are both encouraged to achieve *and* instilled with negative expectations relating to success, conflict seems a likely consequence of these competing pressures. Horner (1972) has discussed some apparent indexes of achievement-related conflicts of American women. These findings include the tendency for those professional women who score high on Horner's measure to choose less attractive and less challenging specialties.

differently from males to situations in which they can accept or reject an opportunity to succeed.

Slovic (1966) found this to be the case for children ranging in age from 6 to 16 years with a game that he had set up at a county fair in the United States. Slovic's game involved a free vending machine with ten switches. Players were told that pushing any but one of the switches, one at a time, would result in their winning candy. But if the one "Disaster" switch were pushed, the game would be terminated and all winnings forfeited. From the player's vantage point then, the game offered an opportunity to be successful, but it also presented an element of risk.

In several respects, female performance showed less risk taking than male performance. Firstly, whereas 735 boys volunteered to play the game, only 312 girls dared to enter Slovic's tent. This particular sex difference increased with age. Secondly, far more boys than girls played the game to its theoretical limit of nine trials. This sex difference also increased with age. In fact, the difference in style of play did not exist at all for children between 6 and 8 years, but it increased in magnitude until it reached statistical significance at about age 11. Somehow, it seems, American girls acquire different dispositions toward risk taking than do American boys. This acquisition requires some years of rearing in a culture that possesses a negative stereotype about female achievement and that apparently treats the two sexes differently during the child-training years.

Other Sex Differences and a Reason for Them

If you reviewed the very rich anthropological literature on sex differences around the world, you might conclude, as did Munroe and Munroe (1975, p. 116), that (1) there are modal sex differences in behavior in every society and (2) every society has some division of labor by sex. These two phenomena, besides being universal, are also probably interrelated in a functional way. But before we consider that interrelationship, we will briefly review some of what is known about behavioral differences between the sexes.

In an earlier chapter of this book we learned that Barry, Bacon, and Child (1957) had found rather consistent differences in the way many societies discriminate between the sexes in childhood-socialization emphases. A later publication by the same team of cross-cultural psychologists (Barry, Bacon, & Child, 1967) was based on ratings of reports in the Human Relations Area Files for 45 societies. The team reported sex differences in every society in nurturance, responsibility, and obedience (with females displaying more of those classes of behavior) and in self-reliance, achievement, and independence (with males displaying more of those).

The correspondence between sex differences in socialization emphases and sex differences in behavior is virtually perfect. That the two sexes behave in ways they are taught to behave is, of course, not surprising, but it still raises interesting questions. For example, have all these societies observed different inborn behavioral tendencies in males and females and shaped their socialization practices to reinforce such biologically determined tendencies? Or are societies' socialization practices merely influenced by certain anatomical differences between males and females, with those practices responsible for behavioral differences? We will return to these questions after considering a few more behavioral differences between the sexes.

Generally speaking, and with few exceptions anywhere in the world, males are more likely than females to initiate sexual activity. Males are more likely to be physically aggressive. Males are more likely to express dominance over females, rather than vice versa; females are more likely to conform, defer, comply, and otherwise submit to an authority figure of either sex, but especially to a male. And, as we saw in the previous chapter, females tend to differ from males in cognitive styles, being more field dependent (or less "psychologically differentiated") than males.

These generalizations derive from many publications, too numerous to be cited here. The Six Cultures Study, supervised by John and Beatrice Whiting and carried out by several anthropology/psychology teams, has resulted in numerous reports. These reports should be consulted for, among other things, recently acquired facts about sex differences in different societies (B. B. Whiting, 1963; Whiting & Whiting, 1975; Whiting & Edwards, 1973).

The last-cited publication is a particularly rich source. It reports observations of children of both sexes in two age groups (3 to 6 years and 7 to 11 years) in Okinawa, India, the Philippines, Mexico, Kenya, and New England. Among the behavior classes for which boys generally outscored girls in these six diverse societies were (1) expressing dominance, (2) responding aggressively to aggressive instigations, and (3) manifesting aggression both physically and verbally. Girls outscored boys on two subclasses of dependency, "seeking help" and "seeking or offering physical contact," but not on a third sub-class, "seeking attention," which was found to be mostly a male form of dependency. A female superiority in nurturance was found, but only among the 7- to 11-year-olds. This same study also showed that the tasks assigned to girls provided the best predictor of the degree to which girls actually displayed "feminine" behavior more than boys. For example, in the Kenyan society—where some child-care and other domestic tasks are assigned to boys—and in the New England town— where tasks assigned to girls are not exclusively stereotypically feminine ones—sex differences in behavior were smaller or less frequent than in the other societies (Whiting & Edwards, 1973).

Risking oversimplification, we can summarize the picture of sex differences in behavior that is presented by anthropology and cross-cultural psychology as showing males to be more self-assertive, achieving, and dominant and females to be more socially responsive, passive, and submissive. How best might this be explained?

Economic and Biological Roots. One key to the explanation is the fact that the behavioral differences just summarized, although nearly universal and almost never reversed, range in magnitude from quite large down to virtually nil. A satisfactory explanation, then, will account both for the universality of direction of difference and the variation in magnitude of the difference.

Such an explanation takes into account economic facts—including division of labor by sex—and socialization practices. Key contributors to this explanation have been Barry, Bacon, and Child (1957), Barry, Child, and Bacon (1959), and Van Leeuwen (1978). Their arguments were reviewed in the preceding chapter in the context of a discussion of sex differences in field independence/dependence, but they can now be amplified and generalized.

The argument begins with an early anthropological finding (Murdock, 1937) that a division of labor by sex is universal (or nearly so) and quite consistent in content. For example, food preparation is done predominantly by females in nearly all societies. Child rearing is usually the responsibility of females. Sometimes it is shared, but in no society is it the modal practice for males to assume the responsibility themselves. Although there are many cross-cultural variations in the content of sexual division of labor, there are, once again, hardly ever significant reversals.

Barry, Bacon, and Child (1957) suggested that this consistent pattern of sex-role differentiation during adulthood represents a set of solutions that societies have invented to deal with what were, for subsistence-level societies, practical problems. These problems are viewed as arising from biologically based *physical* differences (and not behavioral ones) between the sexes, especially the female's lesser overall physical strength and—most of all—her child-bearing function. Different economic roles for males and females, with the latter consigned mostly to close-to-home activities, would have been a functional response.

The next step in the argument is to suggest that differential socialization of the two sexes evolved as a means for preparing children to assume their sex-linked adult roles. Then, the behavioral differences between the sexes could best be viewed as a product of different socialization emphases, with those in turn reflective of, and appropriate training for, different adult activities.

Consistent with this argument is Barry, Child, and Bacon's (1959) finding that large differentiation between the sexes in socialization tends to occur more often in societies with "an economy that places a high premium on superior strength, and superior development of motor skills requiring strength" (p. 330). Also consistent with the argument is that—if sexual differentiation occurs during socialization—girls nearly always receive more training in nurturance, obedience, and responsibility than boys and less in assertiveness, achievement, and independence.

Van Leeuwen's (1978) ecological model, with which we are already familiar, expands the argument so that it can accommodate numerous details about the subsistence mode and variations in degree of sex differences in behavior. Thus, in sedentary, high-food-accumulating societies not only will females be subjected to more training to be nurturant and compliant, but the degree of the difference between the sexes' training will also be very high. In low-food-accumulating societies, such as hunting societies, there will be less division of labor by sex and little need for either sex to be trained to be compliant. Often in such societies, women's contributions to the basic subsistence activity are integral to it. Hence, women's work is valued by the men, who are then not inclined to denigrate women or to insist on subservience from them.

What we have seen in this section is that females do indeed have some behavioral dispositions that are different from those of males. Thanks primarily to cross-cultural research, it is clear that these sex differences are the product of cultural forces, operating through socialization practices and reflective of ecological factors. Both the consistencies in the cross-cultural data and the variations from society to society help us to understand how cultural values have been defined differently for the two sexes and how individuals come to behave in accord with them.[5]

Societal Differences in Attitude toward Sexual Equality

It is probably no accident that active movements for equality of the sexes have taken root and flourished effectively in industrial nations, especially in the United States and Western Europe, and have gone almost unnoticed or have been vociferously scorned in most nonindustrialized societies. In industrialized nations division of labor by sex is not nearly so functional as it is in predominantly subsistence-level societies. Modern technology has produced numerous labor-saving devices, which make possible unprecedented leisure time and make differences in physical strength between the sexes virtually irrelevant. Males who tend to be principally employed outside the home in fact have many hours available each day to spend at home. Hence, they are at least available to perform domestic tasks, including child rearing. Similarly, women in modern societies are no longer so tied to such tasks. Furthermore, family-planning technology, very pervasively employed in industrial societies but not yet very widely accepted elsewhere, has drastically reduced the time and attention that must be devoted to infant care, traditionally the most time-consuming and restricting activity of female adults.

Hence, it is no surprise in industrial societies that sexual differentiation during childhood socialization is minimal (Barry, Bacon, & Child, 1957) or that sex differences in behavior among children are minimal (Whiting & Edwards, 1973). A visitor from Mars dropping into most nonindustrialized nations would have little difficulty detecting the existence of two sexes (how could she fail to note differences in hairstyles, dress, and so on?). But if the visitor arrived in an

---

[5]With regard to contemporary changes in sex roles, Segall (1976) has commented: "In modern technologically sophisticated societies, where labor roles need no longer be differentiated on the basis of sex, sexual differentiation in socialization has become anachronistic. . . . The trend should be toward . . . decreasing differences in behavior between the sexes. What differences remain we ought view as products of differential socialization that [have] historicultural roots but that are less functional than they may once have been" (pp. 176–177).

American university classroom, utter confusion might result. If warned in advance to look for men and women, the visitor might expect the men to be the short-haired ones wearing blue jeans and using four letter Anglo-Saxon expletives. These and other once-reliable sex-distinguishing characteristics would mislead our visitor as often as they would help. Clearly, a degree of cultural homogenization has emerged, albeit with constraints and countertendencies.

In these same societies where a blurring of sex differences in child rearing and in behavior has begun, inequality of economic opportunity remains as an anachronism. Not surprisingly, these societies have seen the emergence of feminist movements as an inevitable response to that inconsistency. No such inconsistency characterizes mostly subsistence-level societies. Where tradition prevails, adult roles remain sex linked, and socialization practices include clear and effective efforts to produce behavioral differences between the sexes that are for the most part accepted as normal, natural, and appropriate.

Of particular interest in this regard are those nonindustrial societies in which certain cultural facts seem to contribute to an unwanted blurring of sexual distinctions. For example, there are societies whose practices result in both boys' and girls' being reared and influenced by female caretakers. Such practices include polygyny, exclusive mother/child sleeping arrangements, and matrilocal residence patterns, all of which enhance father absence and reduce male salience. If these societies also accord social dominance to adult males —as is clearly the case in high-food-accumulating, subsistence-level societies— they also are most likely to have severe male initiation ceremonies during adolescence, including circumcision (Burton & Whiting, 1961; Harrington, 1968; Whiting, 1962).

A persuasive interpretation of the cross-cultural correlation between low male salience during infancy and male initiation ceremonies during later childhood is that the ceremonies represent an institutional response designed to overcome cross-sex identification tendencies in young males. (See Munroe & Munroe, 1975, for a thorough and up-to-date review of studies bearing on cross-sex identification and other societal responses to it. These responses include the couvade [male pseudopregnancy] and other institutions that permit males to display "feminine" behaviors in societies that do not structurally emphasize maleness.)

Societies thus differ in the value attached to the maintenance of differences between the sexes. Some sex distinction is universal, but the content and degree of the distinction vary across cultures. In some societies the distinction is actively being blurred. In others it is simply being maintained. In still others it is under strain, with the pressures acting to diminish it being counteracted by institutional practices designed to reinforce it. How and to what degree societies tolerate or struggle against a blurring of sex distinctions is largely a reflection of the functionality of adult division of labor by sex. Where the economic system functions more smoothly with such a division of labor, acceptance of sexual equality is minimal. Where a sexual division of labor is largely irrelevant to the functioning of the economic system, approval of equality is likely to be high or, at least, increasing.

We have now completed our discussion of cultural differences in values, attitudes, and behavior relating to the sexes. We will turn to some other topics that have also received attention from cross-cultural psychologists interested in cultural differences in behavioral dispositions. For some of them, sex differences will once again crop up. This will be the case, for example, with regard to aggression, the behavioral disposition to be discussed next.

Aggression in Different Cultures

One of the findings on sex differences in behavior already mentioned in this chapter was that, on the average, boys quite consistently manifest more aggression than girls. This sex difference is a cultural universal (or rather, it probably is; although we have no cases to the contrary, obviously not all possible cases have been studied). What about aggression per se? Ignoring sex differences, do we find aggression everywhere and in roughly the same magnitude? Or do cultures vary in the expression of aggression? And, if they vary, is the variation systematically related to certain aspects of culture, such that the relationship will reveal how aggression itself is both caused and controlled?

To determine how much we know about the answers to such questions, we must first review some insights derived from psychological research and theorizing in Euro-American settings. Then we will examine some cross-cultural research.

To begin, let us make clear what is meant here by *aggression*. Following Dollard, Doob, Miller, Mowrer, and Sears (1939), who worked together at the Interdisciplinary Institute of Human Relations at Yale University, we will take aggression to mean "a sequence of behavior, the goal response of which is the injury to the person toward whom it is directed" (p. 9). Implicit in this definition is that the "harm" may be physical or psychological and that the "response" is an overt manifestation of an inferred behavioral disposition, an intention to harm.[6]

For convenience of exposition, I will largely eliminate from consideration here intergroup hostility, or aggression directed to out-groups (as in discrimination against minorities or warfare). This topic will be treated in Chapter Eight, because it requires its own, rather lengthy, exposition.

---

[6]Aronson (1972, p. 144) distinguishes between *intentional* aggression, where infliction of harm is intended, and *instrumental* aggression, where the pursuit of some other goal involves the actor in hurting someone in order to achieve it. Segall (1976, p. 204) treats instrumental aggression as a developmental step on the way toward learning intentional aggression. In any case, it is intentional aggression with which we are concerned here.

Instinct or Product of Learning? The many theories that offer to explain the pervasiveness of aggression fall into two major categories. In one, aggression is viewed as an instinctive, wired-in, primal feature of human nature (see, for example, Lorenz, 1963; Ardrey, 1966; Morris, 1967; Storr, 1968). In the other, aggression is seen as an outcome of learning, primarily through socialization (see, for example, Freud in many, but not all, of his discussions of the issue; Dollard et al., 1939; Berkowitz, 1958; Bandura & Walters, 1963). The weight of the evidence is very clearly in support of the social-learning position. This position and the evidence that supports it have been presented in detail by Segall (1976). His argument derives mostly from ideas originally put forth by Freud, by Dollard and colleagues, and by Berkowitz. It asserts that (1) aggression is both a product of socialization and is controlled by socialization, (2) aggression is one of several possible learned responses to frustration, and (3) the learning of aggressive dispositions is accomplished both by intermittent reinforcement contingent on the aggressive responding of the learner and by observation and imitation of the aggressions of others (Segall, 1976, pp. 199–213).

The relevance of cross-cultural research to these two competing classes of theories of aggression is obvious. Instinct theories would find support in data that tended to show aggression to be manifest to roughly the same extent the world over, regardless of ecocultural variations. Social-learning theories would find support in data that tended to show systematic variations in aggression, correlated with specifiable ecocultural characteristics. (Of course, as is always the case with nature-versus-nurture arguments, a definitive resolution is not possible. But we should expect that cross-cultural evidence will be adduced to support one position more than the other.)

Also supportive of the social-learning approach to understanding aggression would be evidence of cross-cultural variation in parental responses to infants when they display—as do all infants—what has been termed *proto-aggressive* behavior (Segall, 1976, p. 201). Such behavior includes the intense, diffuse thrashings about, crying, and struggling that are characteristic of the relatively helpless infant's mode of signaling needs. When those needs (for water, food, release from pain, and so on) are tended to, the infantile behavior that induced the parental caretaking is also rewarded and thereby strengthened. If the characteristic modes of infant caretaking varied among societies—so that infants in some received more reinforcement for their proto-aggressive behavior—and if such variation were accompanied by a correlated variation in strength of aggressive behavior in children, one feature of social-learning theory would be supported.

Similarly, certain variations in the training of older children would interest social-learning theorists. Suppose, for example, that cultures differed in characteristic degrees of parental consistency in socialization and that this were correlated with variations in aggression. Social-learning theorists would probably consider such a correlation in accord with that part of the theory that views an inconsistent reinforcement schedule as frustrating and potentially aggression inducing.

Perhaps even more to the point would be cultural variations in the use of punishment as a socialization tool. Social-learning theory and research indicate that punishment, while effective in suppressing those particular responses that are punished, inadvertently sets the stage for subsequent aggression. Sometimes this aggression is against the punishers themselves, but more often it is against surrogate authority figures or relatively weak scapegoats. If cultural variations in punishment were related to cultural variations in overt aggression of one kind or another, social-learning theorists would certainly find support in this. And, because of the well-established empirical link between frustration and aggression (Caplan & Paige, 1968; Dollard et al., 1939; Miller, 1941; Miller & Bugelski, 1948), cultures' differences in aggression related to their characteristic levels of inequality of opportunity would also reveal a social-learning mechanism working at the societal level. For these and other reasons, cultural variations in aggressive behavior and in various presumed controlling variables, especially features of socialization practices, should have been the object of much cross-cultural searching.

But there have not been many systematic studies of aggression performed cross-culturally. Most research on this behavioral disposition has been conducted in U.S. laboratories and, more recently, in field studies conducted in the United States. (See Chaffee & McLeod, 1971; Lefkowitz, Eron, Walder, & Husemann, 1977; and Milgram & Shotland, 1973. All three of these are field studies of the impact of televised violence on aggressive behavior of viewers.)

The anthropological literature on aggression has from time to time contained reports of the discovery of an isolated society that appears, to the anthropologist, to be free of aggressive tendencies. But such reports are relatively unsubstantiated and should best be viewed with skepticism. Moreover, should a truly nonaggressive people exist, their existence would clearly be exceptional and would require careful study of their particular conditions of ecology and culture for a possible explanation of this departure from the general existence of aggression around the world. Such careful studies have not been done.

Research in Six Cultures. A beginning has been made in the interdisciplinary Six Cultures Study, portions of which have been devoted to observations of socialization of aggression and of manifest aggression in children. Lambert (1971), for example, has reported differences across the six communities (U.S., Kenyan, Indian, Mexican, Okinawan, and Philippine) in degree of parental punishment for aggression by children against other children. The Mexican parents were maximally strict, while the American (a New England-village sample) were maximally tolerant of peer-directed aggression. Lambert hypothesized that this cross-cultural difference in socialization of childhood aggression reflected the presence or absence of close relatives. He suggested that, the more persons there are nearby with whom a family is interdependent, the less aggression by the family's children is permitted.

With regard to punishment by mothers of childhood aggression directed toward adults (especially toward mothers themselves), the Kenyan, Philippine, and Mexican samples scored high, the Okinawan and U.S. samples were moderate, and the Indian sample was relatively low. The variable that seemed to bear the strongest relation to variations in control of adult-directed aggression was the presence of other adults in the household.

Neither of these socialization variables (control of peer-directed aggression and control of adult-directed aggression) directly predicts manifest aggression by children in these six societies, however. To account for manifest aggression, Lambert has offered a two-stage theory of the shaping of aggressive dispositions. Applied to peer-directed aggression, for example, the first stage presumably makes some children in any culture more active (high social interactors) than other children. Then, in stage two the more active ones acquire whatever cultural values pertain to aggression in their particular society. Hence, in Mexico the more active children should tend to be less aggressive, but in the United States the more active children should tend to be more aggressive (Lambert, 1971, p. 58).

What happens in the presumed-to-exist second stage is, according to this theory, a function of the need to control aggression under conditions of high-density living. Harrington and Whiting (1972, p. 481) reiterate this idea. But, as Munroe and Munroe noted (1975, p. 103), this cross-cultural finding and its interpretation clash somewhat with most findings from Western settings that punitiveness breeds—rather than diminishes—aggression. Munroe and Munroe then reexamined findings from the Six Cultures Study and were struck by the fact that, in the three societies with extended-family households, children displayed *more* aggression. Although this fact eliminates the clash with Western findings, it raises some fascinating questions. As Munroe and Munroe aptly put it:

> The extended family not only treats aggression harshly, but also breeds aggression. Is this because, as first assumed, high density cannot easily tolerate aggression and punishes it on appearance, but the high density is stressful and produces aggression anyway? Or is it because high density cannot tolerate aggression and punishes it, and then the punishment produces aggression? Or is it perhaps because the density first produces the aggression, and the punishment is a reaction to it? [1975, p. 105].

Currently available cross-cultural data do not permit a determination of which of these three mechanisms suggested by Munroe and Munroe is the best. So this question must be considered still open. Nevertheless, the data from the Six Cultures Study, combined with information available in the Human Relations Area Files, provide us with intriguing empirical links among household arrangement, socialization of aggression, and manifest aggression. The mere fact of their covariance indicates that the social-learning theory of aggression, whatever its details, is likely to be needed to account for variations in aggression across societies and, hence, for variations in individual aggression within societies, as well. Future research, it is to be hoped, will reveal the needed details of such a theory.

As this brief review of some relevant studies has shown, we are only at the beginning of what will have to be a systematic cross-cultural analysis. It will be necessary to analyze socialization practices, ecocultural antecedents, institutionalized expressions of aggression, and other potentially related variables if we are to understand this very pervasive behavioral disposition. At present there is more chaos than order. But, as the Six Cultures Study suggests, some order may soon be forthcoming. Nonetheless, the answers we seek from cross-cultural research to questions about aggression are, for the present, pitifully few.

Cultural Factors Relating to Crime

One manifestation of aggression that has received some attention cross-culturally is crime. Criminal behavior includes many kinds of acts and reflects many different motives, including greed, genuine need, compensation for low self-esteem, and probably many others. But most acts that are socially defined as criminal involve the intentional infliction of harm to others, so they satisfy our working definition of aggression. Like other aggressive behaviors, criminal acts occur in all societies.[7] Bacon, Child, and Barry (1963), beginning with a sample of 110 mostly preliterate societies, found 48 for whom ethnographic information in the Human Relations Area Files was adequate to permit reliable ratings of criminal behavior. They examined correlates of crime in general, correlates of theft, and correlates of crimes against persons. Their most striking finding was that both subcategories of crime—and hence crime in general—were more frequent in societies in which opportunity for contact between child and father is minimal (for example, societies with polygynous mother/child households).

The Bacon team related this finding to the tendency of most crimes to be committed by males and to findings (Whiting, Kluckhohn, & Anthony, 1958; Burton & Whiting, 1961) concerning cross-sex identification problems in "low-male-salience" societies. They offered their finding as support for a hypothesis that crime is partly a defense reaction against initial feminine identification in males. Such a hypothesis has been favored by several students of crime and delinquency in the United States (see, for example, Glueck & Glueck, 1950; Rohrer & Edmonson, 1960). It is impressive to find supportive evidence for such a mechanism in a broad cross-cultural sample.

Other findings of Bacon and associates were concerned with the distinguishing correlates of theft on the one hand and personal crime on the other. Three societal characteristics—"level of political integration, social stratification,

---

[7]Incidentally, but not unimportantly, criminal acts are committed very disproportionately by males. The magnitude of this sex difference in Western societies is very great, but it may be diminishing.

and elaboration of social control" (all considered to be indexes of a highly differentiated status system)—were positively correlated with theft and unrelated to personal crime. Also, the greater the value attached to personal property in a society, the more likely was the occurrence of theft (Bacon et al., 1963, p. 297). Personal crime was found to be correlated with several child-training emphases—for example, severity of punishment—that together the authors viewed as indexes of childhood experiences conducive to the development of attitudes of rivalry, distrust, and hostility (p. 298). Thus, two different forms of crime were shown over a sample of 48 societies to have their unique correlates as well as a common relationship with factors likely to encourage compensatory efforts to establish masculine identity. The Bacon, Child, and Barry study, then, is an excellent example of cross-cultural research that has yielded support for a social-learning interpretation of aggression.

Expectation of Reward and Other Temporal Values

A common observation about personalities both within and across cultures is that individuals differ in their tendencies to wait for rewards. Some seem quite able and willing to tolerate delays in reward. Perhaps they anticipate larger ones if they wait. And they have probably learned to trust that the rewards, however delayed, will in fact be forthcoming. Others prefer immediate rewards, however small. Perhaps these people have little reason to expect the rewards to be larger if delayed. And perhaps they lack trust. By this reasoning, preferences for immediate or for delayed reinforcement would be seen as manifestations of variations in expectations. Such variations, in turn, might be expected to vary systematically with childhood experiences with reinforcing agents, most notably parents. To the extent that such experiences vary across cultures, we should anticipate cultural differences in preference for delayed reward.

A series of studies focusing on this topic has been reported by Mischel (1958, 1961a, 1961b). Of Mischel's various findings, perhaps the most provocative are those relating to father absence, a variable we have seen to be related to a large number of behavioral dispositions that vary across cultures. In his 1958 study, done in Trinidad with rural children between the ages of 7 and 9 years, Mischel found children from father-absent homes to be most likely to choose an immediate reward (a small piece of candy) rather than to wait a week for a promised larger one. A cross-cultural comparison within the Trinidad setting (between "Negro" and "East Indian" subgroups) yielded data consistent with this. The subgroup with the higher proportion of father-absent cases preferred immediate rewards more. Within the Negro subgroup, the children whose fathers were absent were more likely to prefer immediate rewards than those whose fathers were present.

In his 1961 study Mischel found a greater preference for delayed reinforcement among Grenadian Negro schoolchildren as compared with

Trinidadian Negroes. This cultural difference could *not* be attributed to differential father absence, although the 1961 findings did replicate the 1958 findings in one respect. *Within* both Trinidad and Grenada, for children aged 8 and 9, father absence was once again related to preference for immediate reward. So, the story becomes more complicated. Father absence is clearly one variable that relates to reward preferences, but there must be other cultural and economic factors that play a role in establishing the kinds of trust and other expectations that will lead an individual to tolerate delay in reward.

Mischel (1961a) has presented evidence that ability to delay gratification is related to strength of achievement motivation, long-term goal direction, and other indexes of individual autonomy. All of these, in Western value terms, are likely to be seen as expressions of "maturity." Therefore, we should reasonably expect that the other cultural and economic factors that contribute to reward preferences are the same ones that earlier in this chapter we found to contribute to the other behavioral dispositions with which delay of gratification are related. It remains for future cross-cultural studies to provide the evidence that this is so.

Studies of reward preferences that show differences among various groups continue to be reported. Price-Williams and Ramirez (1974) found White American fourth-grade schoolchildren to prefer delayed gratification more than Mexican-American children, with Black Americans generally intermediate. Wober and Musoke-Mutanda (1972), working with Ugandan primary-school children, found differences between the sexes and between social classes. In neither of these studies, however, was it possible to relate the performance differences to other possible cultural determinants.

Time-Related Values. Doob (1971) has appropriately warned that results like those reported in this section must be cautiously interpreted. He notes that persons "choosing the lesser of two . . . rewards [may have] intended, not to obtain gratification immediately, but to use the sum to invest in a small business and hence to obtain greater rewards in the future" (p. 100). That warning is contained in a major work by this pioneer cross-cultural psychologist entitled *Patterning of Time*, in which numerous temporal motives and other time-related behaviors are examined in the light of both anthropological and psychological insights.

Doob's book is replete with ideas from which testable hypotheses about cultural influences on time-related behavioral dispositions can be derived. Only a brief sample can be presented here: Social life requires regulation of behavior, and regulation requires a system of time reckoning. Every society will therefore keep track of time and organize activities within time frames. Activities and events will everywhere be subject to scheduling. Hence, delay, waiting, postponing, remembering, anticipation, expecting, abandoning, and similar time-related processes will occur everywhere. All of these temporal matters, however, will relate to the modal beliefs and attitudes that prevail in any society and that each individual acquires by socialization. Subjective estimates of durations may thus be expected to vary, not only among individuals but also across groups. So must all motives and values that relate to time.

In a section of the book that is most directly relevant to cross-cultural psychology (Doob, 1971, pp. 52–100), there are numerous insights pertaining to differences between traditional and industrial societies. For example, "Traditional peoples are likely to pay relatively little attention to the future" (p. 52). Acceptance of ascribed roles is likely to be a corollary of this non-future-oriented attitude. More generally, "The modal temporal perspective of a society reflects and affects a modal philosophy of values pertaining to other behavior" (p. 56). The complex of values known as "modernity" (to be discussed at length in a later chapter of the present book) includes a heightened concern with being on time and with advance planning (p. 81). The more a society's essential activities require coordinated efforts by several persons, the more scheduling and planning will occur (p. 82).

In another section of the book that is relevant to our present concerns (pp. 332–346), it is noted that age grading is a universal dimension of social organization. Thus, reference groups,[8] status, and roles all vary with age and are, therefore, basically temporal values. Individual behavior, then, will vary with age in ways that reflect cultural values. And cultures will vary in the different degrees of prestige attached to various age statuses. This variation, in turn, may relate to modal tendencies to be either tradition oriented or future oriented.

For those who would conduct cross-cultural research on time-related behavioral dispositions, Doob's idea-filled analysis of the patterning of temporal matters is a rich resource from which fruitful empirical studies of cultural influences on temporal values can stem.

Other Behavioral Dispositions

In this chapter we have ranged widely over a variety of motives, values, and behavioral dispositions, seeking cross-cultural differences and pancultural factors that might contribute to their acquisition. Our review was by no means exhaustive. Rather, it dealt with certain classes of behavior (autonomy/conformity, cooperation/competition, achievement motivation, sex-role typing, aggression, and time-related behaviors) that have proven to be especially interesting to cross-cultural psychologists. But there are other classes of behaviors—which presumably reflect important human dispositions, subject to cultural influence—that have attracted some attention from psychologists working in more than one culture. In this section a few of these will be briefly noted.

[8]Reference groups are the groups to which an individual relates himself/herself or that serve as a standard of comparison.

Morality, Humanism, and Kindness

Morality and ethics, traditionally subjects of philosophy, may also be studied from a psychological perspective by focusing on what individuals actually say or do about situations that pose dilemmas because of conflicting values. Psychological morality may be studied developmentally, by examining changes in solutions to moral dilemmas as people grow older and presumably learn their culture's values. A developmental approach to the study of morality is exemplified by some of Piaget's work (1932) and by the work of Kohlberg (1969a, 1969b, 1970). These two men offer stage theories of moral development that can be taken as possible models of the universal unfolding of morality.

Against these models can be measured the developmental trends revealed by empirical research with persons of various ages in any society. Various standardized tests of behavior in situations that pose dilemmas can be administered, and differences in response as a function of age can be compared across cultures. Such research can have several worthwhile ends. It can test the universality of the stage theories. It can reveal possible cultural differences in the definition of moral behavior. And it may demonstrate similar adult-level definitions of morality, accompanied by different rates of progress over age toward the incorporation of that definition in actual behavior.

Oversimplifying matters, one could assert that all societies recognize as morally desirable behavior that is more other-serving than self-serving. And one could add that, in one manner or another, a central concern of child rearing in each society is to instill in children this concern for others. But societies also teach respect for authority, obedience, and some self-aggrandizing behaviors (for example, individual achievement), such that competing behavioral tendencies are likely to emerge among individuals in any society. The particular mix of competing behaviors is likely to vary from society to society. Hence, the prevailing moral dilemmas and their characteristic modes of solution are also likely to vary across societies.

There has been less research done than this argument might suggest. For the most part the research to date is descriptive, revealing similarities or differences in moral behavior across a small number of societies, with minimal efforts to explain those similarities or differences.

An aspect of Kohlberg's model of moral development has recently inspired a cross-cultural study by Bloom (1977), who administered questionnaires to French and American university students and to a sample of adult residents in Hong Kong. Kohlberg had postulated a necessary link between "moral autonomy" (referred to by Bloom as "social principledness" and meant to denote a readiness to differentiate between a conventional and a personal standard of morality) and "social humanism," or a readiness to give priority to human welfare over other, potentially competing, values. Bloom found instead that in all three cultural settings these two dimensions were independent of each other. In short, in all three societies some persons scored high on both dimensions, but many others were high scorers on only one or the other.

Bloom's study shows that there is interest in studying moral development cross-culturally, but the systematic research the topic deserves has not yet begun. Needed are cross-cultural replications of field experiments in helping behavior (for example, see Feldman, 1971, for a report of real-life tests of honesty conducted in the streets, shops, and taxis of Boston, Paris, and Athens). These must be coupled with analyses of ecological, economic, and cultural characteristics of the societies in which the tests are applied. We might well expect concern for the rights of others to vary with other societal characteristics in a meaningful way.

Romantic Love and Affective Relationships

In a very thoughtful essay dealing with certain patterns of personality found to prevail in many subsistence-level societies in Africa, LeVine (1973) contrasted an African pattern of seemingly unemotional behavior toward intimates with the importance Westerners attach to emotional relationships.

Rosenblatt (1966) has shown, for a sample of 18 traditional societies, considerable variation in the importance attached to romantic love. A few African societies were included; they scored low on romantic love as a basis for marriage. His study also provided empirical support for a Freudian-based hypothesis that initial oral indulgence and later severity of oral socialization (because oral needs are presumably related to a general need for affection) would covary with the importance of romantic love in adult life. Rosenblatt found that romantic love was more likely in societies that did not orally indulge their infants and that did severely socialize childhood orality. In short, where oral needs were more frustrated, romantic love was more likely to be employed as a basis for marriage.

Beliefs about Illness

Freudian hypotheses, modified to make them more compatible with contemporary learning theories and sharpened so that they might be subjected to empirical examination, were tested by Whiting and Child (1953) in their classic study of relationships between child-training emphases and adult belief systems. The Freudian concept that attracted the attention of Whiting and Child was *fixation*, or, as Freud originally viewed it, arrested development at one or another putative stage of psychosexual development. In his own treatment of fixation, Freud argued that it could result either from "overindulgence" *or* frustration. Thus, a child might become orally fixated as a result of an extremely permissive feeding schedule *or* as a result of a too rigid one. Whiting and Child, members of a generation of social scientists whose immersion in behavioristic learning theory[9] made them acutely aware of the *contrasting*

---

[9]Whiting and Child were part of the group of psychologists, anthropologists, sociologists, and psychiatrists who composed the Institute for Human Relations at Yale University, where the learning theory of Clark Hull was applied systematically to a variety of issues in human behavior.

effects of reward (indulgence) and nonreward (frustration), found it desirable to modify Freud's fixation notion by postulating opposing effects of indulgence and frustration.

Hence, their learning-theory modification of Freud's ideas produced the two concepts of positive fixation and negative fixation. They argued that the former, a product of indulgence, should lead to a positive evaluation of relevant behaviors. The latter should lead to a negative evaluation. In adulthood, then, behaviors like those that had been subjected to much reward during childhood would be strong and accompanied by positive feelings. But behaviors associated with earlier punishments should be anxiety provoking and otherwise accompanied by negative feelings.

Although they assumed such mechanisms to occur at the individual level, the authors actually tested their modification of Freudian theory at the societal level of analysis. They reasoned that positive or negative aspects of shared belief systems would reflect, respectively, childhood indulgence or severity of socialization of behaviors related to the beliefs. The belief system they investigated had to do with illnesses, their suspected causes, and their preferred therapies. They further reasoned that what a whole society modally tends to believe makes one ill is a good index of anxiety surrounding certain activities, whereas what the society tends to believe can cure illness is an index of behaviors that are surrounded by positive feelings. Thus, Whiting and Child had to predict that, in societies in which feeding training (oral socialization) is strict and severe, oral activities would be likely to appear in the belief system as an illness-causation factor. But in a society in which children are orally indulged, oral activity would more likely be viewed as therapeutic.

Employing data from the Human Relations Area Files, the authors found much stronger evidence for negative fixation than for positive fixation. And the predicted correlations between aspects of child training and illness belief varied in magnitude for the various behavioral arenas studied. The strongest relationships involved weaning and oral explanations for illness (Whiting & Child, 1953). A reanalysis of their data, completed almost 20 years later and employing more sophisticated statistical techniques and computer technology (Guthrie, 1971), has produced questions about the meaningfulness of the relationships uncovered by Whiting and Child. But their study stands as a pioneer example of a cross-cultural approach to the study of shared behavioral dispositions.

Some Concluding Observations

Perhaps the single best generalization that can be made from the material reviewed in this chapter is that in any society there is likely to be a meaningful relationship between child-training emphases and adult behavior. This theory has guided research efforts from Whiting and Child's study in the early 1950s through the Six Cultures Study, which has produced nine major publications, the most recent appearing in 1975 (Whiting & Whiting). Furthermore, it is clear that ecological and economic factors are also important, so that our generalization is probably best expressed in these terms: Children are likely to be induced to behave in ways compatible with adult roles that they will have to assume, with those roles in turn reflective of socioeconomic complexity and social organization. The tenability of this generalization is nowhere better illustrated than in the 1975 report from the Six Cultures Study, but it applies to nearly everything we have covered in the present chapter.

Future cross-cultural research on behavioral dispositions, to be fruitful, must be of a systematic, hypothesis-testing kind; must focus attention on ecological and economic variables, child rearing, child behavior, and adult behavior; and must seek interrelationships among all of these. Conducted in such a manner, the research is likely to succeed in filling in many details, as yet unrecorded, of the network of relationships expressed in this now well-supported generalization.

An implication of the generalization is that motives, beliefs, and values are nowhere static. As ecological systems and social structures change, so must the associated child-rearing systems and the behavioral dispositions they instill. This implication comprises the subject matter of the next chapter, in which research on modernization will be our concern.

References

Ardrey, R. *The Territorial Imperative.* New York: Atheneum, 1966.

Aronson, E. The need for achievement as measured by graphic expression. In J. W. Atkinson (Ed.), *Motives in Fantasy, Action, and Society.* Princeton, N.J.: Van Nostrand, 1958.

Aronson, E. *The Social Animal.* San Francisco: Freeman, 1972.

Asch, S. E. Studies of independence and conformity. *Psychological Monographs*, 1956, *70* (9 Whole No. 416), 1–70.

Atkinson, J. W. (Ed.). *Motives in Fantasy, Action, and Society.* Princeton, N. J.: Van Nostrand, 1958.

Bacon, M. K., Child, I., & Barry, H. III. A cross-cultural study of correlates of crime. *Journal of Abnormal and Social Psychology*, 1963, *66*, 291–300.

Bandura, A., & Walters, R. H. *Social Learning and Personality Development.* New York: Holt, Rinehart & Winston, 1963.

Barry, H. III., Bacon, M. K., & Child, I. L. A cross-cultural survey of some sex differences in socialization. *Journal of Abnormal and Social Psychology*, 1957, *55*, 327–332.

Barry, H. III., Bacon, M. K., & Child, I. L. Definitions, ratings and bibliographic sources of child-training practices of 110 cultures. In C. S. Ford (Ed.), *Cross-Cultural Approaches.* New Haven, Conn.: HRAF Press, 1967. Pp. 293–331.

Barry, H. III., Child, I. L., & Bacon, M. K. Relation of child training to subsistence economy. *American Anthropologist*, 1959, *61*, 51–63.

Becker, E. *The Denial of Death.* New York: Free Press, 1973.

Berkowitz, L. The expression and reduction of hostility. *Psychological Bulletin*, 1958, *55*, 257–283.

Berry, J. W. Independence and conformity in subsistence-level societies. *Journal of Personality and Social Psychology*, 1967, *7*, 415–418.

Berry, J. W. *Human Ecology and Cognitive Style: Comparative Studies in Cultural and Psychological Adaptation.* Beverly Hills, Calif.: Sage, 1976.

Beshai, J. A. Content analysis of Egyptian stories. *Journal of Social Psychology*, 1972, *87*, 197–203.

Bloom, A. H. Two dimensions of moral reasoning: Social principledness and social humanism in cross-cultural perspective. *Journal of Social Psychology*, 1977, *101*, 29–44.

Bradburn, N. M. *n* achievement and father dominance in Turkey. *Journal of Abnormal and Social Psychology*, 1963, *67*, 464–468.

Bradburn, N. M., & Berlew, D. E. Need for achievement and English economic growth. *Economic Development and Cultural Change*, 1961, *10*, 8–20.

Burton, R. V., & Whiting, J. W. M. The absent father and cross-sex identity. *Merrill-Palmer Quarterly*, 1961, *7*, 85–95.

Caplan, N., & Paige, J. M. A study of ghetto rioters. *Scientific American*, 1968, 219(2), 15–21.

Chaffee, S. H., & McLeod, J. M. *Adolescents, parents and television violence.* Paper presented at the American Psychological Association meetings, Washington, September 1971.

Child, I. L., Storm, T., & Veroff, J. Achievement themes in folk tales related to socialization practices. In J. W. Atkinson (Ed.), *Motives in Fantasy, Action, and Society.* Princeton, N.J.: Van Nostrand, 1958. Pp. 479–492.

Davies, E. This is the way Crete went—Not with a bang but a simper. *Psychology Today*, 1969, *3*(6), 43–47.

Dawson, J. L. M. Temne-Arunta hand-eye dominance and cognitive style. *International Journal of Psychology*, 1972, *7*, 219–233.

Dollard, J., Doob, L., Miller, N., Mowrer, O., & Sears, R. *Frustration and Aggression.* New Haven, Conn.: Yale University Press, 1939.

Doob, L. W. *Patterning of Time.* New Haven, Conn., and London: Yale University Press, 1971.

Feldman, R. E. Honesty toward compatriot and foreigner: Field experiments in Paris, Athens, and Boston. In W. W. Lambert & R. Weisbrod (Eds.), *Comparative Perspectives on Social Psychology.* Boston: Little, Brown, 1971. Pp. 321–335.

Feshbach, S. The drive-reducing function of fantasy behavior. *Journal of Abnormal and Social Psychology*, 1955, *50*, 3–11.

Feshbach, S., & Singer, R. *Television and Aggression.* San Francisco: Jossey-Bass, 1971.

Finison, L. J. The application of McClelland's national development model to recent data. *Journal of Social Psychology*, 1976, *98*, 55–59.

Fleming, J. Fear of success imagery in urban Kenya. *Kenya Education Review*, 1975, *2*(2), 121–139.

Gallo, P. S., Jr., & McClintock, C. G. Cooperative and competitive behavior in mixed-motive games. *Journal of Conflict Resolution*, 1965, *9*, 68–78.

Glueck, S., & Glueck, E. *Unraveling Juvenile Delinquency.* New York: Commonwealth Fund, 1950.

Guthrie, G. M. Unexpected correlations and the cross-cultural method. *Journal of Cross-Cultural Psychology*, 1971, *2*, 315–323.

Harrington, C. Sexual differentiation in socialization and some male genital mutilations. *American Anthropologist*, 1968, *70*, 952–956.

Harrington, C., & Whiting, J. W. M. Socialization process and personality. In F. L. K. Hsu (Ed.), *Psychological Anthropology* (Rev. ed.). Cambridge, Mass.: Schenkman, 1972. Pp. 469–508.

Heilbroner, R. L. *An Inquiry into the Human Prospect.* New York: Norton, 1975.

Horner, M. S. Fail: Bright women. *Psychology Today*, 1969, *3*, 36–38, 62.

Horner, M. S. Toward an understanding of achievement-related conflicts in women. *Journal of Social Issues*, 1972, *28*, 157–176.

Horner, M. S., Tresman, D. W., Berans, A. E., & Watson, R. I. *Scoring manual for an empirically derived scoring system for motive to avoid success.* Unpublished manuscript, Harvard University, 1973.

Kohlberg, L. Stage and sequence: The cognitive-development approach to socialization. In D. A. Goslin (Ed.), *Handbook of Socialization Theory and Research.* Chicago: Rand McNally, 1969. Pp. 347–480. (a)

Kohlberg, L. *Stages in the Development of Moral Thought and Action.* New York: Holt, Rinehart & Winston, 1969. (b)

Kohlberg, L. The child as a moral philosopher. In P. Cramer (Ed.), *Readings in Developmental Psychology Today.* Del Mar, Calif.: CRM Books, 1970. Pp. 109–115.

Kohn, M. L. *Class and Conformity: A Study in Values.* Homewood, Ill.: Dorsey, 1969.

Lambert, W. W. Cross-cultural backgrounds to personality development and the socialization of aggression: Findings from the Six Culture Study. In W. W. Lambert & R. Weisbrod (Eds.), *Comparative Perspectives on Social Psychology.* Boston: Little, Brown, 1971. Pp. 49–61.

Lambert, W. W., & Weisbrod, R. (Eds.). *Comparative Perspectives on Social Psychology.* Boston: Little, Brown, 1971.

Lefkowitz, M. M., Eron, L. D., Walder, L. W., & Husemann, L. R. *Growing Up to Be Violent: A Longitudinal Study of the Development of Aggression.* Elmsford, N.Y.: Pergamon, 1977.

LeVine, R. A. *Dreams and Deeds.* Chicago: University of Chicago Press, 1966.

LeVine, R. A. Patterns of personality in Africa. *Ethos*, 1973, *1*, 123–152.

Liebert, R. M., Neale, J. M., & Davidson, E. S. *The Early Window: Effects of TV on Children and Youth.* Elmsford, N.Y.: Pergamon, 1973.

Liebert, R. M., Sobol, M. P., & Davidson, E. S. Catharsis of aggression among institutionalized boys: Fact or anti-fact? In G. A. Comstock, E. A. Rubenstein, & J. P. Murray (Eds.), *Television and Social Behavior.* Vol. 5: *Television's Effects: Further Explorations.* Washington: U.S. Government Printing Office, 1972.

Lorenz, K. *On Aggression.* New York: Harcourt, Brace & World, 1963.

Luce, R. D., & Raiffa, H. *Games and Decisions.* New York: Wiley, 1957.

Madsen, M. C. Cooperative and competitive motivation of children in three Mexican subcultures. *Psychological Reports*, 1967, *20*, 1307–1320.

Madsen, M. C. Developmental and cross-cultural differences in the cooperative and competitive behavior of young children. *Journal of Cross-Cultural Psychology*, 1971, *2*, 365–371.

McClelland, D. C. The use of measures of human motivation in the study of society. In J. W. Atkinson (Ed.), *Motives in Fantasy, Action, and Society.* Princeton, N. J.: Van Nostrand, 1958.

McClelland, D. C. *The Achieving Society.* Princeton, N. J.: Van Nostrand, 1961.

McClelland, D. C. *n* achievement and entrepreneurship: A longitudinal study. *Journal of Personality and Social Psychology*, 1965, *1*, 389–392.

McClelland, D. C. *Motivational Trends in Society.* New York: General Learning Press, 1971.

McClelland, D. C., & Winter, D. G. *Motivating Economic Achievement.* New York: Free Press, 1969.

Milgram, S., & Shotland, R. L. *Television and Anti-Social Behavior.* New York: Academic Press, 1973.

Miller, A. G., & Thomas, R. Cooperation and competition among Blackfoot Indian and urban Canadian children. *Child Development*, 1972, *43*, 1104–1110.

Miller, N. E. The frustration-aggression hypothesis. *Psychological Review*, 1941, *48*, 337–342.

Miller, N. E., & Bugelski, R. Minor studies in aggression: The influence of frustrations imposed by the in-group on attitudes expressed toward out-groups. *Journal of Psychology*, 1948, *25*, 437–442.

Mischel, W. Preference for delayed reinforcement: An experimental study of a cultural observation. *Journal of Abnormal and Social Psychology*, 1958, *56*, 57–61.

Mischel, W. Delay of gratification, need for achievement, and acquiescence in another culture. *Journal of Abnormal and Social Psychology*, 1961, *62*, 543–552. (a)

Mischel, W. Father absence and delay of gratification. *Journal of Abnormal and Social Psychology*, 1961, *63*, 116–124. (b)

Monahan, L., Kuhn, D., & Shaver, P. Intrapsychic versus cultural explanations of the "fear of success" motive. *Journal of Personality and Social Psychology*, 1974, *29*, 60–64.

Morris, C., & Jones, L. V. Value scales and dimensions. *Journal of Abnormal and Social Psychology*, 1955, *51*, 523–535.

Morris, D. *The Naked Ape.* New York: McGraw-Hill, 1967.

Munroe, R. L., & Munroe, R. H. *Cross-Cultural Human Development.* Monterey, Calif.: Brooks/Cole, 1975.

Munroe, R. L., & Munroe, R. H. Cooperation and competition among East African and American children. *Journal of Social Psychology*, 1977, *101*, 145–146.

Murdock, G. P. Comparative data on the division of labor by sex. *Social Forces*, 1937, *15*, 551–553.

Mussen, P. H., & Rutherford, E. Effects of aggressive cartoons on children's aggressive play. *Journal of Abnormal and Social Psychology*, 1961, *62*, 461–464.

Oskamp, S., & Perlman, D. Effects of friendship and disliking on cooperation in a mixed-motive game. *Journal of Conflict Resolution*, 1966, *10*, 221–226.

Peck, R. F. A comparison of the value system of Mexican and American youth. *Interamerican Journal of Psychology*, 1967, *1*, 41–51.

Pepitone, A., Faucheux, C., Moscovi, S., Cesa-Bianchi, M., Magistretti, G., Iacono, G., Asprea, A. M., & Villone, G. The role of self-esteem in competitive choice behavior. *International Journal of Psychology*, 1967, *2*, 147–159.

Piaget, J. [*The Moral Judgment of the Child*] (M. Gabain, trans.). London: Routledge & Kegan Paul, 1932.

Price-Williams, D. R., & Ramirez, M. III. Ethnic differences in delay of gratification. *Journal of Social Psychology*, 1974, *93*, 23–30.

Rohrer, J. H., & Edmonson, M. E. (Eds.). *The Eighth Generation: Cultures and Personalities of New Orleans Negroes.* New York: Harper, 1960.

Rosen, B. C. Socialization and achievement motivation in Brazil. *American Sociological Review*, 1962, *27*, 612–624.

Rosen, B. C., & D'Andrade, R. The psychological origins of achievement motivation. *Sociometry*, 1959, *22*, 185–218.

Rosenblatt, P. C. A cross-cultural study of child rearing and romantic love. *Journal of Personality and Social Psychology*, 1966, *4*, 336–338.

Segall, M. H. *Human Behavior and Public Policy: A Political Psychology*. Elmsford, N. Y.: Pergamon, 1976.

Shapira, A., & Madsen, M. C. Cooperative and competitive behavior of kibbutz and urban children in Israel. *Child Development*, 1969, *40*, 609–617.

Siegel, A. E. Film-mediated fantasy aggression and strength of aggressive drive. *Child Development*, 1956, *27*, 365–378.

Slovic, P. Risk-taking in children: Age and sex differences. *Child Development*, 1966, *37*, 169–176.

Storr, A. *Human Aggression*. New York: Atheneum, 1968.

Southwood, K. E. *Some sources of political disorder: A cross-national analysis.* Unpublished doctoral dissertation, University of Michigan, 1969. (Cited in D. C. McClelland, *Motivational Trends in Society*. New York: General Learning Press, 1971.)

Van Leeuwen, M. S. A cross-cultural examination of psychological differentiation in males and females. *International Journal of Psychology*, 1978, *13*, 87–122.

Weber, M. [*The Protestant Ethic and the Spirit of Capitalism.*] New York: Scribner's, 1930. (Originally published, 1904.)

Wells, W. D. *Television and Aggression: A Replication of an Experimental Field Study*. University of Chicago, 1972. (Mimeographed abstract. Cited in R. M. Liebert, J. M. Neale, & E. S. Davidson, *The Early Window: Effects of TV on Children and Youth*. Elmsford, N. Y.: Pergamon, 1973.)

Whiting, B. B. (Ed.). *Six Cultures: Studies of Child Rearing*. New York: Wiley, 1963.

Whiting, B. B. The Kenyan career woman: Traditional and modern. *Annals of the New York Academy of Sciences*, 1973, *208*, 71–75.

Whiting, B. B., & Edwards, C. P. A cross-cultural analysis of sex differences in the behavior of children aged three through eleven. *Journal of Social Psychology*, 1973, *91*, 171–188.

Whiting, B. B., & Whiting, J. W. M. Task assignment and personality: A consideration of the effects of herding on boys. In W. W. Lambert & R. Weisbrod (Eds.), *Comparative Perspectives on Social Psychology*. Boston: Little, Brown, 1971. Pp. 33–45.

Whiting, B. B., & Whiting, J. W. M. *Children of Six Cultures: A Psycho-Cultural Analysis*. Cambridge, Mass.: Harvard University Press, 1975.

Whiting, J. W. M. Comment. *American Journal of Sociology*, 1962, *67*, 391–393.

Whiting, J. W. M., & Child, I. L. *Child Training and Personality*. New Haven, Conn.: Yale University Press, 1953.

Whiting, J. W. M., Kluckhohn, R., & Anthony, A. The function of male initiation ceremonies at puberty. In E. E. Maccoby, T. Newcomb, & F. L. Hartley (Eds.), *Readings in Social Psychology* (3rd ed.). New York: Holt, 1958. Pp. 359–370.

Whittaker, J. O., & Meade, R. O. Social pressure in the modification and distortion of judgment. *International Journal of Psychology*, 1967, *2*, 109–113.

Wober, M., & Musoke-Mutanda, F. Patience and gratification preferences among Ugandan school children. *Journal of Social Psychology*, 1972, *87*, 141–142.

Zimet, S. G., Wiberg, J. L., & Blom, G. E. Attitudes and values in primers from the U.S. and twelve other countries. *Journal of Social Psychology*, 1971, *84*, 167–174.

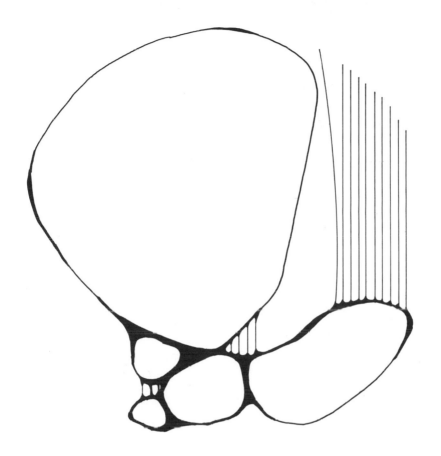

Intercultural
Relations

Part Three

Seven

Cultural Contact and Change

Introduction

In the research reviewed in previous chapters, *culture* was, for the most part, treated as if it were merely "there," serving as an unchanging context in which individual behaviors are acquired and shaped. Viewed as such, culture is a convenient fiction. It is useful for psychologists to treat a particular complex of cultural facts as if it were a fixed state of affairs impinging on people. But the fact is, all cultures are continuously in flux.

In much of the research examined earlier, the pictures of culture we employed were mostly stills, which froze the action. In the present chapter our interest shifts to what might be revealed if we used motion pictures. Rather than depicting *states,* our intent now is to focus on *process.*

This chapter was prepared with the assistance of Larry S. Beyna, a doctoral candidate in the Interdisciplinary Social Science Program at the Maxwell School, Syracuse University.

In the course of examining the process of cultural change, we will consider some of the forces that produce it, most notably contact between cultures. And we will look in detail at some of the most important individual behavioral consequences of cultural change. As the story of cultural contact and change unfolds, we will have occasion to explicate further some familiar sociological concepts, such as *modernization* and *development*. These terms were mentioned in the last chapter, where we discussed Heilbroner's (1975) views on industrial society and McClelland's (for example, 1971) theories linking achievement motivation to economic development. We will also meet a related psychological concept—*acculturation*—to refer to all those behavioral changes that are the consequences of sociocultural change.

Our study will begin with some generalizations about sociocultural change. There follows a discussion of some theories, or models, that have been offered by various students of the process. Their goal has been to depict the inter-relationships between societal change and individual acculturation. Then we will review and analyze several noteworthy efforts by social scientists to define and measure acculturation, most of which have been couched in terms of a movement from *traditionalism* to *modernism*. The chapter concludes with a special topic that relates to cultural change—the psychology of nationalism.

The study of acculturation, which is the focus of this chapter, probably needs no lengthy justification. It should be apparent that, because the goal of cross-cultural psychological research is to discover how human behavior is shaped by culture, study of the impact of *changing* cultures on individual humans promises to be a fruitful strategy for testing the most basic propositions relating culture and behavior.[1] Furthermore, because a majority of the world's societies are undergoing rapid social and economic change, it is of obvious theoretical and practical interest to study people's adjustments to the pressures of this modernization.

Such study also has implications for understanding the behavior of many individuals in so-called modern societies as well. As Kelman (1968) argued at a conference on problems of national development, social change needs to be studied not only in developing nations but also in industrial societies "because the forces toward social change ... manifest themselves wherever there are populations that have been excluded from effective participation in the political process, from a share in the benefits of the national economy, and from meaningful roles in the social structure" (p. 15). Finally, modern societies are subject to continual economic, political, and social changes that demand adjustments from all their members, not just the disadvantaged. (An example is the need to adjust to dwindling supplies of fossil fuels in the industrial world.) Thus, the practical significance of understanding acculturation ought to be obvious.

[1]In this regard, it is noteworthy that the first time the *Journal of Cross-Cultural Psychology* published a special issue focused on a single topic, that topic was the psychological aspects of culture change (see Volume 8, Number 2, June 1977).

Four Preliminary Generalizations about Acculturation Research

As just noted, all cultures are always changing—sometimes rapidly, sometimes imperceptibly, but everywhere continuously. Despite the fact that we often talk of modern nations on the one hand and developing nations on the other, *all* societies are modernizing. Institutions change, technologies are modified, ideologies are amended. And as these change, so do the persons who both invent and respond to them. Hence, acculturation is as fundamental a phenomenon in human existence as socialization. Not only is every one of us shaped by the traditional norms and teachings that prevail in our culture; each of us is subjected to lifelong changing influences. Our first generalization, then, is that the twin processes of cultural change and acculturation are universal and may be studied anywhere.

Secondly, all cultures are in contact with one or more other cultures. No society exists in complete isolation from ideas, institutions, technologies, or values that originated outside its geographical confines. All such cultural aspects are widely dispersed by immigrants, tourists, missionaries, business people, diplomats, films, literature, and numerous other culture carriers. Our second generalization is that culture contact is a source of acculturation everywhere.

The spread of cultural elements among societies in contact is a two-way process. Host cultures influence their visitors and are influenced by them. Therefore, our third generalization must be that a complete study of acculturation should take into account the reciprocal influences that result from cultural contacts. However, as we will see as this chapter unfolds, most attention has been devoted to the influence of the more powerful industrialized societies on subcultural groups within them and on persons in nonindustrial nations.

The fourth generalization, although of less obvious validity, needs to be expressed because it has inspired considerable acculturation research. This is the proposition that certain societies may be more susceptible to behavioral influences from different cultures than other societies. Whether (and, if so, why) some societies are more resistant to cultural contact has been a major topic in acculturation studies.

A corollary to the fourth generalization concerns individual differences *within* societies in susceptibility to acculturative pressures. Much of the research we will examine in this chapter consists of efforts to measure and account for such individual differences.

An Acculturation Model and Some Theories of the Modernizing Process

Figure 7-1 depicts one way of conceptualizing the complex relationships among ecological, social, cultural, and behavioral variables in a society that is in contact with another culture. The focal concern in this depiction is the individual

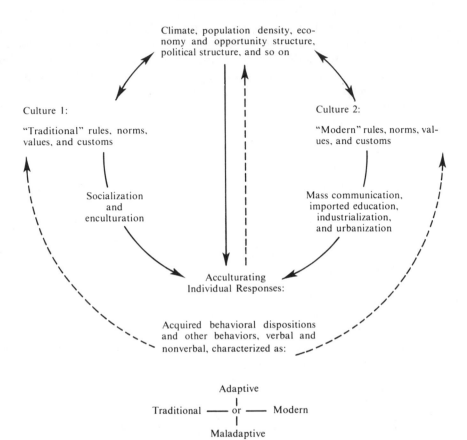

Structural Environment:

Climate, population density, economy and opportunity structure, political structure, and so on

Culture 1:

"Traditional" rules, norms, values, and customs

Culture 2:

"Modern" rules, norms, values, and customs

Socialization and enculturation

Mass communication, imported education, industrialization, and urbanization

Acculturating Individual Responses:

Acquired behavioral dispositions and other behaviors, verbal and nonverbal, characterized as:

Adaptive

Traditional —— or —— Modern

Maladaptive

Figure 7-1. A model of acculturation. The elements at the left, right, and top of this figure are forces affecting the individual. The individual's responses are depicted at the bottom in terms of two continua. Dotted-line arrows indicate the effects of the individual's behavior on other elements. Solid-line arrows indicate influences acting on the individual.

member of the society, whose behavior is of paramount interest to the psychologist. The individual's *acculturation* consists of those changes and adaptations in behavior that presumably occur in response to the sometimes competing forces that originate in the two (or more) cultures impinging on him or her.[2]

---

[2]This model is similar in content to the general ecological framework devised by Berry and presented earlier in this book. The model is also consistent with the spirit of Berry's more specific acculturation model, which will appear in the forthcoming *Handbook of Cross-Cultural Psychology* (see Berry, 1979).

The left-hand side of Figure 7-1 represents the socialization and enculturation processes through which each individual acquires those behavioral dispositions (for example, motives, attitudes, and intentions) that are within the limits imposed by his or her culture's norms and customs and that are consonant with the society's traditional values. Socialization includes all the more or less direct teaching to which the individual is exposed. This teaching involves the inculcation of norms and customs by various socialization agents—parents, teachers, elders, and others—who consciously endeavor to shape the individual according to the cultural model of a "proper" member of society. Enculturation refers to all of the incidental learning that occurs through imitation of elders and others, who—although they may not be trying consciously to teach anything —serve as effective models to be emulated. As a result of the twin processes of socialization and enculturation, the individual acquires his or her personal behavioral reflections of the society's traditional culture.

The right-hand side of Figure 7-1 represents the parallel—potentially competing—process by which the individual is exposed to externally originated models of behavior. Through contact with members of or ideas from another society (a society that is perceived as being "more modern" or otherwise worthy of emulation) the individual is affected by different socialization and enculturation pressures. The teaching agents, or models, in this case may be immigrants, colonizers, missionaries, educators imported from aid-granting nations, and mass-media products exported from relatively developed societies. Purposely or not, these models serve to communicate the societies' prevalent values.

Simultaneously, forces emanating in the structural environment (which itself may be changing in response to competing cultural pressures) impinge on the individual. Hence, Figure 7-1 shows three sets of forces acting to shape individual responses.

The responses that result from these three sets of influences are depicted as involving adjustments in the individual's behavioral dispositions. The responses are shown as falling (at any moment) at some point along a traditional/modern continuum and, simultaneously, at some point along an adaptive/maladaptive continuum. These two are depicted as uncorrelated, because in any traditional society there may be times and situations in which traditional behavior is more adaptive and other times and situations in which modern behavior is more adaptive. (See Foster, 1967, for a fuller discussion of this point, with examples from a transitional Mexican society.)

The two dimensions along which the individual's resultant behavioral dispositions fall are those that have attracted the most attention from students of acculturation. Numerous studies have tried to measure the degree to which individual behaviors are traditional or modern in character. And a number of studies have focused on overt manifestations of psychological conflict, stress, confusion, or other presumed maladies arising out of cultural-contact pressures.

Figure 7-1 also depicts the individual's behavior as influencing his or her own culture, the externally originated culture, and—both directly and indirectly—the environment. These influences are indicated by dotted-line arrows. The direct and indirect influences *on* the individual are indicated by solid-line arrows.

The acculturation process as modeled in Figure 7-1 is comprehensive in that it includes both environmental and cultural forces acting on the individual *and* individual behavioral influences on environment and culture. As such, the model is global. But it is not immediately useful except as a kind of conceptual umbrella. Under it can be sheltered more manageable theories of acculturation that tend to treat *either* influences on the individual *or* individual influences on culture—but not both simultaneously. It is to some examples of theory that we now turn.

Some Acculturation Theories

Godwin (1974) has noted that the theories employed in acculturation (or modernization) studies tend to treat individual personality traits either as independent, mediating, or dependent variables in the process of societal modernization.

Personality as the Independent Variable in Modernization. Some theorists, who focus on the individual as the *agent* of social change, emphasize the presumed necessity for certain individually held attitudes, values, motives, or other dispositions to exist *before* modernizing behavior—and hence societal modernization—can occur. Such theorists usually acknowledge the need for certain economic resources and a favorable economic climate before modernization can occur. But they stress that, without certain psychological attributes in good supply, modernization will not take place.

One example of such theorizing, McClelland's (1971) theory of the role played by achievement motivation in economic development, was discussed in detail in Chapter Six. In an elaboration of McClelland's theory, Pareek (1968) suggested a somewhat more general paradigm in which development is the result of achievement motivation plus a concern for others (labeled "extension motive") minus dependency motivation. Although Pareek's theory is multidirectional, in that it views these motivational patterns both as being generated by the social system and as influencing that system, he emphasizes the latter influence, as does McClelland.

Lerner (1958) has argued for the central importance of a psychological disposition that he terms "empathy." This is a personality trait that presumably enables newly mobile individuals to operate efficiently in a changing social environment. Through empathy, transitional individuals are able to imagine what life is like outside the restrictive realm of their traditional surroundings. Their empathy leads to the desire to experience what has been imagined and to become participating members of the transitional society. For Lerner, participation is manifested in the holding of opinions on public matters. To the degree that such overt behavior is present in a population, the society will be in the process of modernizing.

A final example of a theory that treats personality as the independent variable in social change is Hagen's (1962). Hagen assumes that economic development requires individual movement away from authoritarian, noninnovating personality. His theory postulates that certain members of a traditional society will undergo a loss of relative status in the social order, come to perceive themselves as suffering a loss of respect, and—in response to this perception —enter a period of social retreat. He predicts that their descendants will develop a social, familial climate that favors the development of creativity. The resultant innovators, finally, are viewed in this theory as the necessary agents of economic development.

Personality as the Mediating Variable. In Godwin's (1974) classification of modernization theories, those that propose that the initial and primary thrust toward modernization comes from changes in the opportunity structure usually treat personality variables as mediating between such changes and the resultant modernization. In most such theories, shifts in the economic and political environment are viewed as providing opportunities for individuals to "modernize." But it is only those individuals with the appropriate attitudes, values, and beliefs who can and will respond gainfully to those opportunities. Thus, one or another set of personality traits is seen as facilitating profitable adjustment to changing external conditions.

The difference between these theories and those that employ personality traits as independent variables is primarily one of emphasis. In the independent-variable theories the modernizing individual is imbued with considerable power to shape the opportunity structure as well as to exploit it. In the mediating-variable theories the importance of personality resides in the ability to exploit opportunity, an ability that is conditioned by the existence of personal characteristics.

This mediating-variable approach to acculturation is exemplified by the theories of Kahl (1968), Inkeles and Smith (Inkeles, 1969; Smith & Inkeles, 1966), Doob (1960), and Dawson (1967, 1973). All of these theorists tend to treat the mediating personality as a complex of values, attitudes, and beliefs. And, in most applications of their theoretical position they have concentrated on efforts to measure that syndrome of modernization-tending traits. We will consider some of these efforts later, in a section on the measurement of modernism/traditionalism.

Personality as the Dependent Variable. A dependent-variable approach to the study of acculturation has not been popular, but it is the one Godwin (1974) advocates. Instead of certain "modern" attitudes and behavioral dispositions being treated as causing or helping the individual to produce social change, the individual dispositions would be treated as *consequences* of structural and cultural changes. If the acculturation model shown in Figure 7-1 is read from top to bottom and attention is focused solely on the downward-pointing solid-line arrows, this approach can be seen clearly.

Godwin considers such an approach promising for both theoretical and methodological reasons. He has argued that viewing changes in attitudes and values as the result of behavioral change is in line with the results of much empirical research by social psychologists. He has also argued that it is methodologically difficult to move backward and forward among different levels of analysis (personality, aggregated personality, social structure, and culture) and relatively easy to design tests of a structural change/behavior/ attitude paradigm.

One might ask how important it is whether attitudes "cause" behavior or behavior "causes" attitudes. It could matter for those who want to intervene in the modernization process. On the one hand, McClelland's efforts (McClelland & Winter, 1969) discussed in Chapter Six are predicated on the view that, if one changes attitudes toward personal achievement, behavioral changes will result that ultimately produce modernization at the societal level of analysis. The conception advocated by Godwin, on the other hand, would be more consonant with a policy of restructuring the social environment toward inducing modern behaviors, with the expectation that the appropriate attitudes will subsequently emerge. Be that as it may, Godwin's dependent-variable approach has as yet received little formal application to the study of societal modernization.

These three approaches to the study of modernization vary only in the role they assign to the individual in the modernization process. All three are subsumed by the general model depicted in Figure 7-1. They are alternative partial strategies for designing research on acculturation, rather than complete models of cultural change and acculturation. As Figure 7-1 suggests, a complete model must depict the interrelationships among environmental, social, cultural, and behavioral variables as complex and multilinear. For empirical research to be fruitful, however, it has to take one or another of the partial strategies as its paradigm. Whichever paradigm is employed, psychological research on acculturation will focus on individual behavioral variables, treating them either as independent, mediating, or dependent. A fundamental problem in all such psychological research, then, will be the measurement of these behavioral variables, and it is to this problem we now turn.

The Measurement of Individual Modernism

In this section we consider in detail several examples of attempts to define and measure individual differences in acculturation—that is, variations in individual responses to acculturative opportunities and pressures. Before we do so, however, it is well to discuss briefly some issues of terminology in order to understand just what is being measured.

Diversity of Terms in Acculturation Research. A wide variety of terms have been generated to describe societal change, particularly that occurring among so-called developing nations. Terms such as acculturation, civilization, Europeanization, Westernization, economic development, urbanization, industrialization, detribalization, assimilation, and modernization have particular connotations. But they have all been used to refer to changes in social, political, and economic environments. Often, the same terms are employed to refer to the behavior of individuals who live in those changing environments, and again the term employed carries with it certain emphases.

Some of the terms—especially *civilization, Europeanization, Westernization,* and, to a lesser extent, *modernization*—have a decided aura of ethnocentrism about them, used as they are primarily by Western social scientists studying the behavior of peoples "becoming like us." Similarly, the concept *detribalization* conveys negative affect to people living in some societies. These people contend that the concept *tribe* did not exist until anthropologists visited and—refusing to recognize nations because the societies had features different from those of the anthropologists' own nations—called them tribes. Terms such as *urbanization* and *industrialization*, though neither very ethnocentric nor offensive, seem limited and specialized in meaning. *Assimilation* also has a special usage, limited primarily to studies of immigrants becoming integrated into a host society. Hence, these various terms are employed by some and shunned by others. If used, they are differentially employed in different kinds of situations.

Yet there is a common thread running through them. At the societal level of analysis the terms refer to changes that we will henceforth in this chapter call *modernization*. These changes will include industrialization, urbanization, and other concomitants of sedentary, high-food-accumulating, cash-economy societies. A formal education system, mass communications, and a transportation network are all rapidly appearing nearly everywhere in the world and at an accelerating pace. The fact that such social and cultural features appeared earlier in Western societies is irrelevant for our present purposes. That they are replacing—for better or for worse—nonindustrial, rural, subsistence economies enables us to label the newly appearing features as modern. Our use of this label is meant to convey only the temporal fact of their recent appearance and spread. We do not consider modern as necessarily better, however much those people who are themselves modernizing might believe it to be.

When employed at the individual level of analysis, all of these terms refer to changes in behavior (and presumably underlying attitudes and habits) among people confronted with relatively far-reaching changes in their environments. Some people so confronted maintain some of their old, or traditional, ways of behaving; others adopt new, or modern, ways; and still others may adopt *marginal* behavior, a term meant to denote expressions of psychological stress. All three of these behavioral possibilities may occur in a single individual and are best thought of as defining end points along a continuum. We will employ the term *acculturation* to refer to the process of individual adjustment to changing circumstances and the terms *traditional* and *modern* (as in Figure 7-1) to define the primary continuum along which acculturation takes place.

Modernization, then, will be used in this chapter to refer, in a value-neutral way, to *social* change resulting primarily from cultural contact. Acculturation will be used to refer to the changes in *individual* behavior that accompany and are a part of modernization. As psychologists, we are more interested in acculturation (individual behavior) than in modernization (social change). And it is the measurement of acculturation, conceived basically as movement from traditional to modern behaviors, that is our immediate concern in this section.

Four Approaches to the Measurement of Acculturation

There have been several efforts to assess individual differences in acculturation. Four will be described here, two that stem primarily from a sociological interest in economic development (Kahl, 1968; Smith & Inkeles, 1966) and two originated by psychologists with an obvious interest in individual behavior (Doob, 1957, 1967; Dawson, 1967, 1969).

Kahl's "Modern Values." This approach derives from several assumptions about values:

1. Traditional and modern societies (an idealized dichotomy) differ in many ways, including division of labor, state of technology, degree of urbanization, type of economy, system of social stratification, education and communications, and—most significantly—values.

2. Values may be viewed either as affecting the social and economic development of a nation as a whole or as influencing the behavior of upwardly mobile individuals. Of particular interest in this regard are work-related values.

3. Values, while not directly observable, can be inferred from behavioral observations because they are the "central rules that explain the consistency of words and actions displayed by people under observation" (Kahl, 1968, p. 9).

4. Values, properly assessed, can differentiate among societal groups and can predict behaviors in particular situations.

5. Each traditional/modern value can be treated as a continuous variable that ranges from extreme traditionalism to extreme modernism, and each individual can be located on this continuum, based on his or her responses to questionnaire items.

The value concepts that Kahl chose to employ came from sociological theory—most notably the writings of Talcott Parsons (1951) and Florence Kluckhohn (1949–1950)—and from his own interviews with 25 Brazilians who were either traditional farm laborers or modern office managers. Some of his "modern" values (with their "traditional" counterparts in parentheses) are as follows:

Activism (fatalism). Humans, through science and technology, can control and change the world around them.

Occupational primacy (the primacy of other activities such as recreation). Career success is the highest goal.

Individualism (need for security in the form of close ties with work mates). Independence from work mates is stressed.

Participation in mass media (dependence on local gossip).

Having identified 14 value domains on an a priori basis, Kahl constructed a questionnaire of items that he hoped would reflect them. One statement designed to tap activism read "The secret of happiness is not expecting too much out of life, and being content with what comes your way." Strongly *disagreeing* with this statement constituted the most "modern" response to it.

Employing specific subgroups—for example, factory and white-collar workers—Kahl administered his questionnaire to more than 1300 male respondents in Brazil and Mexico. The outcome was that seven of the original 14 values, a core set reflecting modernism, intercorrelated in nearly identical fashion in both Mexico and Brazil. This suggests that Kahl's operational definition of modernism may be cross-culturally applicable.

Inkeles and Smith's "Overall Modernity." Alex Inkeles and David Smith (Inkeles, 1966, 1969, 1975; Smith & Inkeles, 1966; Inkeles & Smith, 1974) attempted to measure individual modernism and to relate it to certain institutional and experiential variables that play a prominent role in modernization theory. Like Kahl, they began with a conception of modern society as characterized by a complex of traits, including urbanization, high levels of education, and industrialization. They conceptualized the modern individual as one who has acquired behavioral dispositions that permit effective participation in such a society. Inkeles and Smith considered 20 themes potentially relevant to a definition of individual "modernity." Their conception of modernity rested on "thoroughly elaborated theory as to the qualities which modern settings are likely to generate, as well as considerations of personal attributes which are likely to best adapt a man to life in such institutional settings" (Smith and Inkeles, 1966, p. 359). Among the most influential of these settings they considered to be the industrial factory, as it both teaches and requires certain modern ways of arranging things, of thinking, and of feeling.

In *Becoming Modern* (1974), Inkeles and Smith detailed how the factory, through its institutional arrangements and mode of functioning, can be viewed as an agent in the socialization of the individual from traditional to modern. The factory setting provides the modeling, generalization, exemplification, and reward and punishment that operate in the socialization of the modern man.

These authors identified several additional modernism themes, including attitudes toward the family, religion, and social stratification. They also attempted to tap individual modernity from a behavioral perspective by including questions on what the respondents *knew* (information presumably acquired from having behaved in modern ways) and what they *did* (self-reported modern or traditional behavior). For example, respondents were asked to name three newspapers and to demonstrate their ability to read.

Inkeles and Smith administered their questionnaire to large samples of men, aged 18 to 32, in six developing countries: Argentina, Israel, Chile, India, East Pakistan, and Nigeria. In each country, subsamples were chosen to represent degrees of exposure to presumed modernizing influences. Two major groups were cultivators still living in a traditional rural community and former rural dwellers who had had at least three years of experience working in urban industrial factories. A third sample was migrants from the countryside who had just arrived in the city and who were not yet integrated into factory or bureaucratic work settings. A fourth sample, urban *non*industrial workers, was added to test for the effects of simply living in the city versus working in a factory. Additional subsamples based on varying factory experience, amount of education, and type of factory were employed in an effort to permit diverse tests of hypotheses about determinants and consequences of modernity.

Inkeles and Smith concluded that there is "a general factor or syndrome of individual modernity which influences or is reflected in the individual's response to the particular issue with which he is confronted in many different realms of life and in many diverse social relations" (1974, p. 98). Central to this syndrome are the following values and behavioral tendencies listed by Inkeles (1975):

(1) *Openness to new experience*, both with people and with new ways of doing things, such as attempting to control births; (2) the assertion of increasing *independence from the authority of traditional figures*, such as parents or priests, and a shift of allegiance to leaders of government, public affairs, trade unions, cooperatives, and the like; (3) belief in the *efficacy of science and medicine* and a general abandonment of passivity and fatalism in the face of life's difficulties; (4) ambition for oneself and one's children to achieve high *occupational and educational goals*; (5) preferences for punctuality and an interest in carefully *planning* one's affairs in advance; (6) strong interest in and an active participation in *civic and community affairs and local politics*; and (7) an energetic striving to keep up with the news and a preference for *national and international news* over accounts of sports, religion, or local affairs.

Inkeles and Smith asserted that this modernity syndrome was remarkably similar across their six national samples.

To validate their scale, they used the criterion-group method. By this method, the scale is found to be valid if it discriminates accurately between men who are known to be modern and those known to be traditional by some other independent criterion of modernity. According to their theory, men are made modern by certain experiences and exposure to certain influences. The authors could independently identify men who had had more and less of this exposure and experience. If they could show that those with more experience scored as more modern and those with less experience as more traditional, the scale could be considered valid.

Accordingly, Inkeles and Smith (1974) devised a summary index of modernization that was composed of ten main independent variables: years of education, years of urban residence, home/school modernity, mass-media exposure, consumer goods possessed, months of factory experience, father's education, residential urbanism, objective skill, and number of factory benefits.

Men with higher scores on this summary index could be expected to have higher scores on the scale. Inkeles and Smith found that their expectations were consistently met, both within each country and across the six countries.

Doob's Modernization Scales. In his book entitled, with wit and irony, *Becoming More Civilized* (1960), Leonard Doob reported research on acculturation in rapidly changing African societies.

Three questions guided Doob's investigations: (1) What differences can be identified among people in the old society who are having varying degrees of contact with the representatives of a new society? (2) What accounts for these differences? (3) Do these differences stem from psychological differences that were present before contact began, or is it the contact itself that produces such differences?

In his early studies (1957, 1960), Doob reported a large number of a priori and ad hoc hypotheses on how the conditions of culture contact and the characteristics of individuals experiencing it might influence differential learning. Contact was defined operationally as having had Western education or being a leader among one's people (presumably, African leaders have had more contact with Europeans and other modernizing agents). A few of Doob's hypotheses are illustrative: individuals with greater contact feel hostility toward Europeans, show antagonism to traditional authorities, are sensitive to other human beings, and are able to postpone gratification for the sake of future rewards. In these early studies Doob administered numerous tests to samples of African respondents who differed in degree of acculturative contact as he defined it.

In a later article (1967) Doob offered a set of scales devised to measure opinions and attitudes dealing with several modernization themes. Eight scales were designed to tap various modernization themes: (1) *temporal orientation,* an emphasis on the future rather than the present or past; (2) *government,* the belief that the country's present legal government has important beneficial functions to perform for its citizens; (3) *confidence and optimism,* the feeling that life in general is pleasant and that to a significant degree people control their destiny; (4) *patriotism,* strong feelings of attachment and loyalty to the country; (5) *science and determinism,* "correct" knowledge from a scientific viewpoint, and the deterministic conviction that many or most phenomena are intelligible and hence are not to be considered irrational or capricious; (6) *conception of people,* a nonparanoid, generous, trusting conception of human nature; (7) *politics and leaders,* approval of the country's leaders and their specific policies; and (8) *tribalism,* a tendency to deemphasize or discredit traditional values and practices.

Doob's eight scales were administered to 14 African samples characterized by various tribal affiliations, rural or urban residence, and differing educational experiences. Scores on the scales related primarily to education.

Dawson's Traditional versus Modern Attitudes. John Dawson (1973) proposed a multifactor theory of how attitudes change from traditional to modern. These factors included the type of environment and related subsistence economy, the type of socialization (severe or permissive), the degree of social stratification and presence or absence of authority systems, the nature and degree of modern contact, and the degree of culturally determined tolerance for cognitive inconsistency. Dawson viewed change from traditional to modern attitudes as an adaptive process in which the individual in a changing society tends to achieve consistency. His assumption was that attitudinal inconsistency is maladaptive to the individual and that there is pressure to reduce or eliminate it.

In order to measure attitude change in transitional situations—such as in Sierra Leone, the site of some of his research—Dawson developed the Traditional versus Modern Attitude Scale (1967). In general, he expected that individuals would be affected by such Western influences as education, economic change, and modern medicine. Dawson chose 18 concepts as representative of the social organization of Sierra Leone tribal groups. For each of these 18 themes Dawson constructed four statements to reflect traditional, semi-traditional, semimodern, and modern attitudes. Here are Dawson's (1967, p. 84) four statements referring to the concept of the gift:

Traditional
1. The traditional custom of making a gift to someone to welcome them, on special occasions, and for services to people binds people together and makes them friendly toward each other.

Semitraditional
2. The act of giving something to someone is in many ways very good, but it can be carried too far.

Semi-Western
3. Giving someone something has its place, but it can too easily become an endless chase for money and gifts.

Western
4. It should not be necessary to give someone something when he or she does something for you. It should be enough to say thank you; otherwise it might develop into bribery.

To validate his scales, Dawson administered them to three samples of Sierra Leonean men who had had varying exposure to Western influences —illiterate tribal villagers, illiterate mine workers, and mine apprentices with a secondary-school education. A fourth group of university students was also tested. As expected, the scores for the illiterate villagers were high on the Traditional subscale and progressively lower on the Semitraditional, Semi-Western, and Western subscales. By contrast, the university students obtained low Traditional subscale scores and progressively higher scores on the others. The two intermediary groups tended to score in between the villagers and the university students.

In more recent studies (1969, 1972, 1973) Dawson and his associates constructed similar traditional/modern scales for use with Australian aboriginal, Chinese, Japanese, and Eskimo respondent groups. For them, traditionalism/

modernism comprised somewhat *different* sets of attitudes. The traditional/ modern scales were constructed anew for each cultural group. This culture-specific approach of Dawson reflects his concern with the *ecological* and economic environments as factors influencing attitudes and values. Inkeles and Smith and Kahl, in contrast, seem more concerned with the influence of certain modernizing *institutions*, which can, in a sense, be transported across cultures. Dawson's study of traditionalism/modernism, then, is restricted to comparisons among subcultural groups within national and cultural boundaries and does not involve comparisons across countries.

The Cross-Cultural Comparability of Modernism

If the content of modernism varies from culture to culture, perhaps the measurement of modernism should be tailored to meet specific cultural definitions. This issue is an important one for the social scientist interested in studying modernization *cross-culturally*. Schnaiberg (1970) argued for defining modernism in an *absolute*, cross-culturally applicable fashion. Without an absolute definition, Schnaiberg argued, it is impossible to compare cultures in the search for similarities and differences in modernization on a cultural level.

Among the four approaches to the measurement of modernism we have just reviewed, those of Kahl and of Inkeles and Smith clearly reflected the position that Schnaiberg argued. Doob presented his scales in his 1967 article in order to encourage others to use them in cross-cultural studies in Africa; whether he would go so far as to say they are *universally* applicable is uncertain. Dawson, however, was less concerned with comparing the elements of modernism across national boundaries. Instead, his comparisons were restricted to those among cultural groups within a particular area. Despite Doob's and Dawson's less than universal approach to the measurement of modernism, their definitions were based on general theory.

In contrast, Stephenson (1968) argued that modernization is "the movement of persons or groups along a cultural dimension from what is *defined by the cultural norms* as traditional toward what is defined by the same culture as modern" (p. 268; emphasis added). If a particular cultural group does not make a distinction between what is traditional and what is modern, then measurement using an externally derived instrument is meaningless.

Stephenson questioned several assumptions made by those who have attempted to devise a universally applicable definition and measure of modernism: (1) that the modern/traditional distinction is universal across cultures; (2) that all modern cultures are basically similar in content and that all persons who can be said to be becoming modern share the same traits, regardless of their cultural membership or past circumstances; and (3) that change from traditional to modern does occur.

Stephenson developed a scale to measure modernism in a particular society, based on statements made by his Appalachian respondents about what *they* considered modern and traditional values and attitudes. These statements were then sorted by seven judges, knowledgeable in Appalachian culture, along a traditional/modern dimension. An initial 15 items were administered to 130 male and female respondents, and Stephenson settled on six items for his Modernism-Traditionalism Scale. His approach, of course, precludes cross-cultural comparison.

Inkeles and Smith's work is of interest in this regard, because they demonstrated a remarkable similarity in the *structure* of modernism across six rather diverse national samples—Argentina, Israel, Chile, India, East Pakistan, and Nigeria.

Moreover, after examining the work of other students of acculturation (or of "modernity," as Inkeles prefers to label it), Inkeles concluded in 1977 that there is a core of characteristics that properly defines an individual as modern. Inkeles asserted (1977, p. 144) that the core elements probably include "variants on the themes of fatalism, empathy, efficacy, innovativeness, flexibility, achievement orientation, information, . . . active citizenship . . . [and] stress, alienation, and anomie."

This list may, of course, result from several investigators' having sought—and hence measured—the same qualities. But Inkeles prefers to interpret the convergence of findings as real rather than as an artifact of shared methods.

The Emic/Etic Distinction Revisited. A compromise between a culture-specific definition of modernism (for example, by Stephenson) and a cross-culturally universal approach (for example, by Kahl, Inkeles, & Smith and Schnaiberg) can be found in a methodological suggestion made by Berry (1969) with regard to comparing behavior cross-culturally. According to Berry, the problem for a cross-cultural comparison of behavior is this:

> Ideally each behaviour system should be understood in its own terms; each aspect of behaviour must be viewed in relation to its behaviour setting (ecological, cultural and social background). It follows from this that the comparison of behaviour from different behaviour settings is essentially a false enterprise, for we are comparing incomparables [p. 122].

To resolve this dilemma, Berry suggested a three-step approach for comparing behavior across two or more cultures:

1. It must first be demonstrated that the behaviors to be compared are *functionally equivalent* in the two cultures. This means that the behaviors are seen to have developed in response to a problem shared by the two sociocultural groups, even though the behavior in one society may not appear to be related to its counterpart in the other society. According to Berry, "These functional equivalences must pre-exist as naturally occurring phenomena; they are discovered and cannot be created or manipulated by the cross-cultural

psychologist. Without this equivalence, it is suggested, no valid cross-cultural behavioural comparisons may be made" (1969, p. 122).

2. Then, existing descriptive categories and concepts can be applied to the behavior systems in a tentative way (the imposed etic approach), just as Kahl, for example, imposed theoretically derived Western categories onto the content of modernism in his Brazilian and Mexican cultures. But that is only a first approximation. The imposed etic must be modified to the extent that it becomes an adequate description *from within* each of the cultures being studied (the emic approach). Those categories that are shared can then be used to establish new ones that are valid for both systems and that can be expanded into universals (derived etic approach).

3. With a derived etic in hand, the researcher can then devise measuring instruments and techniques that will measure the behavior across cultures and that will meet the requirement of conceptual equivalence.

Berry's suggestion can be seen to be a compromise between the methods of those who want to measure modernism culture-specifically ("emicly") and those who want to measure it cross-culturally ("eticly"). It involves modifying and limiting one's theoretically derived and, perhaps, Western-oriented notions of what should constitute modernism to fit existent notions within the cultures being compared. The final compromise definition of modernism may not be as comprehensive as some might like, but it would be meaningful in all cultures under study. Whether there are any categories that can be found to apply to two or more cultures at the same time—that is, whether there are any value or attitude (or behavior) themes that define modernism/traditionalism in two or more cultures—is an empirical question.

Similarities and Differences in Definitions of Modernism. We have seen how in several separate research efforts the construct called modernism has been operationally defined. However sound each of the various definitions appears to be, it is clear that researchers differ in what aspects of reality they choose to emphasize.

There are, however, *some* similarities among the definitions of modernism in the literature. The following is a list of some common elements and the researchers who have identified them.

> Independence from traditional authority figures: Inkeles and Smith, Dawson
> Belief in the efficacy of science: Inkeles and Smith, Doob, Dawson
> Activism—abandonment of passivity and fatalism: Inkeles and Smith, Kahl, Adinolfi and Klein, Kiray
> Ambition for oneself and one's children: Inkeles and Smith, Kiray
> Interest in civic affairs: Inkeles and Smith, Schnaiberg
> Mass-media participation: Kahl, Schnaiberg
> Low integration with extended relatives: Kahl, Schnaiberg, Dawson
> Individualism: Kahl, Adinolfi and Klein, Dawson
> Emphasis on the future: Doob, Kiray

Trust in one's fellow humans: Kahl, Doob
Low valuation of traditional beliefs and practices: Doob, Dawson
Egalitarian attitude toward family role structure: Kahl, Schnaiberg, Dawson

Two other conceptions of what it is to be traditional and what it is to be modern are those of Foster and of Triandis:

1. Foster (1967) presented a limited-good model of the traditional peasant, who sees all desirable things in life as existing in absolute quantities that are insufficient to fill the needs of everyone. This world view inhibits behavior that would contribute to development. In contrast, there are those individuals who are innovators (who have done new things, such as buy a sewing machine or use chemical fertilizer). Innovators are motivated by the desire for economic profit and for new forms of prestige and status.

2. Triandis (1973) holds that modernism involves a relatively complex view of one's environment. More specifically, the modern individual is sufficiently differentiated in the universalistic forms of exchange (information, money, goods) and relatively less differentiated in the particularistic forms of exchange (love, status, services). The traditional individual is described oppositely.

Thus, we have seen both diversity and communality in various definitions of modernism and differences and similarities in approach to measuring it. On balance, there appears to be considerable agreement among students of acculturation that modernism is best assessed as a syndrome of attitudes, measured by verbal responses to items constructed partly emicly and partly eticly. All of the researchers discussed so far assume that modernism is a viable and measurable construct.

The Construct Validity of Modernism.[3] In his discussion of measuring modernism, Schnaiberg (1970) asked whether it should be treated as a single cluster of personal characteristics—as has been done by those who construct attitude questionnaires—or be broken into separate characteristics with different schedules of development. In other words, does the modernization process involve the simultaneous development of a whole set of identifiable modern traits? Or can it involve the development of some traits without others in a variety of possible patterns? Schnaiberg argued that a theoretical formulation of the modernization process that postulates the co-occurrence of several specific, individually held attitudes and values should be verified empirically.

Kahl's and Inkeles and Smith's approaches, it will be recalled, began with a theoretical definition of what components ought to make up the phenomenon called individual modernism. After measuring their respondents' attitudes and

---

[3]Construct validity, rather than predictive validity, is used almost without exception in the validation of modernism measures. A construct is a hypothetical variable, a syndrome of behaviors thought to be interrelated. Through construct validation, the researcher investigates the empirical reality of the construct—that is, whether or not the hypothesized relationships do in fact exist.

values with their theoretically derived indexes, they found it necessary to eliminate certain concepts from the list. The data simply did not fit their theoretical expectations. Schnaiberg argued that this approach is faulty in that there is no good *theoretical* explanation for the fact that some particular dimensions of modernism should be less well integrated into overall modernism. Unless the theoretically salient dimensions of modernism all covary highly, the concept of modernism, according to Schnaiberg, needs rethinking.

Jones (1977) agreed. She assessed the internal consistency of several modernity scales like those discussed earlier in this chapter and found that they each measure more than one factor. This suggests that a unidimensional concept of modernity does not accord with reality.

In a study of Turkish city and village women, Schnaiberg (1970) found that his own six theoretically derived dimensions of modernism—mass-media consumption, relatively few extended family ties, egalitarian family role structure, low religiosity, extended environmental orientation, and modern production and consumption behavior—did *not* covary equally highly. A factor analysis showed further that among these Turkish women one major factor of modernism was revealed—an emancipation factor.

Schnaiberg has concluded that, although there is some striking unity to what is called modernism and the modernizing process, there are instances that lack such unity, and the explanation is not a simple one. Further, the more specific the behavioral and social situations we want to analyze, the more we need to consider the possible variations in modernism. But the multifaceted nature of modernism may also be taken as a demonstration of the construct validity of the specific scale components. For example, there is a strong relationship in Smith and Inkeles' research between modern responses to items dealing with openness to new experiences, on the one hand, and modern responses to items dealing with the efficacy of science and medicine, on the other. This relationship points to a certain degree of construct validity of these two sets of items. Smith and Inkeles (1966, p. 360) had expected from a theoretical point of view that the two sets of verbal behaviors would be highly and positively correlated.

Further demonstration of construct validity can be accomplished by the "known-groups" method. In this procedure the instrument to be validated is administered to various groups of people who are known (by some other means) to differ in the attribute or behavior under consideration. If the instrument correctly discriminates among these groups of respondents, it can be said to be a valid instrument. Inkeles and Smith, as reported earlier, validated their scales by relating modernism scores to a ten-variable index, which included amount of education, years of urban residence, exposure to mass media, and so on. Dawson and, to some extent, Doob have similarly validated their scales.

The evidence on record from these and other researchers does warrant the conclusion that these several tests of modernism do measure an individual characteristic that can be theoretically related to several other individual and societal variables.

The Utility of Modernism Measures: Do They Predict Modern Behavior?

Modernism measures are useful only to the extent that they relate to behaviors that are of interest to the researcher. Unless modern attitudes reflect real behavioral tendencies, measuring them and demonstrating the measures' construct validity become little more than an academic exercise.

Dawson (1967) has stated that a comprehensive measure of traditional and Western attitudes is needed in order to study, for example, the differential acculturation, or adaptation, of "tribal" people to urban life. He defined this differential acculturation as a "process whereby individuals from different tribal groups, although exposed to similar levels of urban and Western influence, show varying degrees of adaptation to the new conditions and changes in attitudes and values, apparently due to initial differences in their tribal values and organization" (pp. 82–83).

The dependent variables for Dawson are differential adaptation to new conditions, on the one hand, and changes in attitudes and values, on the other. Few psychologists would deny that the more interesting of the two, from both theoretical and applied perspectives, is differential adaptation—that is, differential behavioral responses to modernization. Changes in attitudes and values are interesting primarily to the extent that they have implications for differential adaptation.

Too often, however, students of modernization (Dawson, 1969, included) have settled for assessing only the changes in attitudes and values without much concern for the differential behavioral adaptation. Triandis's work (for example, 1973) on modernity and economic development further illustrates this point. Having developed the construct of "cognitive complexity" as an index of modernity, he argued that with better instruments we should be able to specify which kinds of socialization and education lead to particular kinds of cognitive complexity (and particular forms of modernity). So far, however, more effort has gone into specifying the relationship between modernizing influences and cognitive complexity than between cognitive complexity and particular forms of modern behavior.

Identifying indisputably modern behaviors to relate to modernism is a difficult problem. The more general the attitudes and values that are tapped by an instrument, the more difficult it is to relate attitude-scale scores to specific behaviors.

Values and Success: Little Relationship. Adinolfi and Klein (1972) tried to relate traditional/modern values to more or less specific forms of behavior (that might be labeled modern and traditional). They tested the hypothesis that the value orientations of relatively successful, "coping" farmers in rural Guatemala would differ in interpretable ways from those of unsuccessful, poorly coping farmers.

They used an adaptation of the Harvard Values Orientation Scale, in which it is assumed that all members of a cultural group must orient themselves to one of a finite set of alternative modes of thinking and behaving with regard to certain pancultural human problems. According to the scale, a person's relation to other people is viewed as either lineal, collateral, or individualistic. People are seen as either subject to the whims of nature or in control over certain aspects of their natural environment. Emphasis is placed on the past, present, or future. And a stress is placed on either constructive activity or the attainment of leisure and passivity. The test itself presents situations and alternative responses that involve preference for a person who demonstrates one or more of these values in the situation. Coping effectiveness was measured with an index in which total income, amount of land worked, style of house inhabited, and degree of literacy were measured.

Adinolfi and Klein measured the values of those Guatemalan couples (with children between 6 and 14 years of age) who had the highest and the lowest scores on the coping effectiveness index. They found that, in general, the major value orientations of *all* the respondents (high- and low-coping couples) included being subject to the whims of nature, preferring an individualistic interpersonal orientation, focusing primarily on the present rather than the past or future, and stressing constructive activity. When high- and low-coping females were compared, no significant relationship between values and coping effectiveness was found. As for males, high "copers" were significantly more individualistic than the low copers, but no other significant differences were found. It appears that there is little relationship between at least some of the values used to distinguish traditional from modern attitudes and some supposedly related behaviors.

A fairly extensive study of the relationship between individual variables and societal modernization was made by Guthrie (1970) and his associates. They administered a long interview—part of which contained some of Smith and Inkeles's modernity items—to respondents identified as "big people" and "little people" in four towns (and their barrios) that varied in distance from Manila in the Philippines. Of the three independent variables—proximity to Manila, sex, and social status—only social status was found to be associated with differences in outlook. Big people (those who were better off economically) were more modern than little people. Interestingly, however, even a majority of little people had rather modern attitudes.

Guthrie argued that people with modern attitudes and values often maintain traditional patterns of behavior. Therefore, the correspondence between modernism, as currently defined and measured, and modern behaviors is less direct than some might expect, he contended. Guthrie was addressing his comments specifically to those who propose that traditionalism poses an obstacle to development or, conversely, that modernism leads to individual behaviors that contribute to development. Issues of causality aside, there is still little evidence to support even the less powerful proposition that modern attitudes *reflect* or *predict* modern behavior.

Attitudes and Behavior: No Easy Link. If we are ultimately interested in behavior, then perhaps the measurement of modern attitudes and values is too indirect. The cross-cultural research points strongly to Western education as a primary producer of modern attitudes (see, for example, Schnaiberg, 1970; Doob, 1960; Armer & Youtz, 1970). But perhaps learning to express oneself *as* a relatively modern individual is something very different from learning to behave in definably modern ways. It may be possible that an individual can acquire one without the other.

Several students of the modernization process have argued that individuals in transitional societies are able to compartmentalize their behaviors and attitudes comfortably into some that are modern and others that remain traditional. For example, Singer (1966) noted that the ability of many Indians to reconcile modern attitudes and behaviors in their workplace with traditional caste and religious beliefs and practices at home is difficult for the Westerner to comprehend. A person's behavior, it is felt, should be consistent from one realm to another. Indians, however, seemed to be much more tolerant of role conflict. Perhaps our Western expectation that people's verbal behavior and their other behavior be logically consistent is not so applicable elsewhere.

Behavioristic Approaches to the Study of Modernization

It may well be that trying to measure modern behavioral tendencies (and trying to explain their causes) indirectly by the measurement of attitudes of modernism may be a less promising strategy than was once thought. With respect to determining what causes development-related behavior, Guthrie (1970) wrote:

> Faced with the unproductive activities of many individuals in a poorly developed area, one is often prompted to ask, "Why don't they. . . ?" The answer often comes in a form which describes the behavior under consideration or invokes an inferred inner quality, "They don't because they are conservative, or ignorant, or poor." When they examine the matter further, we are led to conclude that there is no satisfactory answer to, "Why don't they. . . ?" There is no way to rule out alternative answers. A question which can, at least theoretically, be answered is "What changes need to be made so that they will. . . ?" In this way we are looking at behavior as determined by factors in the individual's history and his present environment. The latter, at least, can be manipulated in various ways to test the validity of an assertion that change in a given factor can lead to change in a specific cultural practice [p. 110].*

*From *The Psychology of Modernization in the Rural Philippines,* by G. M. Guthrie. Copyright 1970 by the Ateneo de Manila University Press. Reprinted by permission.

In his persuasive book, Guthrie argued in favor of an experimental approach to ferreting out the causes of that individual behavior that contributes to development. He proposed, for example, that Philippine barrios be randomly assigned to various types of development programs in order to determine which external conditions and reinforcement contingencies lead to particular forms of "modern," or "adaptive," behavior on the part of residents. Research like this, focused on behavior other than verbal expressions of attitude, would be a welcome trend.

Concluding Comments on the Measurement of Modernism

After reviewing many of the same attempts to measure individual modernism that we have considered at length here, Brislin, Lonner, and Thorndike (1973) commented that the modernism measurers "dealt with a 'traditional-modern' continuum as if everyone knows what it is" (p. 199). Our own review suggests that this is only partly true. Although many students of modernism indeed began with a priori conceptions of the characteristics of modern men and women, the scales they have emerged with were largely empirically determined. We saw that some reliably measurable aspects of modernism were unique to particular groups. But we also saw considerable communality in the content of modern values and attitudes—including independence from traditional authority figures, belief in the efficacy of science, personal ambition and achievement motivation, a future-looking temporal orientation, and similar points of view. That is an encouraging state of affairs to those who conceive of modernism as a pancultural dimension and who would try to measure it anywhere with a more or less standardized instrument. But even this empirical success must be viewed with caution. "Even the most rough instrument can yield data which can potentially force people into categories of [the investigator's] convenience, and not necessarily into categories that reflect reality" (Brislin, Lonner, & Thorndike, 1973, p. 200).

We have seen that some students of modernism have urged a more behavioral approach to its measurement. Rather than beginning with attitudes and values that seem a priori to be modern, one could instead start with a large sample of persons who are comparable in some ways (all members of a particular ethnic group residing in a particular "developing nation") and different in many others (degree of education, nature of occupation, and so on). Then, one could make numerous behavioral observations of all of them, including such "items" as how they spend their money, what they know, and how they spend their leisure time, as well as what they believe about a wide variety of issues. Each individual so observed would receive many scores that could later be summarized on the basis of an empirically determined weighting procedure, based on the interrelationships among all the items.

By this essentially classical psychometric procedure, the concept of modernism would be purely operationally defined, because it would be composed only of those items that interrelated. Its content would probably vary from behavior setting to behavior setting. But, as Doob properly pointed out in his pioneering work on the psychology of acculturation (1960), most of what we have to learn about modernism will best be based on observations made within societies, rather than on comparisons across societies.

However successful the measurement of modernism turns out to be, it is only a tool to be employed for the investigation of substantive hypotheses about the individual behavioral changes that accompany social modernization. In the next section of this chapter we will consider some studies that have this more substantive focus.

Some Empirical Studies of Modernism

On the Maintenance of Traditional Beliefs by Modernists

It has been observed that, not surprisingly, people who are becoming more modern in some ways retain many traditional behaviors and beliefs. One of the more interesting demonstrations of this phenomenon has been provided in a study of supernatural beliefs (witchcraft, ghosts, spirits, and so on) among Ghanaian university students (Jahoda, 1970). On seven of ten items designed to assess acceptance of such beliefs, a clear majority of 280 students expressed at least qualified acceptance.

But even more interesting—and considerably more enlightening—were Jahoda's findings relating acceptance of supernatural beliefs to age and to individual differences in modernism and field independence. With regard to age generally, younger students (less than 25 years of age) were found to hold more supernatural beliefs than older ones. Among the younger students modernism was not correlated with holding such beliefs. But among the older students the less modern ones were more likely to hold the traditional beliefs. Also, among the younger students the holding of supernatural beliefs was not correlated with field independence. But among the older ones the more field independent individuals were the ones who most often subscribed to traditional beliefs.

This complex pattern of age differences was explained by Jahoda as follows: First he noted that the older students, whose entry into the university was delayed, had received their earlier education at a time in Ghana's development when anything traditional was evaluated negatively by the modernizing elite. Hence, in that generation of modernizing Ghanaians only field-independent (nonconformist) individuals might be expected to hold on to traditional "superstitions." With a general increase in self-confidence in the next "generation" of Ghanaians, there developed a partial rejection of foreign values and a reassertion of indigenous ones. The intellectual climate changed, enabling younger Ghanaians, including more conformist ones, to express approval of traditional beliefs. In short, for the younger students, whether individually more modern or not, the holding of a belief in supernatural phenomena—*provided* the belief was perceived as traditionally Ghanaian—would be merely to subscribe to a prevailing norm.

Jahoda's observations and findings are a clear demonstration of what may be a pervasive phenomenon of modernization. Earlier, less sophisticated modernism may involve rejection of anything that smacks of tradition, whereas later, more sophisticated modernism may include a reassertion of indigenous values. Certainly his findings are consistent with this possibility.

On the Key Role of Formal Education

In their thorough review of psychological development in diverse cultures, Munroe and Munroe (1975) give prominence to the contrast between traditional and modern (Western-influenced) societies. They especially note developmental differences in cognition, competitiveness, achievement, and self-orientation, all of which they attribute to purposeful training. Much of this training occurs in socialization; but they note that socialization practices are supported by "special institutional arrangements," one of which is a formal educational system (p. 150).

Participation in a formal educational system is so obviously a means for acquiring modern behavioral dispositions that the amount of schooling thus far completed is often employed as an independent variable in research on individual differences in acculturation. In Doob's (1960) series of hypotheses comparing three categories of persons in modernizing nations—"the unchanged, the changing, and the changed" — the categories were in fact defined by amount of education.

In most so-called developing nations, whether a child enters the formal schooling programs (and in most such nations participation is both optional and costly) and how far the child progresses virtually determine which of two contrasting life-styles—traditional or modern—will be pursued during adulthood. Aspects of modernity impinge on nearly everyone in a modernizing society. But for those persons with no or little formal education such aspects remain essentially foreign. And for those with larger amounts of education almost the reverse is the case; for them, traditional practices are likely to seem foreign.

Generational gaps, while present in all societies, are nowhere more dramatic than in the developing nations, where it is common for students to report that it is nearly impossible to communicate with their uneducated parents.[4] In such settings school vacations are in many respects like a trip to a foreign land.

---

[4]Even *within* generations, communication difficulties between formally educated and nonformally educated individuals create striking problems of human relations. See, for example, Okot p'Bitek's (1966) dramatic poem, *Song of Lawino*, for an artistic insight into such problems in an East African setting.

Thus, it may be merely documenting the obvious to demonstrate that the amount of formal schooling correlates with individual modernism, but such documentation has been provided by several studies. LeCompte and LeCompte (1970) found that first-year secondary-school students in Turkey expressed more traditional attitudes than third-year students. Feldman (1972) reported a similar finding from Kenya. Dawson (1967, 1969), working with Sierra Leonean persons no longer in school, found that those who expressed the most traditional attitudes were those who had the least amount of education. Traditionalism declined as educational accomplishments increased, but only up through secondary education. (Individuals who had been to college expressed *more* traditional attitudes than those who had stopped at secondary school, a finding that is interesting to relate to the findings of Jahoda, 1970, in Ghana, reviewed in the preceding section of this chapter.)

It would obviously be reasonable to expect that, if a school in a developing country is managed and staffed by persons from a more modern one, the impact of education on the students' modernism would be enhanced. LeCompte and LeCompte in their (1970) study in Turkey compared girls attending an American missionary school with girls attending a Turkish government school and found higher scores on a modernism scale among the former.

Sex Differences. Some provocative sex differences in modernism and some interesting interactions between sex and education have also been reported. To understand them, it is perhaps well to note first that females in developing countries are in general more sheltered than males and less likely to be schooled—or, if schooled, more likely to drop out at a lower level. By the same token a modernizing experience, as is epitomized by formal education, is likely to be a more dramatically liberating experience for females, provided that the effects of the education are not effectively counteracted by traditional, authoritarian upbringing.

Some relevant findings include those of Omari (1960), who found female secondary students in Ghana to express more modern attitudes toward marriage and family than male students. Doob (1960) reported more modern attitudes among females than among males for both Zulu and Jamaican respondents to his acculturation measures. Feldman (1972), working among the Gusii in Kenya, also found that female secondary-school students expressed more modern attitudes.

On the other hand, in a study of "superstitions" among Lebanese Arab students in Beirut, Za'rour (1972) found female secondary students to be more superstitious than male students, particularly among those of the Moslem faith. Za'rour suggested that these sex differences could be explained by the fact that girls are more exposed than boys to traditional beliefs and practices maintained by uneducated female elders and that all women, even educated ones, remain largely under male domination in this essentially conservative and authoritarian culture.

Language as a Factor. Formal schooling usually employs a Western language (notably English or French) as the medium of instruction. Thus, not only the content of education produces modernizing but also, perhaps, the language in which it occurs. When individuals acquire the modern language while retaining their traditional one, they may even hold contrasting sets of attitudes, each couched in a different language.

Indeed, there is some evidence, not wholly consistent, that educated persons express different degrees of modernism depending on the language of the questionnaire by which their attitudes are assessed. This was the case in a study by Doob (1957) of bilingual Ganda, Luo, Zulu, and Afrikaaner respondents in Uganda and South Africa. When queried in their native language (as were a randomly selected half of Doob's respondents), individuals in all four of these ethnic groups assented more to questionnaire items designed to tap traditional values. However, Doob (1958) did not replicate this finding in Jamaica. Botha (1968) found the language-of-questionnaire effect for bilingual Arabic-French students in Lebanon but did not find it for bilingual Arabic-English students in the same country. Feldman (1972) found among the more modern of his Gusii secondary-school students in Kenya that those who received a questionnaire in their traditional language expressed more traditional attitudes. This was not the case for less modern-scoring students, however, for whom the language of the questionnaire did not matter.

While these findings concerning the language of the modernism question-naire are primarily of methodological interest, they do support a substantive hypothesis like that suggested by Botha (1968). He suggested that language carries with it a set of cultural values that the language user necessarily adopts, even inadvertently, whenever the language is used. Hence, not only what is learned in school but also the language in which it is learned may contribute importantly to the modernizing effect of formal education. In any event, there can be little doubt that formal education is a key factor in individual modernism. Many other factors contribute, but no other single one is of similar import.

On Conflict and Acculturative Stress

One of the oldest and most widely accepted generalizations about acculturation, among laypersons and specialists alike, is that individuals exposed to a rapidly changing culture find that exposure psychologically disruptive. Subjected often to conflicting values—for example, modern ones at school, traditional ones at home—they are thought to be living a schizophrenic-like existence in two conflicting cultures or, as it is sometimes metaphorically expressed, in two different historical periods. The image of *The Lonely African* (Turnbull, 1962), poised precariously with one foot in the pre-European-contact 19th century and the other in a heavily European-influenced present day, is a case in point.

Such pictures of acculturative stress are probably exaggerated and ethnocentric. They ignore the fact that, to many individuals experiencing culture change, elements of the contact culture are often not even perceived as foreign, because they have "been there" throughout the lifetimes of those individuals. Consider, for example, pizza pie and frankfurters. To most American children these seem to be indigenous aspects of their culture, not the foreign imports that they in fact are. Similarly, to the educated, affluent Kenyan dwelling in the burgeoning metropolis of Nairobi, skyscrapers, traffic jams, movies, radio and television, Kentucky Fried Chicken—and, yes, even pizza pie and frankfurters—seem indigenously Kenyan. So, in any culture-contact situation, elements of culture originating from outside may often very easily be assimilated, with no disruptive consequences necessarily flowing from them.

Still, the potential for some conflict and acculturative stress must exist in every culture-contact situation, particularly when the "old" and "new" cultural elements relate to contradictory values. When traditional parental values contradict values conveyed in formal educational settings, first-generation schooled individuals may certainly be expected to display manifestations of attitude conflict. Some of Dawson's research in Hong Kong relates to this issue (see, for example, Dawson, Whitney, & Lau Tak-san, 1972). Another form of stress that has often been reported is "culture-shock" among medium-term visitors to a foreign land (such as Peace Corps volunteers). Spradley and Phillips (1972) reported an interesting study of self-reports of volunteers concerning foreign values to which they found difficulty adjusting.

But surely acculturative stress varies as a function of (1) the acculturative pressures brought to bear on a community, (2) certain traditional features of that community, and (3) certain characteristics of individuals. That these cultural and individual variables must be taken into account in an attempt to predict when and how culture contact may be stressful was argued cogently by Berry and Annis (1974). Just as we have done here, these authors argued that it is not correct to expect that culture contact always produces acculturative stress.

Conditions Associated with Stress. Empirical research to determine the cultural and individual variables that relate to acculturative stress is clearly called for. Berry and Annis in their 1974 paper reported one such study done among three Amerindian groups in Canada, the high-food-accumulating Tsimshian, the medium-food-accumulating Carrier, and the low-food-accumulating Cree. Relatively traditional and relatively acculturated samples from each of these groups were studied. Berry and Annis's first hypothesis concerned points (1) and (2) enumerated above: acculturative stress would be greater in communities where the gap between tradition and the imposed culture (in this case, Euro-Canadian) was greater. As they put it, "The psychological distress is . . . a function of the length of the journey and the insistence that the journey be undertaken" (p. 388).

With regard to this hypothesis, they found evidence for some acculturative stress (assessed by different measures, including a psychosomatic-symptom checklist, a "marginality" scale, and a "deviance" scale) in all Amerindian communities, compared with a sample of Euro-Canadians residing in a small Euro-Canadian village (Westport, Ontario). But the patterning of differences *among* the Amerindian communities supported the hypothesis. Most acculturative stress was found in the Cree, whose traditional life-style is most discrepant from that of Euro-Canadian culture.

Berry and Annis's second hypothesis concerned individual differences. They reasoned that individuals who for whatever reason had attained a degree of separateness from their traditional fellows and an independent cognitive style (psychological differentiation) would be less susceptible to the stresses of culture contact. Data bearing on this hypothesis were partly paradoxical. *Across* samples, the Cree were on the average more psychologically differentiated and, as we just saw, more subject to acculturative stress than the other two groups. *Within* all samples, however, the more psychologically differentiated (field-independent) individuals were the least susceptible to acculturative stress. Thus, Berry and Annis's two hypotheses received empirical support. And a beginning has been made toward understanding the conditions, both at the cultural and individual levels of analysis, under which stress is to be expected in a culture-contact situation.

Before leaving this topic, it should be noted that the psychiatric literature has long dealt with possible relationships involving cultural factors and mental illness. This literature contains some evidence of an association, *possibly* causal in nature, between cultural change and mental illness. For example, Bloom (1973), working among Eskimo psychiatric patients, found most of them to be women migrants, neurotically affected by conflicting values. Similar studies have been reported from New Guinea (Burton-Bradley, 1973), Malaysia (Hartog, 1973), Australia (Kiloh, 1975), and other places where migration from a traditional to a modern setting is a common phenomenon. But the interpretation of findings in such studies is an exceedingly subjective matter, and the proposition that culture conflict *causes* mental illness is an extremely dubious one.

Psychological Concomitants of Nationalism

One way in which modernization is occurring in many parts of the world involves the creation of nation-states, relatively large and complex geopolitical entities composed of many smaller, often tribal, units. As Doob (1962) pointed out, the continent of Africa (in its sub-Saharan portion alone) contains approximately 700 traditional societies structurally integrated into fewer than 50 nations. For individuals to function effectively as citizens of such nations requires the acquisition of behavior patterns different from those that enabled them to perform adaptively as members of small traditional societies, linked by kinship, language, common life-styles, and other similarities.

One fundamental change required involves the acquisition of a sense of loyalty to the nation and an identification with it. With regard to Africa, Doob (1962) suggested "It is most difficult to create this psychological groundwork for nationalism, for distinctive qualities must come to be associated with the synthetic entity of the nation, loyalty must be aroused and deep convictions must be stirred" (p. 152). Such feelings certainly exist with regard to the traditional society, within which one finds compatriots who are so similar that it is easy to identify with them. Nations, on the other hand, do not correspond with ethnicity. In Africa nations are often composed of many such groups, and their boundaries—in many cases drawn by outsiders meeting in political confer-ences—cut across ethnic territories. Identification with the nation, then, takes time and requires individual changes in attitudes.

Kelman (1976) defined nationalism as an ideology that provides a justification for the creation or existence of a nation-state, a definition of its particular population, and a prescription of the relationship of its included individuals to that state. Kelman recognized that often a population is considered a nation only by virtue of the fact that it is part of the state, not because the population is an already interrelated group of people aware of their interrelationship. When the population is ethnically diverse, a process of nation building must go on. Moreover, as Kelman put it, "The mere existence of common cultural elements among members of a collectivity is not enough to define them as a nation. They must also have the consciousness that these common elements represent special bonds that tie them to one another" (1976, pp. 9–10).

In this, Kelman echoed views expressed years before by one of the founders of social psychology, Floyd Allport, who asserted: "The main criteria of nationality are psychological. There are certain traditions, historical perspec-tives, and principles possessed in common by the members of every national group which are both the evidence and the substance of their nationality. If an individual shares these ideas with the others of his group, and like the others is loyal to them, he belongs to their nation" (1933, p. 138).

The psychological counterpart to national ideology, then, is national consciousness. Numerous political scientists and psychologists have theorized about both the social forces required to stimulate national consciousness and the psychological forces it taps. With regard to the latter issue, Kelman (1976) proposed that two powerful psychological dispositions—the need for self-protection and the need for self-transcendence—together can compose the motivational basis for individual identification with a nation-state. At the social level, political leadership and institutional forces of one kind or another are required to mobilize those psychological dispositions and to mold them into national consciousness. How best to create national consciousness is an intriguing question for which few answers yet exist.

A Case Study of Nationalism in Sub-Saharan Africa

Individual reactions to nation-building efforts in a new African nation were studied by Segall, Doornbos, and Davis (1976) during Uganda's first decade of national independence. The study was an attempt to examine, at the individual level of analysis, the possible emergence of national identity.

Nation building, as we have just seen, is a sociopolitical process that merely begins with the declaration of national independence. It also involves a psychological process that must take place in the minds of many individuals. Less obvious perhaps than the political and economic aspects of nation building, its psychological components are nevertheless fundamental. A nation is not merely a geopolitical fact; it is also a state of mind.

Segall, Doornbos, and Davis studied the self-identification patterns of several hundred men in one traditional society that is part of Uganda, which had attained its political independence in 1962. The persons studied were all Banyankore, a distinct Ugandan subgroup united by language (one of many spoken in Uganda) and many customs (some of them unique to Banyankore). Throughout most of their lifetimes the Banyankore had been officially designated subjects in a kingdom—Ankole.

The questions addressed by the research included: What changes in self-perception occur as the Banyankore become integrated into Uganda? What personal events correlate with the acceptance of national citizenship? What tactics available to central-government leaders foster national integration? Is suppression of traditional identity frames, as in the abolition of a so-called "tribal" monarchy, effective? Does national integration require a decline in "primordial" group identity?

The research was begun in 1965 and continued until 1968. During that period Uganda's central government enacted a constitution that provided the opportunity for a natural experiment—an effort to measure its effects by comparing data from before and after the constitution was instituted. The same survey instrument was employed in both cases.

Both surveys involved a face-to-face interview with samples of Banyankore men, 227 before 1967 and 115 after. The form and content of the interview were dictated by relevant characteristics of Ankole society.

The Primacy of Banyankore Identity. Respondents were given several opportunities to reveal how they thought of themselves. These opportunities encompassed a number of question formats, ranging from open-ended to highly structured inquiries. "Munyankore" (a person of Ankole) was a consistently popular response over all item formats.

When, at the outset of the interview, respondents were asked simply "What are you?" approximately 40% first said "I am a Munyankore" (34% in the first survey and 46% in the second). The only response to exceed "Munyankore" in popularity was "I am a person," and then only in the first wave. If the first response to "What are you?" is the best index of salience of reference terms, *Munyankore* stands out in bold relief as the single most salient aspect of social identity. In addition, respondents were encouraged to give as many answers as they liked. Considering *all* responses, more people said "Munyankore" than anything else (approximately 60% of the samples).

Munyankore might be expected to be a rare response to a question designed to elicit normative attitudes. When asked "How should the Banyankore think of themselves?" most respondents (over 60%) said "as Ugandans." Nevertheless, about 25% of them said that they *should* think of themselves as Banyankore (24% in the first survey and 27% in the second). Clearly, then, most Banyankore seemed to think of themselves as Banyankore, and a surprisingly large number justified thinking of themselves as such.

In more structured portions of the interview, where they were asked to rank all applicable descriptive terms, they ranked *Munyankore* so high that this term earned the highest composite rank in both surveys. Regardless of how the question was posed, *Munyankore* is what most people seemed to consider themselves.

Another clear conclusion was that few Banyankore had by 1968 come to think of themselves as Ugandan. Hardly anyone said that he was a Ugandan in response to "What are you?" The phrase "I am a Ugandan" can hardly be said to have been on the tongue tip of the typical Munyankore.

On the other hand it is equally clear that the Banyankore know that they are Ugandan, that they ascribe "importance" to that status, and that most of them acknowledge the propriety of thinking of themselves as Ugandan. About two-thirds of all respondents said that Banyankore *should* think of themselves as *Ugandan*, and both samples gave high ratings to Ugandan on both the ranking and pair-comparison tasks. Indeed, these ratings were about as high as those given to *Munyankore*. So, the typical Munyankore man seemed to know that it was appropriate to identify as a Ugandan and value his Ugandanness as a status to be accorded value, but he had yet to think of himself *as* a Ugandan.

Individual Differences in Identity in Ankole. It appeared reasonable to the authors of this study that "sense of Ugandanness" might be positively correlated with educational level. But *Ugandan* was not systematically related to educational level. Rather, the better educated Banyankore were more *personalistic*. In response to "What are you?" lesser educated respondents tended to say "I am a Munyankore" and better educated respondents said either "I am a person" or cited their occupations. With increasing education there was a decline in salience of *Munyankore* but no change in salience of *Ugandan*. It was concluded that the more exposure a man has to broadening influences, the less investment he makes in his corporate identity—whether "tribal" *or* national—and the more he thinks of himself as a unique personality. Accordingly, it appears that education per se cannot be expected to make national identity more salient.

Education related to rankings in some surprising ways. *Ugandan* was ranked higher by better educated respondents than by lesser educated respondents, but so was *Munyankore*. Thus, a sense of Munyankoreness and a sense of Ugandanness seemed not to be in psychological opposition. With increased levels of education, *both* terms were given higher rankings.

The authors concluded that education enhances awareness of the importance of the nation but doesn't reduce the judged importance of the "tribal" reference term. The educated man does not trade one group identity for another but, rather, discovers himself in the process of becoming enlightened. This might be due to the fact that education as practiced thus far in developing nations like Uganda has been a privilege enjoyed by a select few, one that drastically enhances one's economic and social potential. High achievement academically has meant entry into the elite, and the prestige accompanying that status would, not surprisingly, reinforce personalistic thinking. As educational opportunities increase, increased national identity might well become a major by-product of education.

Persistence of Banyankore Identity. If the abolition of the Ankole monarchy and other features of the 1967 constitution were intended to lessen the Banyankore's sense of identity as Banyankore, those tactics failed. In the post-1967 survey, the Banyankore revealed that they were at least as conscious of their Ankole identity as they had been prior to the 1967 constitutional change. The salience of Munyankoreness (as assessed by first responses to "What are you?") was even *greater* in 1968 than prior to 1967. The salience of Ugandanness remained stable—and very low. The awareness of the desirability of "thinking Ugandan" (as assessed by responses to "How should the Banyankore think of themselves?") was not greater after 1967 than it had been before 1967.

Ranking and pair-comparison data revealed no interwave differences, either. *Munyankore* was ranked highest in both waves, with *Ugandan* ranked near it both times. No significant differences in scale value resulted from interwave comparisons.

Thus, there was no evidence that Banyankoreness declined or that Ugandanness increased during the months following the enactment of the 1967 constitution. The removal of the tribal king did not result in a decline of traditional identifications.

Nothing in the data suggested that the Banyankore will ever become anything but hyphenated Ugandans. But it also appears that the strength of their identity as Banyankore is not an impediment to national integration. As the one grows, so might the other. This conclusion suggests some propositions for leaders who would seek to encourage nationalism without conflicting with the dynamics of personal identity in a new nation composed of salient, tribal subgroups.

Some Implications for Nation-Building Leadership. Group attachments are mirrored in the social self. Any relationship in which an individual is involved—whether with family, fellow congregationists, coworkers, nation, or language group—contributes to self-identity. But some attachments are more meaningful than others.

Social identity has often been considered a problem in new states because people's basic identifications are with subnational units, such as linguistic, ethnic, racial, or regional collectives. It is implied that a lack of national identity may have serious consequences for the state. Where there is no considerable feeling of belonging to the national framework, it is argued, the state may lack the necessary cohesion even for the smooth functioning of routine governmental operations.

In Africa, particularly, subnational identities are considered to be of considerable tenacity. This, it is now eminently clear, proved to be the case for the Banyankore in Uganda. Subnational identities there are rooted in Ankole ethnicity and involve profound attachments. One might therefore fear that subnational units all over Africa will outlive the national structures superimposed on them. Europe has known cases where such ethnic attachments have continued to be of pervasive impact—in Northern Ireland, for example—and there is no a priori basis for ensuring that the process will be any different in Africa. On the contrary, because overarching governmental structures are relatively new in Africa and subnational structures well established, there is ample reason to expect subnational identities to persist.

However, one can challenge the view that primordial attachments must be severed in order to produce integration into new membership units. Leaders of many new states in Africa encourage their people to think of themselves as citizens of these states *rather than* as members of particular sectional groups. Some leaders have even constitutionally forbidden any reference to ethnic membership. And scholars have frequently echoed these proscriptions. But in the view of Segall and his associates the very findings that have led to such policies—namely, evidence of the potency of ethnic identities—are justification enough for questioning these strategies. To argue that it would be either possible *or* necessary for the Banyankore to become assimilated to the extent that they are no longer Banyankore is probably incorrect. The research suggests that it would be wrong to opt for *assimilation* (which presupposes a blurring of constituent cultures) instead of *integration* (which does not).

Summary and Conclusions

In this chapter we have been concerned primarily with the influence of cultural *change* on behavior. All cultures are constantly changing, and all people are thus faced with the need to adapt their behaviors to suit new conditions in their social environment. But we concentrated primarily on newer nations, where intercultural contact of one kind or another has set the stage for rapid and profound acculturative influences. Our focus was on developing modernism, that psychological process by which individuals acquire behavior patterns that seem necessary for coping in the technologically developing nation-states in which more and more of the world's population lives.

We considered some basic generalizations about cultural change and some theories of the psychological changes that accompany it. We examined several approaches to the measurement of individual modernism and reviewed a few examples of empirical research relating individual differences in modernism to education and other potential modernizing forces.

In the final section of the chapter we considered the psychology of nation building, primarily by reviewing one case study that showed that a sense of national identity can develop—however slowly—alongside more ethnically rooted "primordial" identities.

If there is a central theme in the diverse content of this chapter, it is that human beings are remarkably flexible. Although their personalities are shaped from early childhood by socialization—with the result that they internalize the values and norms of their own more primary groupings—they can also acquire new responses as the culture around them changes. Value conflicts and acculturative stress sometimes result, but they are the exception, not the rule. As was true of the studies of the Banyankore-Ugandans (Segall et al., 1976) and of the Ghanaian university students (Jahoda, 1970), there is apparently room in any person's psychological makeup for alternative values, ideas, and attitudes, just as long as the alternatives are not unavoidably conflicting.

People's culture, then, regardless of the origin or age of its components, is something to which they relate positively and from which they derive guidance for their own attitudes and behaviors.

In the next chapter we will consider people's relationship to cultures perceived of as *not* their own. As we shall see, in-group and out-group attitudes are but two sides of the same coin.

References

Adinolfi, A., & Klein, R. The value orientations of Guatemalan subsistence farmers: Measurement and implications. *Journal of Social Psychology*, 1972, *87*, 13–20.

Allport, F. *Institutional Behavior*. Chapel Hill: University of North Carolina Press, 1933.

Armer, M., & Schnaiberg, A. Measuring individual modernity: A near myth. *American Sociological Review*, 1972, *37*, 301–316.

Armer, M., & Youtz, R. Formal education and individual modernity in an African society. *American Journal of Sociology*, 1970, *76*, 604–626.

Berry, J. W. On cross-cultural comparability. *International Journal of Psychology*, 1969, *4*, 119–128.

Berry, J. W. Psychology of social change. In H. Triandis & R. Brislin (Eds.). *Handbook of Cross-Cultural Psychology* (Vol. 5). Boston: Allyn & Bacon, 1979.

Berry, J. W., & Annis, R. C. Acculturative stress: The role of ecology, culture and differentiation. *Journal of Cross-Cultural Psychology*, 1974, *5*, 382–406.

Bloom, J. Migration and psychopathology of Eskimo women. *American Journal of Psychiatry*, 1973, *130*, 446–449.

Botha, E. Verbally expressed values of bilinguals. *Journal of Social Psychology*, 1968, *75*, 159–164.

Brislin, R. W., Lonner, W. J., & Thorndike, R. W. *Cross-Cultural Research Methods*. New York: Wiley, 1973.

Burton-Bradley, B. G. New Guinian psychiatry and acculturation. *International Journal of Social Psychiatry*, 1973, *19*, 44–49.

Dawson, J. L. M. Traditional vs. Western attitudes in West Africa: The construction, validation, and application of a measuring device. *British Journal of Social and Clinical Psychology*, 1967, *6*, 81–96.

Dawson, J. L. M. Attitude change and conflict among Australian aborigines. *Australian Journal of Psychology*, 1969, *21*, 101–116.

Dawson, J. L. M. Effects of ecology and subjective culture on individual traditional-modern attitude change, achievement motivation, and potential for economic development in the Japanese and Eskimo societies. *International Journal of Psychology*, 1973, *8*, 215–225.

Dawson, J. L. M., Whitney, R. E., & Lau Tak-san, R. Attitude conflict, GSR, and traditional-modern attitude change among Hong Kong Chinese. *Journal of Social Psychology*, 1972, *88*, 163–176.

Doob, L. W. An introduction to the psychology of acculturation. *Journal of Social Psychology*, 1957, *45*, 143–160.

Doob, L. W. The effect of Jamaican Patois on attitude and recall. *American Anthropologist*, 1958, *60*, 574–575.

Doob, L. W. *Becoming More Civilized: A Psychological Exploration*. New Haven, Conn.: Yale University Press, 1960.

Doob, L. W. From tribalism to nationalism in Africa. *Journal of International Affairs*, 1962, *16*(2), 144–155.

Doob, L. W. Scales for assaying psychological modernization in Africa. *Public Opinion Quarterly*, 1967, *31*, 414–421.

Feldman, R. H. *The effect of education on traditional-modern attitudes among the Gusii of Kenya*. Unpublished thesis, Syracuse University, 1972.

Foster, G. M. *Tzintzuntzan: Mexican Peasants in a Changing World*. Boston: Little, Brown, 1967.

Geertz, C. The integrative revolution: Primordial sentiments and civil politics in the new states. In C. Geertz (Ed.), *Old Societies and New States*. Glencoe, Ill.: Free Press, 1963.

Godwin, R. K. Two theory theoretical triangles: The relationships between personality variables and modernization. *Journal of Developing Areas*, 1974, *8*, 181–198.

Guthrie, G. M. *The Psychology of Modernization in the Rural Philippines*. Institute of Philippines Culture Papers, No. 8. Quezon City: Ateneo de Manila University Press, 1970.

Guthrie, G. M. A social-psychological analysis of modernization in the Philippines. *Journal of Cross-Cultural Psychology*, 1977, *8*, 177–206.

Hagen, E. E. *On the Theory of Social Change*. Homewood, Ill.: Dorsey Press, 1962.

Hartog, J. 96 Malay psychiatric patients: Characteristics and preliminary epidemiology. *International Journal of Psychiatry*, 1973, *19*, 49–59.

Heilbroner, R. L. *An Inquiry into the Human Prospect*. New York: Norton, 1975.

Inkeles, A. The modernization of men. In M. Weiner (Ed.), *Modernization: The Dynamics of Growth*. New York: Basic Books, 1966. Pp. 138–150.

Inkeles, A. Making men modern: On the causes and consequences of individual change in six developing countries. *American Journal of Sociology*, 1969, *75*, 208–225.

Inkeles, A. *Individual modernity in different ethnic and religious groups: Data from a six-nation study*. Paper presented at the Conference on Issues in Cross-Cultural Research, New York Academy of Sciences, New York, October 1975. (Mimeographed)

Inkeles, A. Understanding and misunderstanding individual modernity. *Journal of Cross-Cultural Psychology*, 1977, *8*, 135–176.

Inkeles, A., & Smith, D. H. *Becoming Modern*. Cambridge, Mass.: Harvard University Press, 1974.

Jahoda, G. Supernatural beliefs and changing cognitive structures among Ghanaian university students. *Journal of Cross-Cultural Psychology*, 1970, *1*, 115–130.

Jones, P. A. The validity of traditional-modern attitude measures. *Journal of Cross-Cultural Psychology*, 1977, *8*, 207–239.

Kahl, J. *The Measurement of Modernism: A Study of Values in Brazil and Mexico*. Austin: University of Texas Press, 1968.

Kelman, H. D. Social psychology and national development: Background of the Ibadan Conference. *Journal of Social Issues*, 1968, *24*(2), 9–20.

Kelman, H. D. *Sources of attachment to the nation-state: An analysis of the social-psychological dimensions of nationalism*. Third Annual Floyd Allport Lecture, The Maxwell School, Syracuse University, 1976.

Kiloh, L. G. Psychiatry among the Australian aborigines. *British Journal of Psychiatry*, 1975, *126*, 1–10.

Kiray, M. B. Values, social stratification and development. *Journal of Social Issues*, 1968, *24*(2), 87–100.

Kluckhohn, F. R. Dominant and substitute profiles of culture and orientation: Their significance for the analysis of social stratification. *Social Forces*, 1949–1950, *28*, 376–393.

LeCompte, W., & LeCompte, G. Effects of education and intercultural contact on traditional attitudes in Turkey. *Journal of Social Psychology*, 1970, *80*, 11–21.

Lerner, D. *The Passing of Traditional Society: Modernizing the Middle East*. Glencoe, Ill.: Free Press, 1958.

McClelland, D. C. *Motivational Trends in Society*. New York: General Learning Press, 1971.

McClelland, D. C., & Winter, D. G. *Motivating Economic Achievement*. Glencoe, Ill.: Free Press, 1969.

Munroe, R. L., & Munroe, R. H. *Cross-Cultural Human Development*. Monterey, Calif.: Brooks/Cole, 1975.

Omari, T. P. Changing attitudes of students in West African society toward marriage and family relationships. *British Journal of Sociology*, 1960, *11*, 197–210.

Pareek, U. A motivational paradigm of development. *Journal of Social Issues*, 1968, *24*(2), 115–122.

Parsons, T. *The Social System*. New York: Free Press, 1951.

p'Bitek, O. *Song of Lawino*. Nairobi, Kenya: East African Publishing House, 1966.

Pye, L. W. *Aspects of Political Development*. Boston: Little, Brown, 1966.

Schnaiberg, A. Measuring modernism: Theoretical and empirical explanations. *American Journal of Sociology*, 1970, *76*, 399–425.

Segall, M. H. Acquiescence and "identification with the aggressor" among acculturating Africans. *Journal of Social Psychology*, 1963, *61*, 247–262.

Segall, M. H., Doornbos, M., & Davis, C. *Political Identity: A Case Study From Uganda*. Syracuse, N.Y.: Maxwell Foreign and Comparative Studies/East Africa XXIV, 1976.

Singer, M. The modernization of religious beliefs. In M. Weiner (Ed.), *Modernization: The Dynamics of Growth*. New York: Basic Books, 1966. Pp. 55–67.

Smith, D. H., & Inkeles, A. The OM Scale: A comparative socio-psychological measure of individual modernity. *Sociometry*, 1966, *29*, 353–377.

Spradley, J. P., & Phillips, M. Culture and stress: A quantitative analysis. *American Anthropologist*, 1972, *74*, 518–529.

Stephenson, J. B. Is everyone going modern? A critique and a suggestion for measuring modernism. *American Journal of Sociology*, 1968, *74*, 264–275.

Triandis, H. G. Subjective culture and economic development. *International Journal of Psychology*, 1973, *8*, 163–180.

Turnbull, C. *The Lonely African*. New York: Simon & Schuster, 1962.

Za'rour, G. I. Superstitions among certain groups of Lebanese Arab students in Beirut. *Journal of Cross-Cultural Psychology*, 1972, *3*, 273–282.

Eight

The Individual
in Relation to
Out-Group Cultures

A Small World

Despite the fact that the most pressing problems confronting humankind are global in scope, most people continue to identify primarily with relatively small groups. An awareness is beginning to grow that energy consumption, population growth, hunger, and the need for more equable economic development can be faced only as unitary, worldwide challenges. And a new consciousness is spreading, underscored by photographs of a tiny earth taken by cameras borne aloft into space, that the globe is an integral surface occupied by a single human species, sharing a single fate. Yet the old consciousness persists, as we saw in the previous chapter, fueling a loyalty to the ethnic or national segment and impeding concern for the whole.

The segments to which we relate most positively are, of course, our own cultures. This relation is the overarching social fact of human existence. *Why* we act in this way has been implicitly demonstrated in all the research discussed in this book. Our perceptions, our views of the world, our values, our life-styles—all of these fundamental personal traits—are largely conditioned by our particular cultures. The contents of our cultures are internalized by each of us; we *are*, in a sense, our own cultures. That we identify with our cultures is thus inevitable.

Despite this inevitability, we must become more than a loyal member of a single society if we are to survive in the shrinking world we inhabit. To avoid the impending catastrophes of which we are increasingly being warned, more and more of us must transcend our own cultures. We must develop—at a minimum—empathy with others and—at best—as profound an identification with the whole human race as most of us presently invest in our own tribe. As will be confirmed in this chapter, such a state of affairs is not likely anytime soon.

Nevertheless, research into individuals' relations with in-groups and out-groups can at least illuminate the magnitude of the problem and may even facilitate the difficult process of enhancing global consciousness. In the previous chapter, especially in the section on the psychology of nationalism, we examined psychological ties that bind individuals to the smaller groups to which they belong and from which they derive much of their sense of self. In the present chapter we will examine the "other side of the coin," the impediments to investing similar affect in other groups, groups perceived by us as *not* us.

Ethnocentrism

The core concept in our attempt to understand out-group attitudes is *ethnocentrism*, first employed in an analysis of individual links with one's own and neighboring groups by William Graham Sumner (1906) in his classic sociological treatise, *Folkways*. The concept embraces both positive feelings toward one's own group (the in-group, in Sumner's terminology) and negative feelings toward others (out-groups); indeed, in Sumner's insightful theorizing, each feeds on the other.

> The relation of comradeship and peace in the we-group and that of hostility and war toward others-groups are correlative to each other. The exigencies of war with outsiders are what make peace inside, lest internal discord should weaken the we-group for war. These exigencies also make government and law in the in-group, in order to prevent quarrels and enforce discipline. . . . *Ethnocentrism* is the technical name for this view of things in which one's own group is the center of everything, and all others are scaled and rated with reference to it. . . . Each group nourishes its own pride and vanity, boasts itself superior, exalts its own divinities, and looks with contempt on outsiders. Each group thinks its own folkways [the contemporary equivalent is *customs*] the only right ones, and if it observes that other groups have other folkways, these excite its scorn [1906, pp. 12–13].

Thus did Sumner postulate a universal syndrome of behavioral dispositions in which positive links with the in-group are reinforced by negative attitudes and behaviors toward out-groups. Cross-cultural research can serve to test the universality of such a syndrome. It can also illustrate the ways in which behaviors directed toward the in-group and out-groups interrelate. In turn, Sumner's theory, whether or not it proves to be accurate in detail, can help in the interpretation of whatever findings emerge from cross-cultural research on intergroup relations. Throughout the balance of this chapter, which will be devoted to empirical research done cross-culturally, we will have frequent occasion to refer to Sumner's ideas on ethnocentrism.

The Ugandan Case Study

Before we review a number of studies that deal with ethnocentrism in many different societies, we will take an intensive look at some further findings that emerged from the Segall, Doornbos, and Davis (1976) study examined in the last chapter. These findings have to do with the Banyankore's attitudes toward certain non-Banyankore—but Ugandan—groups. The relevant data were originally collected as part of an effort to find out how the Banyankore distinguish themselves from their neighbors, because this distinction was felt by the authors to be an aspect of the group identification itself. But the data, not included in their 1976 monograph, serve as well to illustrate ethnocentrism, so we will look closely at them here.

The authors adopted the Sumnerian position that a social group acquires part of its definition in reference to other groups from which, in one way or another, it is subjectively set apart. Significant other groups for the Banyankore include traditional "tribal" groups residing on Ankole's borders—the Baganda, Batoro, Bakiga, and Banyarwanda. Nearby are other groups, including the Banyoro, and slightly farther away are sets of groups known collectively as the Congolese and Nilotics. All of these groups except for the Banyarwanda and Congolese are part of modern Uganda. But they are still out-groups for the Banyankore, as witnessed by the salience attached to Banyankoreness that we saw in Chapter Seven.

Within Ankole itself, complicating the picture of in-group/out-group definition, there is the historically significant distinction between Bairu and Bahima (singular, Mwiru and Muhima). Bairu make up more than 95% of Ankole's population, with the balance being Bahima. Bairu are traditionally agriculturalists; Bahima are herdsmen. These subgroups differ in geographic origin, physical type, and ethnolinguistic category (Bahima are classified anthropologically as Nilo-Hamitic, Bairu as Bantu). They also differ in political status, because the Bahima were traditionally overlords and the Bairu serfs.

Banyankore Attitudes toward Their In-Group

Given this complexity, Segall, Doornbos, and Davis (1976) were interested not only in the Banyankore's attitudes toward non-Banyankore out-groups but also in the way in which they defined their in-group. Toward this end, the men in both sampling waves (before and after the 1967 constitutional changes) were asked five preliminary questions, purposely redundant, in order to elicit as full a picture as possible about Banyankore as an in-group. The five questions were asked in sequence to create a probing effect.

The first question was "What does the term *Munyankore* mean?" The form and content of this question was expected to produce a straightforward reply, such as "Someone who lives in (or was born in) Ankole," because the literal translation of the term is "a person of Ankole." In fact, 85% of the first-wave sample and 86% of the second wave so replied.

The second question was "Who are the Banyankore?" To this, 46% and 71%, respectively, responded "Natives (or inhabitants) of Ankole"—the same kind of response made popularly to the earlier question. But 42% in the first wave and 21% in the second singled out particular people, saying either "Bairu," "Bahima," or "Africans." Of these discriminative responses, *Africans* is of marginal interest since so few non-Africans (primarily Asian shopkeepers) live in Ankole. Responses of major interest, given the concerns of this research, were *Bairu* and *Bahima*. These were given by 34% in the first wave and 16% in the second. Because no one responded in terms of religion, occupation, or any other intra-Ankole subgroup, it is striking that so many respondents, particularly in the first wave, said that Bairu or Bahima are the Banyankore.

If this question (Who are the Banyankore?) may be considered a semiprojective test—one that provided an occasion for Bahima/Bairu ethnocentrism to emerge in a not very subtle, but nonetheless indirect, fashion—then these responses may be interpreted as indexes of intra-Ankole ethnocentrism. To say that only Bairu or Bahima are the Banyankore—when Banyankore, objectively defined, includes both—is to express decidedly parochial attitudes. But in general, intra-Ankole ethnicity was found *not* to be salient or subjectively very important. That only 16% of respondents singled out Bahima or Bairu as Banyankore after 1967 (compared with 34% prior to 1967) suggests that intra-Ankole ethnocentrism was on the wane.

"How does someone (a stranger) recognize a Munyankore?" The third question, because it asked *how*, might have been expected to elicit descriptions of a Munyankore—how he looks, how he speaks, or how he behaves. In fact, in the first wave 53% said "By the language he speaks," while 24% said "By the way he looks" (and 11% rather evaded the question by stating that, although a native could recognize a Munyankore, a stranger could not). The remaining 12% of responses were scattered among dress, diet, occupation, and behavior. In the second wave, the percentage specifying language as the essential cue rose to 72%, while the percentage specifying physical appearance remained near 25%. Clearly then, language—which is shared by Bahima and Bairu and distinguishes them from non-Banyankore—was thought of by most people as *the* distinguishing characteristic of a Munyankore. But nearly one-quarter replied in terms of physical features, which distinguish Banyankore from some of their out-group neighbors but also Bahima from Bairu.

This last point also suggests that intra-Ankole ethnocentrism, although increasingly countered by interethnic tolerance, was not laid to rest in 1967. Differences in stature and physiognomy, which distinguish Bahima from Bairu, were frequently cited by informants. That such responses were no less frequent in the second wave than in the first, coupled with the interwave increase in language responses, suggests a continuing ethnic awareness accompanied by a spreading tendency to grant full Munyankore status to both ethnic categories— in spite of the ethnic awareness.

Respondents were then asked "Is anyone who lives in Ankole a Munyank-ore?" Most respondents said "Yes"—92% of the first wave and 70% of the second. The negative replies (contributed by 8% and 30%, respectively) were hardly ever accompanied by specifications of who the non-Munyankore residents of Ankole might be. Moreover, no one singled out Bahima or Bairu as non-Munyankore.

"Precisely what does a man have to be to be called a Munyankore?" was the final in-group question. Most responses in both waves belonged in the categories *native born, Runyankore speaker,* and *resident.* These three categories accounted for 80% of the first-wave and 87% of the second-wave responses.

Considering responses to all five questions, it was found that (1) nearly everyone in both samples defined a Munyankore as a person who was born or lives in Ankole, with some stress—more so in the second wave—on birthplace as the defining characteristic; (2) although most people repeated those definitions when asked who the Banyankore are, a few specified Bahima or Bairu; (3) language (and, to a lesser extent, physical features) was most often cited as the distinguishing characteristic of a Munyankore; and (4) a few people —particularly better-educated ones—recognized that not all Ankole residents were Banyankore, and—when pressed—most respondents stated that one had to be born a Munyankore (or its functional equivalent, a speaker of Runyankore) to be considered a Munyankore. Thus, although the responses revealed a lingering consciousness of intra-Ankole ethnicity, there were widely spread expressions of a growing willingness to grant Munyankoreness to all Banyankore.

Let us now turn to data that reveal Banyankore perceptions of and attitudes toward their neighbors.

Banyankore Attitudes toward Out-Groups

After answering the five in-group questions, respondents were asked to indicate the names of people who are most like the Banyankore, people whom the Banyankore like best, people whom the Banyankore dislike, and people with whom the Banyankore intermarry. These four questions were also asked in sequence and they yielded multiple responses.

Likes and Dislikes. Many respondents cited more than one non-Banyankore group in response to the questions pertaining to groups liked and disliked. Of initial interest are the first responses made to these questions. The tribal name mentioned most often in response to both questions taken together was Baganda. Slightly more than a quarter of all respondents in both waves cited the Baganda first as the tribe liked best; and 20% and 33%, respectively, mentioned the Baganda as the people whom the Banyankore disliked. Only one group, the Bakiga, was mentioned more often as best liked, and no other group was mentioned as often as disliked. It would have to be concluded, therefore, that the Baganda are the most salient out-group. There are approximately as many Banyankore who think of them first as the best-liked out-group as there are those who think of them first as a disliked out-group.

Toward the Bakiga there was a clearly positive attitude. They were by far the most often cited first as best liked (by 38% and 37%, respectively) and were almost never cited as disliked. The Batoro were also rather popular (best liked by 21% and 17%) and almost never disliked. Thus, the Bakiga, Baganda, and Batoro stand out as groups cited first as best liked. Only one of these, the Baganda, was cited with any appreciable frequency as disliked. Interestingly, the positive responses toward the Baganda came mainly from lesser educated men; most of the negative answers were from better educated respondents.

At the other end of the scale were three out-groups that were relatively frequently cited first as disliked. These were the Nilotics—a category that included several northern Ugandan tribes—(25% and 13%), the Banyarwanda (18% and 19%), and the Congolese (5% and 10%). Hardly anyone mentioned any of these groups as best liked.

Perceived Similarity of Various Out-Groups. Two of the questions may be considered to provide evidence about how similar various out-groups appear to the Banyankore themselves. One question does this directly by asking "Who are most like the Banyankore?" The other gets at it indirectly by inquiring "With whom do the Banyankore intermarry?"

Responses to the former question were very numerous, with about half of the respondents in each wave making two responses and a third making three.

The Bakiga stand out. Half of the first-wave respondents and 60% of the second wave cited them first as the people who are most like the Banyankore. Counting second and third responses as well, eight out of every ten respondents named the Bakiga as most similar to themselves. The only other group that was anywhere nearly as often cited was the Batoro, named by nearly half (but by fewer than 20% as a *first* response). The Baganda were also named with some frequency, but less so even than the Batoro. When persons did make multiple responses, they tended to say "Bakiga, Batoro, and Baganda" in that order. If only two groups were cited, most often they were the Bakiga and Batoro, and, if only one was cited, it was the Bakiga. The only other group that received a noticeable number of mentions was the Banyoro, usually as a second or third response.

Thus, the hierarchy of perceived similarity that resulted was Bakiga,

Batoro, Baganda, and Banyoro, with Banyarwanda and Bahima following, but not very closely. The first four are, in fact, not only the Banyankore's closest neighbors but also culturally and linguistically most closely related to the majority Bairu population of Ankole.

When asked to name the groups with whom they intermarry, the men most frequently said again "Bakiga, Batoro, and Baganda." If only two groups were mentioned, they were most often the Bakiga and Batoro; and if only one was cited, it was the Bakiga. *Baganda* was a more popular response in the second wave than in the first, surpassing *Batoro* in the second wave and, over both waves, equaling *Batoro* in popularity. Still, *Bakiga* stood out very clearly in the first wave and in both waves combined. The results of this question, then, confirm the results of the more direct effort to secure subjective estimates of similarity.

So, the Bakiga were not only the best-liked group but were also perceived as most similar and were thought to provide more marriage partners than any other out-group. The latter two points may be redundant; they might also explain why the Bakiga are the best liked.

Putting all of this together, it seems safe to conclude that on the basis of responses to several different questions the Banyankore have revealed that they perceive their closest neighbors as similar, likable, and marriageable. Their favorite neighbors in all three respects are the Bakiga. Toward the Baganda there is ambivalence at the societal level, in that lesser educated Banyankore like them and see them as similar and marriageable, while better educated do not. The Batoro are viewed in much the same way as the Bakiga, but by fewer people. The Banyoro, farther away geographically than the Bakiga, Batoro, or Baganda, are also liked and thought of as similar but hardly ever cited as marriage partners. Other groups, more distant (but known) and culturally less similar— the Nilotics, Congolese, and Banyarwanda—are far less often seen as similar and seldom thought of as marriage partners. This pattern af attitudes and perceptions is summarized in the map and chart in Figure 8-1.

With one notable exception, proximity seems to be the key to how out-groups are perceived and reacted to. The exception is the Baganda; the attitude toward this group probably reflects not proximity but the history of contact between the Baganda and the Banyankore. Once the Banyankore's overlords (during the early 20th century, when Baganda were employed by the British colonial authorities as "chiefs") and once the Banyankore's enemies in territorial warfare, the Baganda seem to enjoy the respect of the elderly (and lesser educated) and the resentment of the young.

With the special case of the Baganda aside, the people best known are the people best liked, perceived as most similar, and most often taken as marriage partners. And those peoples who live one group removed are the negatively valued out-groups. What should be underscored is that the pattern is probably no different from the one found practically everywhere. Typically, one's closest neighbors—unless seen as enemies, troublemakers, or the like—are one's positively valenced out-groups. And negative attitudes are more likely to be

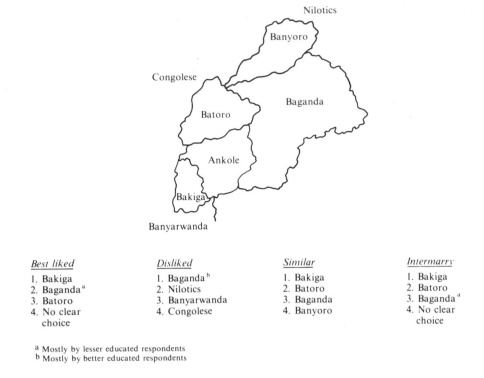

Best liked	*Disliked*	*Similar*	*Intermarry*
1. Bakiga	1. Baganda[b]	1. Bakiga	1. Bakiga
2. Baganda[a]	2. Nilotics	2. Batoro	2. Batoro
3. Batoro	3. Banyarwanda	3. Baganda	3. Baganda[a]
4. No clear	4. Congolese	4. Banyoro	4. No clear
choice			choice

[a] Mostly by lesser educated respondents
[b] Mostly by better educated respondents

Figure 8-1. Ankole and neighboring peoples

applied to well-known, but more distant, neighbors. The really distant ones, hardly known and historically insignificant, are usually spared both negative and positive affect. The only people who, in this sense, matter to the Banyankore are those people whom they know. Among these, the ones they perceive as most like themselves are liked. Those whom they perceive as different from themselves, they dislike.

Intergroup Attraction and Perception on a Broader Canvas

The case study just considered is just that. As such, it gives us a detailed look at a particular instance of intergroup relations, but it cannot serve to test general hypotheses. To do the latter, studies employing a large number of groups are required. Such studies are rare, but there is one excellent one involving, interestingly, 30 groups in East Africa (Uganda, Kenya, and Tanzania). The study includes groups already familiar to us—namely, the

Baganda, Banyoro, Batoro, and Banyankore, all of whom were part of the Ugandan case study just reviewed. Also included are some Kenyan groups—for example, the Kikuyu and Masai—who have been mentioned from time to time in earlier parts of this book. The larger study has been reported by Brewer and Campbell (1976), and we now turn to it.

Ethnocentrism in East Africa

The Brewer and Campbell study was designed to test some of the many hypotheses about intergroup attitudes and perceptions that can be derived from Sumner's (1906) very rich theory of ethnocentrism. Contained in that theory are predictions concerning the characteristics of out-groups that are most likely to be targets of hostility, the role of proximity and cultural similarity in shaping attitudes toward out-groups, the content of stereotypes that are likely to develop for particular in-group/out-group pairs, and the significance of contact between groups as a determinant of mutual perceptions and attitudes, to mention only a few.

Other theories of intergroup relations provide still more hypotheses, not all of them consistent with those derivable from Sumner's ethnocentrism theory. In a systematic compilation of relevant hypotheses, LeVine and Campbell (1972) listed 331 testable propositions, including 253 correlational hypotheses derived from Sumner. Many of the latter refer to attitudes and behaviors that, in the strictest reading of Sumner, would be hypothesized to be universally present and interrelated. The Brewer and Campbell (1976) study was an attempt to test some of these hypotheses.

Data were collected in 1965 among the 30 East African societies, 10 each in Uganda, Kenya, and Tanzania, with 50 individuals questioned in each society by a native speaker. For each society, respondents were queried about their own group and 13 others, nine living within their country and four from neighboring countries.

The standardized interview contained (1) questions relating to social distance (Bogardus, 1925, 1928)—for example, "Would you willingly agree to become related to a ———— by marriage?" (2) questions on familiarity—for example, "Do you know any ———— ? Do you speak their language?" (3) open-ended questions eliciting "good" and "bad" traits about 13 out-groups; (4) a structured list of traits to be assigned to the one group that the respondent thought each trait fit best; and (5) direct questions seeking the most liked, the most disliked, and the most and least similar out-group.

The findings that emerged from this study were many and complex. But they are worth reviewing in some detail, because they provide the best available information on the dynamics of intergroup attraction and perception yet assembled. They will be presented and discussed here in a manner that will permit us to consider what now appear to be the fundamental features of intergroup relations.

1. Affect between Groups. Brewer and Campbell found, over all 30 societies, that measures of *liking* for particular groups, of *social distance* assigned to them, and of *familiarity* toward them were highly intercorrelated. Specifically, liking correlated .63 with social distance and .54 with familiarity, and social distance correlated .77 with familiarity. This pattern of intercorrelations justified speaking of a single dimension of intergroup affect, described by the authors as "desirability of close interpersonal relations" and presumed to underlie the three separate measures of liking, social distance, and personal familiarity.

Their four-item scale of social distance was of interest in its own right. In most of the 30 societies the items scaled in the following order: (1) willingness to share a meal with; (2) willingness to work with; (3) willingness to have as a neighbor; and (4) willingness to become related by marriage. In other words, in these East African societies the least degree of intimacy, subjectively speaking, is offered by sharing a meal and the most by permitting intermarriage. That the items *scaled* means that an individual who named an out-group in response to the intermarriage social-distance item probably named that group in response to the three other items. If a group was named in response to only three items, it was probably to the items other than the intermarriage one.

Most individuals followed this orderly pattern of responding to the four-item set, so that the scale proved to be highly reliable and valid. Part of this success stemmed from the fact that many respondents gave all-yes or all-no answers to the entire set, but this does not detract from the detection of a consistent pattern of social-distance attitudes. And, as we have just seen, the measure of social distance correlated highly with both liking and familiarity, adding further credence to the social-distance measure as an index of intergroup affect.

After combining measures of social distance, liking, and familiarity into a single index of intergroup attraction, Brewer and Campbell were in a position to ask what factual characteristics of out-groups seemed to determine their score on that index. They found, first, that affect for out-groups covaried most strongly with *opportunity for contact* by individuals within the in-group with out-group members. Positive affect (that is, low social distance and high liking and familiarity) was most likely to be assigned to groups that were similar in culture and language to the in-group and that enjoyed geographic proximity to it. In other words most individuals in any group felt closest to those groups that were nearer, better known, and culturally most like their own group.

The overriding importance of the contact variable is underscored by the fact that the most positive ratings of intergroup attraction were given to groups with whom *traditionally* there had been much contact and interaction. Even when overt conflict had recently occurred between two "familiar" groups, the psychological distance was relatively small and the mutual attraction high.

Another variable relating to intergroup attraction was the perceived (and actual) level of modernity (urbanization, economic advancement, and so on) of particular out-groups. But with regard to this variable the relationship was a bit complex. Groups perceived as nonadvanced, "backward," and otherwise of low status were generally assigned high social distance and were otherwise treated as unattractive. This part of the relationship between status and attractiveness was straightforward. But high-status groups such as the economically favored Chagga of Tanzania, Baganda of Uganda, and Kikuyu of Kenya, toward all of whom *respect* was high, were found to earn either high *or* low attractiveness scores depending on the degree to which they were culturally similar to a particular in-group. Brewer and Campbell suggested that high-status groups may serve either as "models of a desired status" or as "visible targets for resentment" (or both). And their findings regarding such groups suggest that they will be emulated and found attractive if they are culturally similar but resented and rejected if not. Hence, the impact of perceived status on attractiveness was found to be mediated by cultural similarity, underscoring once more the overriding importance of that variable.

One final point about intergroup attraction: within each in-group the affect directed toward any other group was quite consistent and general. While individual differences relating to education and urbanization existed, the norms of attractiveness toward out-groups were found to be widely shared. This fact clearly suggests that the attractiveness assigned to particular out-groups is part of the cultural content of any in-group, content that is acquired through socialization and enculturation early in life and is subject to minimal modification as a result of individual experience.

2. *The Reciprocity of Intergroup Affect.* It was generally found by Brewer and Campbell that, if group X liked group Y, group Y liked group X. In other words intergroup attraction, and lack thereof, were usually reciprocated. In a sense this follows from what we have already learned—because attraction appears to be determined primarily by cultural similarity, it follows that similar groups will be attracted to each other and dissimilar ones will find each other relatively unattractive. Nevertheless, the empirical finding of reciprocity is an important one in its own right and has significant theoretical implications. For one, it suggests that, in general, a group that invests negative affect in another group is not necessarily being perverse or hostile in a willy-nilly fashion. It is likely to be the target of similar feelings directed toward it from that other group. It is further likely to find "justification" for its own negative feelings toward that group in its "mistreatment of us." The mutuality of negative intergroup affect thus makes the negative affect virtually self-reinforcing and hence rather tenacious.

What we have seen thus far from the Brewer and Campbell findings reveals a process in which cultural similarity (both perceived and actual) generates in any given *pair* of groups shared, reciprocated feelings—positive for similar groups, negative for dissimilar ones. The most intriguing implication of this process may be that to change an existing intergroup relationship presently characterized by negative affect to more positive feelings would require changes in the behavior of one or both groups—each toward the model provided by the other—together with a mutual perception of increasing similarity. Just as long as either group perceives the other as different, it will not like the other, the other will reciprocate the dislike, and the intergroup affect will remain negative. Perhaps, then, there is some optimism about improving intergroup affective relations inherent in cultural contact, modernization, and other similar processes that, as we saw in Chapter Seven, are tending to produce cultural homogenization. We shall return to this speculative point later in this chapter.

   3. Intergroup Perceptions. Although one might expect that liked groups would be perceived as possessing mostly positive traits and disliked groups as possessing negative ones, the facts revealed by Brewer and Campbell in this regard were not that simple. The contents of intergroup perceptions, unlike intergroup attraction, could not be represented by a single dimension of "acceptability/rejection." To account for their findings regarding intergroup perceptions, the authors needed three dimensions, which they labeled *trust/ conflict*, *attraction/repulsion*, and *admiration/disrespect*.[1] In other words, to adequately depict the pattern of perceptions by each in-group of all out-groups required a three-dimensional conceptual space. On the resultant three-dimensional map of these perceptions, the distance between any group and any other group would vary from time to time, depending on which of the three dimensions was, for whatever reason, salient at the time.

   The theoretical import of this complex pattern is that Sumner's (1906) model of intergroup perceptions, "convergent ethnocentrism," is somewhat altered. Whereas Sumner held that each in-group and its allies would be perceived as positive in all respects and that all out-groups would be located in a negative sector, Brewer and Campbell found this to be true only when "all bases of distinction between 'us' and 'them' are highly correlated" (1976, p. 144). The East African data revealed that Sumner's model is an extreme variation within numerous patterns of intergroup relations. It occurs, according to the authors' own theorizing, when (1) contact opportunities are low, (2) environmental survival threats require extremely high internal cooperation and in-group loyalty, or (3) ethnic discrimination is legally or otherwise encouraged. In the absence of such conditions—which is most often the case—there is "flexibility in adapting patterns of alliance to correspond to differing functional requirements" (p. 145).

   Consistent with these findings is the likelihood that an individual in any in-group can like a particular out-group at certain times or in certain respects and negatively evaluate it at other times or in other respects. Cognitive consistency seems not to be necessary in intergroup attraction and perception.

---

[1]Brewer and Campbell sometimes termed these three dimensions *evaluation* (peaceful and cooperative versus quarrelsome and dishonest), *achievement* (dynamic, hard-working, and advanced versus lazy and backward), and *attraction* (liked and similar versus disliked, dissimilar, and "ugly").

For many people, of course, such consistency will prevail. But the findings of this study suggest that many other individuals, perhaps those who generally reveal a high degree of psychological differentiation, are equipped psychologically to handle complex, inconsistent intergroup attitudes.

The contact variable, which we saw earlier to be important in determining intergroup attraction, was also importantly related to the content of intergroup perceptions. For individuals with little or no familiarity with an out-group, the perceptions of it tended to be more simplistic, consistent, and based largely on reputational stereotypes. Individuals better acquainted with an out-group held more idiosyncratic, less consistent—but not necessarily more positive— perceptions.

4. Perceptions of the In-Group Itself. The aspect of Sumner's theory that received the clearest empirical support from this study concerns high self-regard: "Each group nourishes its own pride and vanity, boasts itself superior, exalts its own divinities" (1906, p. 13). As we have just seen, negative perception of out-groups is not universal; but positive perception of in-groups may well be. Brewer and Campbell found that all in-groups in their study rated themselves more favorably than they were rated by others. Specifically, "The facet of ethnocentrism that comes closest to universality is the tendency to regard own group members as more honorable and trustworthy than others" (1976, p. 143).

The degree to which those positive in-group perceptions were held varied somewhat with the regard in which in-groups were held by other groups. Such positive self-regard was maximal for groups granted either high or low respect by other groups, and it somewhat diminished among moderately respected groups. That especially low- and high-status groups should hold themselves in such high self-regard led the authors to hypothesize that these Sumnerian ethnocentric feelings "may reflect high self-esteem associated with achievement and positive regard from others, or a defensive self-esteem associated with rejection and/or threat" (p. 143).

5. A Recapitulation. Based on data from 30 East African societies, it could be concluded that (1) persons generally like their own groups best and perceive them in a most positive light; (2) the degree of attraction felt toward other groups is fundamentally a cultural fact, internalized by individuals; (3) intergroup attractiveness tends to be reciprocal; (4) intergroup attraction depends on opportunity for intergroup contact, which, in turn, reflects cultural similarity and proximity; (5) out-groups perceived as "backward" enjoy, generally, low attractiveness, whereas groups perceived as "advanced" enjoy high attractiveness *if* they are culturally similar to the in-group of the perceiver; (6) the content of perceptions of out-groups cannot be predicted solely on the basis of their attractiveness, which is only one of three dimensions that apparently underlie those perceptions (the others having to do with trustworthiness and achievement); and (7) opportunity for contact relates to intergroup perceptions but in a complex manner: the perceptions tend to be stereotyped for individuals with little opportunity for contact, but varied and idiosyncratic among individuals who know more about the out-groups in question.

All of these findings are more or less consistent with Sumner's ethnocentrism theory—"more," regarding in-group perceptions and intergroup attraction, "less," with regard to intergroup perception. And perhaps the most important variable determining intergroup relations that has been revealed by this study is intercultural similarity.

That these findings were produced by a large-scale study involving 30 distinct ethnic groups makes it likely that they are reliable, replicable data. It is, of course, highly desirable that they be replicated, preferably in some other part of the world. Until that happens, we can tentatively conclude that intergroup attraction and perception are, in general if not in every detail, products of cultural similarity and status, with the former more important than the latter.

Additional Insights from Other Cross-Cultural Studies

Thus far in this chapter we have dealt with only one case study and one large-scale, hypothesis-testing study. Let us now move further afield.

Stereotyped Out-Group Perceptions

Sumner's ethnocentrism theory also serves as a source of hypotheses about *stereotyping*, the psychological process by which out-groups are ascribed characteristics that serve to justify the social distance at which they are held. In Sumner's view, because out-groups are treated badly, verbal descriptions of them should tend to be dominated by negatively valued characteristics, in order that the hostility might be legitimized. To make an out-group appear deserving of animosity, one must focus on its negative characteristics, even inventing some if necessary. Such invention, however, is seldom necessary, because one can always find some difference in "their" behavior as compared with "ours"; and because ours is moral and good, theirs "must be" immoral and bad.

Since, as we have seen, not every out-group is held at a large social distance, Sumner's view is somewhat exaggerated. Not every out-group will be characterized solely, or even predominantly, by negative stereotypes. But such stereotyping should often take place, particularly with relatively unknown and culturally different groups toward whom low levels of attraction prevail.

Ethnocentrism theory also leads to the prediction that stereotyping will be a mutual, reciprocal process between any two groups aware of each other. Any pair of interacting groups that share a mutual antagonism should possess stereotypes of each other that are complementary. The stereotypes may reflect real, noticed, and acknowledged differences in modal behavior patterns, with the differences described in positive terms for each in-group and in negative terms for each out-group. Because every language is rich in both positive and negative adjectives, it is usually possible to treat any noticed difference between us and them in our favor. On the one hand, if they appear typically to work harder than we, we can describe them as "compulsive." They, in turn, can describe us as "lazy." If, on the other hand, we work harder than they, we can describe ourselves as "industrious," and they can describe themselves as "relaxed."

The final predicted dynamic is a tendency to exaggerate the degree to which any such negatively described out-group trait is possessed by out-group members, attributing it to all, or most, whether fairly or not.

A Classic U.S. Study of Stereotyping. These various ideas lead to a set of expectations about the content of stereotypes, ideas that in recent years have been subjected to empirical test in cross-cultural studies. Many of these are essentially replications of a classic study done in the United States with college students, who selected terms from an adjective checklist and assigned them to numerous out-groups, some known, some not (Katz & Braly, 1933).

The Katz and Braly findings were dominated by much agreement in the assignment of negative traits to any but the core-cultural White Protestant in-group. Other U.S. studies over the years showed similar patterns (see, for example, Blake & Dennis, 1943; Gilbert, 1951; Schoenfeld, 1942; Vinacke, 1956). By 1971 a review of the literature spanning more than four decades (Cauthen, Robinson, & Krauss, 1971) could conclude that in the United States the content of stereotypes remained very stable, with most groups described in much the same way they had been described by Katz and Braly's respondents. Another consistency in findings was that, the greater the social distance between any two groups, the greater the difference between self-stereotype and out-group stereotype. Still another was that individuals who are members of groups stereotyped by others accept at least part of the stereotype as characteristic of their own group, if not of themselves personally.

Cross-Cultural Studies: No Black and White. Cross-cultural studies contain findings that are consistent with these earlier U.S. studies, but they also have particular features. In Hawaii, Kurokawa (1971) administered an 84-item checklist to 100 White, 100 Black, and 100 Japanese-American respondents (adults, college students, and schoolchildren), who were to select five terms that best applied to each of those ethnic groups. Among the high-agreement assignments were: for Whites, materialistic and pleasure-loving; for Blacks, musical, aggressive, and straightforward; and for Japanese-Americans, industrious, ambitious, loyal to family, and quiet. Kurokawa derived a hypothesis from Katz and Braly (1933) that the dominant White group would be endowed primarily with positive traits, whereas both minority groups would be ascribed predominantly negative traits. The hypothesis was not fully supported. In some settings, at least, positive traits are assigned to minority groups.

India, where at least vestiges of a caste system persist, was the setting of a study (Anant, 1970) that confirms the tendency of in-group members—in such settings, at least—to accept stereotypes of their own group held by others. In Anant's study, 239 urban-dwelling and educated respondents from five groups (the Brahmin, Kshatriya, Vaishya, and Sudra castes and the Harijans, or "untouchables") selected five from 88 traits to assign to their own and other groups. Anant found that there was little difference between the traits attributed to a group by its own members and those attributed to it by others. But the number of favorable traits attributed to a caste by its own members was greater than the number of such traits attributed to it by others, a fact that is consistent with findings from many other studies on stereotyping.

Of course, a caste system is a very rigid social arrangement, characterized by formal discrimination and generally understood and "accepted" trait attributions. Not surprisingly, then, in Anant's (1970) study, the proportion of favorable to unfavorable traits assigned to castes decreased steadily as one moved down the caste hierarchy, with the highest proportion of favorable traits assigned to the Kshatriyas, still the economically and politically dominant group in India.

The Influence of Contact on Stereotypes. In another study by Anant (1971), 137 college-educated Indian respondents chose 5 from 88 terms to apply to 15 non-Indian ethnic groups (for example, Germans, Canadians, Russians, Americans). Besides obtaining the usual finding that people will display stereotyping behavior by assigning traits to groups in an interpersonally consistent manner, Anant found that favorable traits were least likely to be attributed to groups neighboring India (for example, Pakistanis, Chinese, Burmese, and Ceylonese). Favorable traits were assigned most frequently to groups with whom Indians typically have had little contact (such as Germans, Canadians, and Russians).

In this study, then, opportunity for contact seemed to be negatively correlated with favorable perception. Of course, as the author suggested, contact may not be a critical factor in national stereotypes held by educated Indians, who may instead base their stereotypes on contemporary sociopolitical factors.

It may well be that contact influences the clarity and valence (positive/negative) of stereotypes for individual respondents, in at least some social settings. Triandis and Vassiliou (1967), working in Greece with both Greek respondents and Americans living there, selected trait attributions of Greeks and Americans that could be compared with attributions made by persons living in their own country and having little contact with nationals of the other country. They found that Americans living in Greece had clearer stereotypes of Greeks than did Americans who had little contact with Greeks. Also, the American respondents were more likely to describe the Greeks as similar to themselves *if* the Americans were living in Greece and thus enjoying contact. But the same did not hold for Greek respondents, for whom contact with Americans did *not* correlate with higher clarity or increased "correspondence" of stereotypes.

Thus, Triandis and Vassiliou's Greek respondents behaved rather like Anant's (1971) Indian respondents, for whom opportunity for contact did not seem to affect the content of the stereotypes they held.

However, Reigrotski and Anderson (1959), in a report of a multinational study of stereotyping, showed clearly that the prevalent finding is for both clarity and content of national stereotypes to be determined by international contact. Respondents from nations that enjoy much contact with other nations were found to be less likely to bias their own-group descriptions in a favorable direction, more likely to attribute favorable characteristics to members of other nations, and more likely to describe their own group in ways that corresponded with descriptions provided by outsiders.

Although contact seems in general to influence stereotypes, there certainly are circumstances under which, as Anant (1971) suggested, sociopolitical factors matter more. Following the Nigerian civil war, Ogunlade (1971) had 100 university students from western Nigeria assign 10 adjectives from a list of 63 to each of 10 national groups (Americans, Russians, French, Chinese, and so forth), some of which had supported the federal Nigerian government (as did most people in western Nigeria) and some of which had been supporters of the secessionist Biafrans. Quite clearly, the nations that supported the federal side were described predominantly by positive adjectives, whereas the reverse was true for nations thought to have supported the rebels.

The Role of Power. Lindgren and Tebcherani (1971) have argued that contact between groups interacts with their relative power in determining the accuracy of the perception each has of the other. The researchers used a measure of *empathy* (rather than a typical stereotype paradigm) in which individual respondents from two groups (Arab and American male students at the American University in Beirut) described themselves and a "typical" member of the other group. Lindgren and Tebcherani found that Arab students described the typical American more as the American students described themselves than vice versa. This finding was considered by the authors to be consistent with the view that relatively low-power Arabs would be more sensitive to, more aware of, and more accepting of the Americans' views of themselves than the Americans would be of the Arab self-perceptions. But the authors acknowledged that their finding could also be accounted for by a (possible) tendency for the Americans to be more open and self-revealing, thus giving more accurate self-descriptions and permitting the Arab observers to predict better how the Americans would describe themselves. In any case, the fact that the two groups were not of equal status seemed to relate to the nonparallel nature of the empathy skills revealed.

A different kind of parallelism in stereotypes is often, although not always, found. Particularly when two groups are in a state of conflict or tension, each tends to hold a view of the other that contrasts markedly with the view each holds of itself. Bronfenbrenner (1961) documented this for the United States and the

Soviet Union at a time when the Cold War was intense, and he called the phenomenon the "mirror-image hypothesis." More recently, Haque (1973) applied the Katz and Braly technique with Indian and Pakistani respondents and found this kind of parallelism. Specifically, *both* the Indians and Pakistanis tended to describe themselves as peace loving, trustworthy, religious, kind, idealistic, democratic, and hospitable. And *both* described the other as cruel, threatening, selfish, war mongering, greedy, and cheating. It may be that the mirror-image phenomenon is stronger when two groups are in a heightened state of intergroup tension. The phenomenon is very likely to exist when this condition prevails.

The Relationship of Stereotyping to Other Dimensions of Intergroup Attraction

Social Distance. In theory, at least, the content of stereotypes should be predictable from other knowledge about the relationship between the groups involved. As was argued earlier, groups that maintain low social distance between each other should tend to hold relatively favorable stereotypes of each other. Social distance and stereotyping should be correlated. But the empirical data do not always correspond to this expectation. Thus, in their East African study Brewer and Campbell (1976) reported: "Although disliked outgroups are generally distrusted and negatively evaluated, outgroups given positive attraction ratings are not consistently assigned positively evaluated characteristics" (p. 143).

Sometimes, of course, the situation is complicated by existing social norms governing interactions among groups. Especially when intergroup relations are subject to legal sanctions, as in the notorious case of South Africa with its *apartheid* laws, we should expect some complications. In that troubled multiethnic society, Viljoen (1974) sought to determine the degree of relationship between stereotypes and social distance that prevailed for African and Indian students toward English-speaking Whites, Afrikaans-speaking Whites, "Coloreds," Jews, and their own two groups. For one of the two politically dominant White groups, the English-speaking Whites, these respondents held an overall positive stereotype *and* asserted that they would welcome relatively close social contact with them. For the other, the Afrikaans-speaking Whites, an overall negative stereotype was accompanied by remote social distance.

Thus, with respect to the African and Indian reactions to the two White groups, social distance and stereotyping were correlated. But both respondent groups revealed feelings of closer social distance toward other non-White ethnic groups than to the English-speaking Whites, even though the stereotype of that group was more positive than the self-stereotype of either respondent group or of the Coloreds. In this respect, then, the correlation between stereotype and social distance broke down.

Prejudice and Authoritarianism. Data from South Africa are also relevant to the issue of the relationship between prejudice (high social distance and low attraction, accompanied by discrimination when power permits) and the personality trait known as *authoritarianism*.

In the United States, and based largely on the work of Adorno, Frenkel-Brunswik, Levinson, and Sanford (1950), prejudice and authoritarianism have been found in general to be correlated.[2] That is, individuals who scored high on the researchers' measure of authoritarianism (approving of rigid moral standards, strong policing, and the like) tended to express high degrees of prejudice against minority groups.

This had led some theorists to argue that such prejudice is best viewed as an outward manifestation of a personality syndrome, indexed by scores on the authoritarianism measure, the F-scale. However, working both in the U.S. South and in South Africa, Pettigrew (1959, 1960) acquired data that challenge this notion, at least for settings in which discrimination and other features of ethnic or racial prejudice are sanctioned. In such settings, Pettigrew expected to find what he termed "other-directed" prejudice, behavior that might best be understood as conformity with prevailing norms and sanctions. In fact, in his Southern study (Pettigrew, 1959) he found that manifest prejudice against Blacks by Whites was not correlated with F-scale scores any more highly than in other regions. But it was correlated highly with such measures of generalized tendency to conform as regularity of church attendance. Nor was anti-Black prejudice correlated with anti-Semitism in that setting, as authoritarianism theory would predict (and is, more generally speaking, the case in other parts of the United States).

When Pettigrew moved his research project to South Africa, where the sanctions against Blacks were even more rigid than in the southern region of the United States during the 1950s, he again found that anti-Black prejudice was not particularly highly correlated to F-scale scores (Pettigrew, 1960). More than a decade later, Lambley (1973) confirmed Pettigrew's findings with a sample of 190 White undergraduates taking introductory psychology at an English-speaking university in South Africa. He found correlations of approximately .4 between authoritarianism and anti-Black prejudice, .4 between authoritarianism and social distance, and .45 between prejudice and social distance. Also working among English-speaking Whites in South Africa and using similar measures,

---

[2]Research reported in the 1950s on the role of "the authoritarian personality syndrome" in ethnic prejudice yielded findings that did not go unchallenged during the next quarter-century. As Christie (1978) has pointed out, there were certain methodological flaws in the original research and some findings that could not subsequently be replicated, probably because changing historical forces influencing discrimination came into play. Nevertheless, as an explanation for some portion of what is known about individual differences in manifest prejudice, the ideas of Adorno and colleagues (1950) are still tenable. As Christie has characterized it, "The current view of the authoritarian personality is that the creature exists, but it needs the proper conditions before it is lured from its lair" (1978, p. 93).

Orpen (1971) found *no* significant correlations among the measures. Orpen's study was done in a setting where, as he put it, "the prevailing cultural norms explicitly sanction prejudiced ideas" (p. 301) and where individuals are encouraged to be intolerant irrespective of personality.[3]

Dogmatism. Another personality dimension that, in the United States at least, has been found to be correlated with ethnic prejudice is *dogmatism* as measured by Rokeach (1960). This hypothetical personality trait is meant to characterize an individual whose cognitive processes tend to be "rigid" and who thus might be expected to be prone to simplistic, stereotypic thinking and to other symptoms of prejudice. As was the case for authoritarianism, however, there is reason to expect that in the highly prejudiced climate of South Africa manifest prejudice would be independent of dogmatism.

To test this expectation, Orpen and Rookledge (1972) administered Rokeach's Dogmatism Scale, a measure of anti-Black prejudice, and a social-distance scale to 72 White English-speaking secondary school students of urban, middle-class background. They found that only about 5% of the variance in prejudice in this sample could be accounted for by individual differences in dogmatism. Rather, political-party preference predicted prejudice. Respondents who preferred South Africa's overtly White-supremacist party were significantly more anti-Black on both the prejudice and social-distance scales than respondents who preferred either of two moderately integrationist parties, even though party preference was not related to dogmatism scores. Once again Orpen has demonstrated that, in settings characterized by sanctioned discrimination and other norms that encourage prejudice, sociocultural factors outweigh personality factors in shaping individual intergroup attitudes.

Agreement on Beliefs. From several sources we have learned that persons from groups perceived by us as similar to us are likely to be evaluated positively, whereas dissimilar persons tend to be disliked, maintained at a relatively large social distance, and assigned negative stereotypes. The author of the Dogmatism Scale, Rokeach, has in fact argued that perceived dissimilarity of belief systems is a root cause of ethnic prejudice and in cases of racial prejudice may outweigh race per se in determining intergroup acceptance. Research done in the United States has shown that an individual's acceptance by a respondent depends sometimes on his alleged values (see, for example, Rokeach, Smith, & Evans, 1960), sometimes more on his ethnicity (Triandis, 1961), and often on both.

Stein, Hardyck, and Smith (1965) told White American high school students that certain stimulus persons were either White or Black and held beliefs that were either consonant or not with the respondent's own beliefs. They

---

[3]Lambley (1973) refers to another of Orpen's findings, this among Afrikaans-speaking Whites. An obtained correlation between F-scale score and a measure of anti-Black attitudes was significantly positive. This respondent group, however, was both more prejudiced and more authoritarian than either Lambley's English-speaking sample or Orpen's.

found that belief consonance determined the perception of the stimulus person more than his or her race. But allegedly "Negro" stimulus persons to whom the experimenters attributed consonance of beliefs were described by respondents as less like themselves than were allegedly White stimulus persons of similarly attributed consonant beliefs. Also, in a condition in which no information about beliefs was provided, acceptance of stimulus persons was based on race. In the American setting race thus was salient, serving as a kind of assumed sign of different beliefs, perhaps. But perceived belief congruence did seem in this study to be of primary importance.

Social Norms. Returning once again to South Africa, where race is socially salient to a degree not exceeded anywhere else in the world, belief congruence/ dissonance must be expected to be less important when compared with race than it was found to be in the United States. This is precisely what Orpen and Pors (1972) found for 54 White middle-class Afrikaans-speaking teenage schoolchildren. First, these respondents completed a personal-values questionnaire. For each respondent, a set of four stimulus teenagers was created, two of them White and two non-White, to whom either consonant or dissonant values were attributed by the experimenter, taking into account the respondent's own values. These four stimuli were presented two months later, at which time the respondents read the descriptions of the four stimulus persons, then completed a social-distance scale for each and indicated the extent to which they considered each stimulus person to be similar to themselves.

The last-named measure revealed that both the White *like* and non-White *like* stimuli were perceived as more similar than either the White or non-White *unlike* stimuli. This indicated that the experimenters' manipulation of attributed values had been successful. In the main findings, however, race was more important than belief congruence in determining social distance. In fact, the social distance indicated for a stimulus labeled "Colored Teenager," with no description of beliefs provided, was not different from the social distance indicated by the same respondents to either the non-White *like* or the non-White *unlike* stimulus.

These results do not, of course, make untenable Rokeach's hypothesis that prejudice has as a root cause the perception of others as different from self in beliefs and values. Rather, they suggest that the social setting determines individual reactions to both race and belief. The basic *psychological* determinant of social distance does seem to be perceived similarity. But, when social norms of racial discrimination prevail, they seem capable of overriding individual, psychological dispositions.

With regard to this last point, it may well be that social-interaction norms based on race have to be very strong indeed to effectively override the perceived similarity. In one more study by Orpen (1972), conducted in Rhodesia where there is a heightened sense of race but where social policy falls short of *apartheid*, a sample of White teenagers (about 40 each of both sexes) was found to evaluate a stranger's likability and desirability as a work partner largely on the basis of attitude similarity, whether the stranger was allegedly White or "African." Thus, the initial contention that persons or groups perceived to be similar to "us" will enjoy greater acceptability than persons perceived to be different seems to be a powerful principle of the psychology of intergroup relations.

A study from Israel by Pirojnikoff, Hadar, and Hadar (1971) bears out this last statement. The study was designed primarily to test the hypothesis that kibbutz-dwelling Israelis would be more tolerant toward out-groups and less dogmatic (Rokeach) than urban Israelis. The tolerance measure was a social-distance scale (Bogardus). Two groups of Los Angeles respondents—one Jewish, one not—were also employed. Both Israeli groups were found to be significantly less dogmatic than the U.S. groups, and on that measure the urban Israeli sample was more dogmatic than the kibbutz-dwellers. On the social-distance measure, however, there was no significant difference between the two Israeli samples; but both together were found to be *less* willing to interact with out-group members than were the American samples. The authors suggested that their findings may have reflected a general Israeli reluctance to interact with persons whom they assume to hold dissimilar beliefs.

What Is an In-Group?

In considerable research by Triandis and various associates the concept of "subjective culture" (or values, beliefs, norms, and other shared cognitions of a people) has been employed as a heuristic device for treating some of the kinds of questions dealt with in this section of the present chapter. For example, asserting that "each culture cuts the pie of experience differently," Triandis (1975) derives from this generalization the expectation that definitions of what constitutes an in-group member will vary from culture to culture, despite the fact that all cultures will, somehow, have an in-group.

A study by Triandis, Vassiliou, and Nassiakou (1968) described the Greek definition of the in-group and showed how different it is from an American definition. The former is more personal in character in that it includes family members, friends, and even foreign tourists, but not persons one doesn't know, *even* if they happen to be Greek. By contrast, Americans do not typically consider foreign tourists part of the in-group; but all Americans, even those unknown personally, are usually included.

This is not to say, however, that co-nationality does not matter to Greeks. In an earlier study (Triandis & Triandis, 1962), a part of which focused on norms governing social distance in Greece and in the United States, it was found that—whereas Americans emphasized race to a degree not present in Greece— the Greeks emphasized religion and nationality. Despite some differences across these two studies, they both reported differences across the two cultures in in-group definition. Thus, what Triandis's work has shown is that the detailed content of in-group definition and the guidelines of behavior toward persons so defined vary across cultures. A relationship that is considered intimate in one culture and available only to a highly valued in-group member may, therefore, be considered more casual in another culture and available to a larger category of persons (Triandis, 1975).

Some Conclusions and Tentative Prescriptions

Our review and discussion of cross-cultural studies of intergroup relations have not been exhaustive, but we have probably seen enough to draw some conclusions and to suggest, cautiously, how intergroup relations might be improved. What surely has stood out is the importance of perceived similarity and of opportunities for equal-status contact in enhancing intergroup attraction and diminishing intergroup social distance. Another salient generalization is that, whatever psychological factors influence individuals in their intergroup relations (namely, authoritarianism, dogmatism, field dependence, and so forth), individual behavior vis-à-vis out-groups is very much subject to institutionalized norms and other forms of social control or influence.

We have also seen that in-group identification (which was dealt with mostly in Chapter Seven) and intergroup distance tend to be dynamically related parts of a whole syndrome of ethnocentric behaviors, much as Sumner argued in 1906. In this light we can better understand the Ugandan case study with which we dealt so intensively in the present and preceding chapters. The cultural identity of the Banyankore that we found to be so strong can now be recognized as socially functional, as it is for any in-group, in that it provides a psychological home base and hence a sense of belonging to individuals confronted with a myriad of possible memberships, some of them in groupings so large and abstract that they probably possess little psychological meaning. By the same token, when individuals locate themselves in a relatively small collectivity that has meaning as an in-group, they can probably also identify comfortably with a larger collectivity that includes the smaller one (for example, Uganda for the Banyankore) or is functionally linked with it.

But the Banyankore's identification as such (and other strong in-group identifications in any part of the world) is one side of a coin, the reverse being a potential for divisiveness and alienation from out-groups. For the Banyankore, whom we can now recognize to be no more ethnocentric than other groups, we found the likability and social distance of out-groups to be correlated with cultural similarity, proximity, and opportunity for contact.

From the Brewer and Campbell (1976) study done in Uganda, Kenya, and Tanzania and from the other cross-cultural studies of stereotyping and social distance, we can draw consistent conclusions. People everywhere seem to hold their own group in highest regard, and that regard diminishes as perceived similarity diminishes.

If we accept all of these findings as providing, tentatively at least, an answer to the question "Why does mankind persist in behaving ethnocentrically and parochially?" then a prescription for breaking down the barriers to a more global consciousness follows clearly. Ways must be found and efforts expended to increase equal-status contacts and to maximize the probability of experiences that will demonstrate and accentuate similarities, rather than differences.

But, of course, equal-status contacts are not very likely between groups of unequal status! Hence, more equitable distribution of opportunities is a prerequisite for equal-status contacts. The relatively deprived (and this applies both to so-called "backward" groups within multiethnic societies and to whole nations, such as the economically less-developed Third World nations) must be assisted in their efforts to "close the gap." In short, they must become less deprived and, as a consequence, more similar. Until that happens, such groups will continue to be perceived as different, and hence less good, thereby "deserving" to be held at large degrees of social distance.

In settings where ethnic discrimination is institutionally sanctioned, one of the effects of that discrimination, of course, is to accentuate and even exacerbate economic, social, and cultural differences. So, in such settings political and legal changes are absolutely necessary. Laws that force groups to remain separate from, and hence different from, their neighbors must be replaced by laws that force the opposite. Experience in the United States has shown that initial opposition to such reversals in the law is soon replaced by acceptance of them, just as Pettigrew's concept of the other-directed nature of much prejudice would suggest.[4]

Leadership of an enlightened nature must accompany such legal changes, of course. The Kenyan case, to cite only one example, bears this out. Prior to the attainment of independence from Great Britain, Kenya was torn by racial strife. With insistence from the late President Jomo Kenyatta, himself detained in prison for years by the British for his alleged role in the Mau Mau emergency, Kenya has become a model of a multiracial, multiethnic African society. Although "tribal" identities remain salient in Kenya (recall Brewer & Campbell's 1976 report), tolerance and interaction are the hallmarks of daily life there. Just as people accepted, believed in, and behaved in accordance with a "color bar" before independence, people today accept, believe in, and behave in accordance with laws that prohibit racial or ethnic discrimination. As Kenyans themselves are proud to point out, Kenya's way of dealing with its multiethnicity should be emulated by other nations of similar complexity. As this is being written, one hopes that even Rhodesia may see its "problem" in this light.

It was suggested at the outset of this chapter that parochial loyalties are tenacious and not easily modified, as they will have to be if we are to contend with our global survival problems. It was also suggested that cross-cultural research into intergroup relations can both illuminate the magnitude of this

---

[4]See Segall, 1976, pp. 111–154, for a more thorough discussion of intergroup relations in the United States.

difficulty and offer some guidelines for dealing with it. The research we have reviewed has, I hope, served both those functions. What we have seen both in this and the preceding chapter has demonstrated once again the potency of cultural forces in shaping human behavior. It is cultural identity that binds individuals to their own groups; it is cultural similarity that permits those same individuals to accept and interact with persons from other groups. Just as persons within groups can deemphasize existing differences and instead emphasize what they have in common with others—even to the extent of suppressing selfish desires in order to cooperate with others—so can they do so with other groups.[5] In effect, by so doing, they are merely expanding the definition of their in-group.

Nothing that we saw in this chapter makes such a phenomenon appear impossible. But it will require a quantum leap in good will, and even that will not be enough unless it is accompanied by enlightened leadership and social policy that provide the requisite economic and normative setting in which such good will can flourish. Should this state of affairs come to pass, a new, global culture will in effect have been created, one to which an increasingly large portion of humankind will relate. But even this need not destroy loyalties, allegiances, and identifications based on smaller, traditional cultures. Complete cultural homogenization need not be feared. In any event, it is nowhere near as fearsome as the cultural parochialism and ethnocentrism from which we will be departing.

References

Adorno, T. W., Frenkel-Brunswik, E., Levinson, D. J., & Sanford, N. *The Authoritarian Personality.* New York: Harper, 1950.

Anant, S. S. Self- and mutual perception of salient personality traits of different caste groups. *Journal of Cross-Cultural Psychology,* 1970, *1,* 41–52.

Anant, S. S. Ethnic stereotypes of educated North Indians. *Journal of Social Psychology,* 1971, *85,* 137–138.

Blake, R., & Dennis, W. Development of stereotypes concerning the Negro. *Journal of Abnormal and Social Psychology,* 1943, *38,* 525–531.

Bogardus, E. S. Measuring social distances. *Journal of Applied Sociology,* 1925, *9,* 299–308.

Bogardus, E. S. *Immigration and Race Attitudes.* Lexington, Mass.: Heath, 1928.

Brewer, M. B., & Campbell, D. T. *Ethnocentrism and Intergroup Attitudes.* New York: Wiley, 1976.

[5]Groups, of course, may have real differences of opinion on various issues of profound meaning to them. Nations may dispute boundaries, ethnic groups may contend over power distributions, and other "real" conflicts may divide groups. Some students of intergroup relations have studied various forms of training (partly derived from "group-dynamics" techniques) to manage or even resolve such conflicts. For example, there is a fascinating series of reports by Leonard Doob and colleagues of training programs applied to border disputes in the Horn of Africa involving Ethiopia, Somalia, and Kenya, interethnic disputes in Crete between Greeks and Turks, and interreligious conflict in Northern Ireland between Catholics and Protestants (Doob, 1970, 1971, 1974a, 1974b; Doob & Foltz, 1973, 1974).

Bronfenbrenner, U. The mirror image in Soviet-American relations: A social psychological report. *Journal of Social Issues,* 1961, *17,* 45–56.

Cauthen, N. R., Robinson, I. E., & Krauss, H. H. Stereotypes: A review of the literature 1926–1968. *Journal of Social Psychology,* 1971, *84,* 103–125.

Christie, R. Reconsiderations [of] *The Authoritarian Personality. Human Nature,* 1978, *1*(4), 90–93.

Doob, L. W. (Ed.). *Resolving Conflict in Africa: The Fermeda Workshop.* New Haven, Conn.: Yale University Press, 1970.

Doob, L. W. The impact of the Fermeda workshop on the conflicts in the Horn of Africa. *International Journal of Group Tensions,* 1971, *1,* 91–101.

Doob, L. W. The analysis and resolution of international disputes. *Journal of Psychology,* 1974, *86,* 313–326. (a)

Doob, L. W. A Cyprus workshop: An exercise in intervention methodology. *Journal of Social Psychology,* 1974, *94,* 161–178. (b)

Doob, L. W., & Foltz, W. J. The Belfast Workshop. *Journal of Conflict Resolution,* 1973, *17,* 489–512.

Doob, L. W., & Foltz, W. J. The impact of a workshop upon grass-roots leaders in Belfast. *Journal of Conflict Resolution,* 1974, *18,* 237–256.

Gilbert, G. M. Stereotypes' persistence and change among college students. *Journal of Abnormal and Social Psychology,* 1951, *46,* 245–254.

Haque, A. Mirror Image hypothesis in the context of Indo-Pakistan conflict. *Pakistan Journal of Psychology,* 1973. (Abstract in *Newsletter of the International Association of Cross-Cultural Psychology.*)

Katz, D., & Braly, K. W. Racial stereotypes of 100 college students. *Journal of Abnormal and Social Psychology,* 1933, *28,* 280–290.

Kurokawa, M. Mutual perceptions of racial images: White, black, and Japanese American. *Journal of Social Issues,* 1971, *27*(4), 213–235.

Lambley, P. Authoritarianism and prejudice in South African student samples. *Journal of Social Psychology,* 1973, *91,* 341–342.

LeVine, R. A., & Campbell, D. T. *Ethnocentrism: Theories of Conflict, Ethnic Attitudes and Group Behavior.* New York: Wiley, 1972.

Lindgren, H. C., & Tebcherani, A. Arab and American auto- and heterostereotypes: A cross-cultural study of empathy. *Journal of Cross-Cultural Psychology,* 1971, *2,* 173–180.

Ogunlade, J. A. National stereotypes of university students in Western Nigeria. *Journal of Social Psychology,* 1971, *85,* 309–310.

Orpen, C. Authoritarianism and racial attitudes among English-speaking South Africans. *Journal of Social Psychology,* 1971, *84,* 301–302.

Orpen, C. The effect of race and similar attitudes on interpersonal attraction among White Rhodesians. *Journal of Social Psychology,* 1972, *86,* 143–145.

Orpen, C., & Pors, H. Race and belief: A test of Rokeach's theory in an authoritarian culture. *International Journal of Psychology,* 1972, *7,* 53–56.

Orpen, C., & Rookledge, Q. Dogmatism and prejudice in white South Africa. *Journal of Social Psychology,* 1972, *86,* 151–153.

Pettigrew, T. F. Regional differences in anti-Negro prejudice. *Journal of Abnormal and Social Psychology,* 1959, *59,* 28–36.

Pettigrew, T. F. Social distance attitudes of South African students. *Social Forces,* 1960, *38,* 246–253.

Pirojnikoff, L. A., Hadar, I., & Hadar, A. Dogmatism and social distance: A cross-cultural study. *Journal of Social Psychology*, 1971, *85*, 187–193.

Reigrotski, E., & Anderson, N. National stereotypes and foreign contacts. *Public Opinion Quarterly*, 1959, *23*, 515–528.

Rokeach, M. (Ed.). *The Open and Closed Mind*. New York: Basic Books, 1960.

Rokeach, M., Smith, P. W., & Evans, R. I. Two kinds of prejudice or one? In M. Rokeach (Ed.), *The Open and Closed Mind*. New York: Basic Books, 1960. Pp. 132–168.

Schoenfeld, N. An experimental study of some problems relating to stereotypes. *Archives of Psychology*, 1942, *38*(Whole No. 270).

Segall, M. H. *Human Behavior and Public Policy: A Political Psychology*. Elmsford, N.Y.: Pergamon, 1976.

Segall, M. H., Doornbos, M., & Davis, C. *Political Identity: A Case Study from Uganda*. Syracuse, N.Y.: Maxwell Foreign and Comparative Studies/East Africa XXIV, 1976.

Stein, D. D., Hardyck, J. A., & Smith, M. B. Race and belief—an open and shut case. *Journal of Personality and Social Psychology*, 1965, *1*, 281–289.

Sumner, W. G. *Folkways*. Boston: Ginn, 1906.

Triandis, H. C. A note on Rokeach's theory of prejudice. *Journal of Abnormal and Social Psychology*, 1961, *62*, 184–186.

Triandis, H. C. Social psychology and cultural analysis. *Journal for the Theory of Social Behaviour*, 1975, *5*, 81–106.

Triandis, H. C., & Triandis, L. M. A cross-cultural study of social distance. *Psychological Monographs*, 1962, *76*(21, Whole No. 540).

Triandis, H. C., & Vassiliou, V. Frequency of contact and stereotyping. *Journal of Personality and Social Psychology*, 1967, *7*, 316–328.

Triandis, H. C., Vassiliou, V., & Nassiakou, M. Three cross-cultural studies of subjective culture. *Journal of Personality and Social Psychology*, 1968, *8*(4, Pt. 2). (Monograph supplement)

Viljoen, H. G. Relationship between stereotypes and social distance. *Journal of Social Psychology*, 1974, *92*, 313–314.

Vinacke, W. E. Explorations in the dynamics of stereotyping. *Journal of Social Psychology*, 1956, *43*, 105–132.

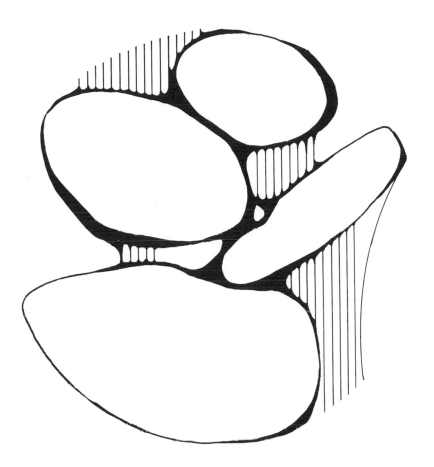

A Conclusion

Nine

A Summing Up and Postscripts

Many chapters ago, we embarked on an introduction to the scientific study of human behavior, a study that necessarily emphasized the ways in which social and cultural forces shape it. We began our introductory exploration of cross-cultural psychology by asserting that one *must* study human behavior in its cultural context; the remainder of our exploration was designed to demonstrate the validity of this assertion.

We began with a stage-setting discussion of *socialization* and *enculturation*, the twin processes by which people everywhere learn from other people how to behave in acceptable ways. We saw that what is learned by these processes can conveniently be termed *culture*. From the writings of the cross-cultural psychologist John Berry we acquired a useful conceptual framework for understanding how all of this happens, a framework in which are interlinked the natural environment (*ecology*), that part of the environment that is of human origin (*culture*), and individual development (*behavior*).

In several chapters we considered in detail the ways in which ecology and culture influence basic psychological processes, including perception, cognition, motives, attitudes, and values. The empirical research considered in Chapters Four, Five, and Six should have left little doubt that each human being, despite his or her uniqueness, is very much a cultural product. People perceive, understand, believe, and feel in ways that are shaped by the cultural context in which the accident of their own birth has occurred. Even before acquiring language, developing individuals are learning the ways of their own culture. With the acquisition of language comes an even more profound immersion in those ways.

In later chapters we moved beyond basic psychological processes and considered some more complex topics that served further to illustrate the impact of culture on human behavior. We considered changes in behavior that are occasioned by changes in culture. Under that rubric we examined the impact of cultural contact on acculturating individuals and considered intensively the processes of cultural identification, of which nationalism and modernism are examples. In the final substantive chapter we looked at some of the implications of cultural identification for intergroup relations, and we found the Sumnerian concept of *ethnocentrism* a useful guide to the growing cross-cultural literature on intergroup attraction and perception.

Throughout this exploration of cross-cultural psychology, we tried to remain attentive to methodological issues that are particularly acute for research in cultures other than one's own. Those issues were first discussed in Chapter Three, but they surfaced time and again as we considered the various kinds of studies done and the theories invented by cross-cultural psychologists to account for what they believe their research has taught them.

All these things considered, we have accomplished the limited purpose with which we began. We have become "introduced" to the relatively new but rapidly growing field known as cross-cultural psychology.

The student who has been awakened by this limited introduction to the fascinating findings that continue to be produced by cross-cultural research should consult the journals that report them, journals that were the source of most of the contents of this book and that will be the source of later books by other writers. For, like any discipline, cross-cultural psychology is ever growing, and ever changing. In time, the salient features of the cross-cultural psychology to which readers of this book have been introduced will be less salient, and a reintroduction will be necessary. To maintain an acquaintance with cross-cultural psychology, then, the student should monitor the *Journal of Cross-Cultural Psychology*, the *International Journal of Psychology*, and the *Journal of Social Psychology*—the three major repositories of accumulating findings in the field. The interested student should also consult the multivolumed *Handbook of Cross-Cultural Psychology* now being prepared by an international team of cross-cultural psychologists, many of whose names are already familiar to readers of this book. And, finally, the interested student should recognize that the many other books mentioned in the present textbook contain far more information about cross-cultural psychology than could possibly have been presented in a single introduction. Those books, too, merit reading in their entirety.

Prepared by this introduction to cross-cultural psychology, the student might also benefit from periodic conferences organized by such scientific bodies as the International Association of Cross-Cultural Psychology and the Society for Cross-Cultural Research. University faculty members involved in cross-cultural psychology or in psychological anthropology are likely to know about meeting sites and dates. The student fortunate enough to be located near a meeting of these groups would be well advised to inquire about attending as a student observer.

Finally, for the student who develops aspirations of becoming a cross-cultural psychologist, there are increasing opportunities for graduate study under the supervision of many of the scholars whose work is described in this book. Happily, most of them are alive and well and working at a university, pursuing their cross-cultural research and training graduate students to do more of the same. Among the North American centers for graduate training in psychology including cross-cultural research are Northwestern University (Evanston, Illinois), Queens University (Kingston, Ontario), York University (Toronto, Ontario), the University of Illinois, the University of Pennsylvania, Pennsylvania State University, Syracuse University, and Harvard University. In addition, there is the East-West Center in Hawaii and, in Asia, the University of Hong Kong. In Europe, the University of Geneva and the University of Strathclyde (Scotland) have facilities and personnel devoted to cross-cultural research. A continuing trend is the emergence of psychologists indigenous to many developing countries—in Latin America and Africa, for example—with centers for research based in universities in those countries. Opportunities thus exist in growing number for students who want to enlarge their introductory knowledge of cross-cultural psychology and acquire the research skills that can enable them to make their own contributions to this growing field.

There *will* be major contributions to cross-cultural psychology, and in the not too distant future. If this book has suggested that much has been learned about the influences of culture on human behavior, surely it has also suggested that the surface has only been scratched. We have come a long way from the turn-of-the-century beginnings that were described in Chapter Two. But in another way we have not yet gone very far. The forward movements in understanding, the gradual movement away from doctrines of instinct and of racially determined behaviors, the improvements in research methodology, the very recognition of the fact of cultural influence—all of these significant gains must be balanced by our continuing inability to solve the real human problems that knowledge of cross-cultural psychology *ought* to have helped us solve. Yet we know that it hasn't; the problems remain.

There is, thus, work to be done, work of an applied nature by which what is already known is employed in efforts to ameliorate the human condition, and work of a basic nature by which we improve and expand what is known. The final message of this introduction to cross-cultural psychology, then, is an invitation to the newly introduced to become better acquainted with this young, promising, stimulating, and rewarding endeavor, the study of human behavior in global perspective.

Name Index

Subject Index